CHAOS, COSMOS, AND SAINT-EXUPÉRY'S PILOT-HERO: A STUDY IN MYTHOPOEIA

CHAOS, COSMOS, AND SAINT-EXUPÉRY'S PILOT-HERO: A STUDY IN MYTHOPOEIA

by

John R. Harris

SCRANTON: UNIVERSITY OF SCRANTON PRESS

Library of Congress Cataloging-In-Publication Data

Harris, John R., 1953-
   Chaos, cosmos, and Saint-Exupéry's pilot hero : a study in
mythopoeia / by John R. Harris.
         p.   cm.
   Includes bibliographical references and index.
   ISBN 0-940866-75-7 (hc). – ISBN 0-940866-76-5 (pb)
   1. Saint-Exupéry, Antoine de, 1900-1944–Ethics.   I. Title.
PQ2637.A274Z735   1999
848' .91209–dc21   98-52501
                                                              CIP

University of Scranton Press
Chicago Distribution Center
11030 S. Langley
Chicago IL   60628

PRINTED IN THE UNITED STATES OF AMERICA

CONTENTS

PREFACE

This work was originally undertaken at the soliciting of Father Rousseau at the University of Scranton Press, who had read an article of mine about Saint-Exupéry in the Winter 1990 edition of *Christianity and Literature*. The ensuing years saw both Scranton's and my own circumstances change radically, due to financial strains in either case. At one point, my professional situation required me to reside in three different states during a single year. Father Rousseau's advice that I address the book to a general audience of inquisitive, well-read people always remained with me, however. Indeed, as my personal situation became more stressful, I may say that I found greater solace in treating Saint-Exupéry as a fellow human being suffering through uncertain times rather than just another literary figure whose work has occasioned another scholarly analysis.

Now my toil (at least with the book manuscript) has come to the happiest of endings: reunion with my worthy editor and with the University of Scranton Press. I can scarcely begrudge the project, in retrospect, for forcing me beyond the literary scholar's typical aloofness. The manuscript has profited from our struggle, and so have I. (It remains to be seen what kind of profit the University of Scranton Press may incur!)

So important is the broad philosophical focus of this book to me that I have tried never to take for granted the reader's knowledge of Saint-Exupéry's novels. Though once extremely popular in this country, and though still readily available in English translation, Saint-Exupéry has unquestionably lost that immediate relevance which he enjoyed during his lifetime, and also that certain trendiness which he enjoyed posthumously through the fifties and sixties. I hope that the reader will discover in him a deeper, less fragile relevance after perusing my study.

To that end, I have sought to avoid citations in French. For secondary sources, I have employed English translations wherever they existed; and where they did not exist, I have supplied my own. I was more reluctant to banish Saint-Exupéry's French from the text, since his style is not only quite distinctive, but somewhat controversial. Nevertheless, I ultimately yielded to the guiding principle of serving a general audience (a principle which Saint-Exupéry himself would surely have understood and endorsed: no stylist was ever more contemptuous of artful effects when they obscure moral edification).

I have appeased my conscience by including the French text of Saint-Exupéry's remarks in endnotes. These notes represent passages from personal correspondence as well as published novels: *all* that has been cited directly from Saint-Exupéry's hand may be found there. The English translations appearing in the body of the chapters are entirely my own. The highly readable translations which already exist often diverge from the French, due (in the most extreme cases) to the hurrying along of Saint-Exupéry's work for an eager American public. My renditions tend to be as literal as good sense will allow—perhaps to the detriment of stylistic elegance. Since close readings of the sort which I have offered rely upon a fairly literal understanding of the text, I have felt obliged to do my own translating. Any errors of translation or interpretation occurring in these passages are thus solely my responsibility.

Finally, I must explain why I have not drawn any citations of Saint-Exupéry from the Quesnel and Autrand Pléiade edition, even though this work is an updated and expanded version of the Caillois text. My problem is that the more recent edition is *so* expanded—the complete works, no less—that it has run into two volumes, and *so* updated that the Gallimard publishers cannot confide to me the approximate day when we may expect Messrs. Quesnel and Autrand to have volume two ready. I have, however, cited repeatedly the most useful introduction to volume one.

CHAPTER 1

FROM AESTHETICS TO ETHICS

I.

The decade following the disappearance of Antoine de Saint-Exupéry during the final days of World War II, presumably in a fatal crash of his P-38 fighter, saw a proliferation of volumes published by friends and comrades. Tonio or Saint-Ex, as his intimates variously styled him, was as enigmatic as Ernest Hemingway, T. E. Lawrence, and most of the few other literary figures who shared his passionate belief in life-risking action as the only true validation—a list which might include Lord Byron, and even Archilochus. Something about such people fascinates those who survive them. Their defenders and detractors, both numerous, rush into print with equally numerous unique assessments of them based upon "direct encounters" (which may range from a shared childhood to a single brush in a noisy bistro). The opening scene of David Lean's *Lawrence of Arabia*, where mourners at the great man's funeral fall to bickering about his true stature, well portrays the ambivalence of public opinion about these figures. If anything, the flurry of interpretations simply feeds an evolving legend rather than setting the facts straight; for the "fact" is that the enigmatic characters in question are contradictory—as are all of us, of course, but they even more so.

Action can carry us only so far. Beyond that point, we either learn to worship truth meditatively, having given up on executing it in an incorrigibly deceptive world, or we tune out all the insufferable cognitive dissonance and perform *beaux gestes* as uncritically as Don

1

Quixote charged his windmills. Very few of us insist upon a synthesis of thought and act in each moment of living; and all of these few become magnificently frustrated, denied the comforts of resignation by their conscience and the cock-sureness of holy crusade by their hapless sanity. We may say virtually anything about their philosophy that we like and be correct. Whatever we say will also be incorrect, however, because we will have imposed upon their system a coherence which they themselves rejected. In Saint-Exupéry's own words, "A tree is not first a seed, then a shoot, then a pliant trunk, then dead wood. We must avoid dividing it to understand it. A tree is that power which slowly weds the heavens" (*Citadelle* 513–14).[1] Living coherence resides in the striving after coherence, not in a column of logically conciliable but inflexible terms.

An observation of this sort often concludes the argument of Saint-Exupéry's apologists. Without disregarding their testimonials, I do not intend to join them in offering still another interpretation of Saint-Exupéry as pilot, author, soldier, philosopher—as a complete phenomenon, in short. The contributors to Tavernier's volume demonstrate as a group just how tendentious such an undertaking is bound to become, with the univocal grief of Saint-Exupéry's intimates being rudely succeeded by the uneasy estimates of literary critics. This unusual collection anticipates the judgment in Major's more recent work that "since about the fifties, we keep witnessing either Saint-Exupéry's annexation or his total rejection, often motivated by the interpretation of 'edifying author' with which he is adorned" (256).

More recently still—almost as I write—the grudging notice paid in certain circles to the fiftieth anniversary of Saint-Exupéry's death hints that literary analysis remains as politically guided as ever. Mavis Gallant's review of two new biographies prepared for the occasion seems to tolerate none of their shortcomings so little as their choice of subject. Feminists are conspicuous among those who would cheerfully see Saint-Exupéry's name struck from every reading list; yet his denigrating view of women was typical of his time, and he had more than the typical reasons for being emotionally complex. At most, he might be called an innocent victim of circumstance. Schiff sensitively concludes that "his oeuvre can be read as a requiem to the male bonds of which he was deprived" (34), and Robinson offers an account of his highly unsettled social life after leaving home (12–21). Seldom has a person so politically centrist and broadly companionable been assailed from so many sides.

As a result, today's critical community may end up making of Saint-Exupéry a footnote to existentialism, and a figure who is otherwise best passed over. The broader reading public warmly but quite mistakenly regards him as a children's author, few of its members suspecting that even *Le Petit Prince* attempts to express the author's evolving philosophy of life. Since merely choosing Antoine de Saint-Exupéry as the topic of a book has become politically charged, I wish to devote this first chapter to explaining my interest in him as fully as space allows.

On one point, all of Saint-Exupéry's comrades, critics, and analysts have always agreed: his books, essays, anecdotes, conversation, and most certainly his philosophy insisted upon the marriage of thought and act. Many commentators have naturally studied his life as a means of penetrating his literature; for not only did he lead an extraordinarily active life, especially for a man of ideas, but his authorship was itself more an active search for answers than a leisurely courtship of the Muses. In Ouellet's words, "The exceptionally narrow lines of rapport established between thought and the acts which constantly nourished it have converged upon a complete identification of the author with his work" (7); while Pélissier, reacting to an earlier criticism that Saint-Exupéry was more pilot than author, insisted, "I cannot see how it would be possible to establish a distinction between one and the other" (17).

Saint-Exupéry himself often invited the identification of his writing with his life, and apparently had little patience with any author whose work failed to have practical relevance. Alluding to André Breton and the surrealists, he once wrote, "If I wish to dazzle, if I am vain, if, for lack of an internal life and a sense of pride, I judge myself according to the effect I produce, then I invent a complicated little rebus and show it off" (*Carnets* 74).[2] Obviously, he saw his own literary vocation as starkly contrasting to such exhibitionism. He insisted that, for him, "écrire est une conséquence" (LJ 35)—that is to say, his writing resulted from his direct encounter with life. How, then, may one study such an author's contribution without tracing the course of his life?

Major announces in his introduction an intent to evaluate Saint-Exupéry's work with a New Critical focus upon the literary text itself rather than upon "functions which are alien to it" (10). He incidentally emerges, in my opinion, with a much better grasp of Saint-Exupéry's personal beliefs and character than do most of those who pay primary attention to textually extrinsic factors. After all, a person's tastes and values can often be better gauged from a pencil sketch than from a résumé. Carlo François has likewise claimed of Saint-Exupéry's aesthetic motive that "it captures and holds up for display the quite intricate correspondences which unite the creative phenomenon's extremely varied modes" (18). These distinguished critics concur that Saint-Exupéry makes of the text a universe unto itself, the quality of whose rules is to be judged by their intrinsic coherence rather than by historical or cultural circumstance.

With some crucial adjustments, I propose to continue in the scholarly tradition of Major and François, examining the formal properties of Saint-Exupéry's fiction. I am no strict formalist, however, and in fact my primary adjustment will be to study such properties as they relate to the recurring moral message's validity—an extrinsic factor to the New Critic, perhaps, but scarcely to Saint-Exupéry. Of course, there is a school of thought which claims that a beautiful life *is* a good life, so that if we concentrate on adumbrating intricate but end-oriented structures in our behavior as we would in composing a story, we will not go far wrong. Major tends to read Saint-Exupéry this way, and with just cause; but his own critical method is excessively committed to minimizing points of incoherence and emphasizing points of harmony, I think.

For the dissonant notes in Saint-Exupéry, though not many, are recurrent and fascinating. They tell the whole story of his failure to tell life's story—to validate through an imagined sequence a code of conduct for daily living. One might say that the *trompe l'oeil* structures of Saint-Exupéry's novels cry out to be deconstructed. Like many of my generation in whom graduate school sought to inculcate Derrida, I have concluded (perhaps perversely, but I hope sensibly) that the most helpful critical strategy is an eclectic one. I do not believe that all works need, reward, or even permit deconstructing. I do not share the political agenda often avowed by those who practice the method. I must say that Saint-Exupéry's politics do not particularly concern me.

For the fact remains that, New Criticism or not, *this* author may be found most palpably in his writing. The text *was* his life in each instance—not a reminiscence or encapsulation of it, but a living struggle with an obstacle. The reality of these struggles was at least equal to that of his aeronautic adventures, and could just as well serve to explain why he flew as his flying might explain the content of his books. Mme. de Vogüé, alias Pierre Chevrier, was quite right to insist of her renowned friend, "The moralist always dominates the novelist" (44): but for Saint-Exupéry, after all, the moral truth by which men can live is necessarily a certain imaginative and moving arrangement of events. "Truth . . . truth is what simplifies the world, and not what creates chaos," Beucler reports him as saying often (142).

Hence I do not offer a historically informed assurance of the man's honesty or sanity or spirituality. I make the suggestion, instead, that his authorship achieved the status of an act unto itself, and belongs far more significantly to him than his taste in food or the ground-in social prejudices of his milieu. For that matter, the striving to put all of oneself into all of one's conscious acts may be the surest proof that one is honest and sane and spiritual at the same time. But is it possible to have these three qualities at once—if it is no longer so in our postmodern labyrinth, was it ever? Deconstruction has alerted us to how systems may contradict themselves within their theoretical foundation. Saint-Exupéry's system, with its many aesthetic and ethical polarities, is no stranger to irreconcilable axioms.

Solon said it to Croesus: a life contemplated cannot be a life in action—a life lived cannot be living life. To desire otherwise is honest and sane and spiritual: it always was and it always will be. People who are not trying to write their life stories as they live do not seek consistency and hence do not keep promises or undertake challenges. They may well be remembering (as Derrida would have us do) that no commitment has unconditional validity: they are certainly not remembering (as Saint-Exupéry would have us do) that one should try to forget the flimsiness of the conditions underlying any commitment. For such enlightened relativists, floating aloof from the snares of narrative, every day begins a new book, not a new chapter in a begun book. Heaven help those of us who must live in their midst—heaven help us all in the postmodern labyrinth.

Nevertheless, it is truly impossible to complete the book of life which the qualities of strong character force us to undertake. Derrida recognizes this well, though he places his emphasis elsewhere:

> If meaning is meaningful only within a totality, could it come forth if the totality were not animated by the anticipation of an end, or by an intentionality which, moreover, does not necessarily and primarily belong to a consciousness? If there are structures, they are possible only on the basis of the fundamental structure which permits totality to open and overflow itself such that it *takes on meaning* by anticipating a *telos* which here must be understood in its most indeterminate form. (*Writing and Difference* 26)

The assumptions which make order possible, then, are self-deluding, or at least run a grave risk of being erroneous (if, in some other dimension, their validity may somehow, someday, be assessed). Frank Kermode made the same point rather more clearly in his Mary Flexner lectures more than three decades ago: "Men, like poets, rush 'into the middest,' *in medias res*, when they are born; they also die *in medias res*, and to make sense of their span they need fictive concords with origins and ends, such as give meaning to lives and to poems" (7). To impose coherence, one must jump to the end and work back—but none of us in this world really knows where the Great End, the terminal objective, resides.

Pascal believed that making such risky assumptions was less risky than not making them, however (*la nécessité du parie*); and Saint-Exupéry, along with every other moralist who ever was, agreed. Building character requires the apparently futile undertaking of positing ends. No one ever resisted acknowledging this futility as heroically as Saint-Exupéry, the author and the man. All of his protagonists struggle against palpable chaos, a disorder of things symbolized (but only symbolized, for the greater disorder is human) by storms, deserts, seas, and the various entropic forces of nature. Their struggle is heroic, as was his, because they and he in every instance refuse to surrender to the evidence of the senses, the unorchestrated kicks and slaps of mindless energy. Even if meaning is nowhere but in their own hearts (precisely the deconstructive view, if the logical mind may be substituted for the heart), they nevertheless fight to impose it upon a meaningless world. After all, where no objective referents exist, who is victimized when one wills one's own set of referents into being? A victim is someone wronged, and no one can be wronged before right and wrong exist.

Yet the futility of such a struggle is perhaps most apparent when the hero meets with material success. He invariably looks more glorious fighting for vague ideals than enforcing them as law. If being right is the winner's prize, then why do we feel so much sympathy for the oppressed? Right and wrong, it turns out, have something ahistorical about them. Castaways on an island seldom simply relapse into an arbitrary order dictated by raw brutality (in a "realist" novel, yes—but seldom in reality). Saint-Exupéry's heroes won their battles with increasing thoroughness in his books. His side defeated the Nazis, as well, or what should have been his side—the side for which he died, like so many of his heroes. During the years when these various victories were most assured, however, he was astute enough to notice that he had not won (either on the page or in the field) the peace worth winning. The triumphant order of his books and of Western society had grown merely arbitrary. Pieces of chaos had been used to construct a wall against chaos, which makes even less sense than senselessness. It certainly does not make *honest* sense.

If the essential nature of chaos is to be in unpredictable motion, then how can its elements contribute to harmony? If human beings themselves are nothing more than products of a fragile, arbitrary order imposed somehow upon the great swirl of things, then whence do they draw their ability to *create* order? Or if they merely mimic an inherited order, how did their order's founding hero get the idea for a foundation?

Deconstruction, as commonly practiced, moves no farther toward answering such questions than did the preceding philosophy of the absurd. To be sure, some of existentialism's most vocal proponents were as romantically blind to the impossibility of self-creation as was Saint-Exupéry. "War and construction," wrote Sartre of Saint-Exupéry's novels (yet with a naiveté all his own), "heroism and work, doing, having, and being, the human condition . . . these are the principal literary and philosophical themes of today" (327 at n.9).

Major, who cites this passage (261), argues more generally throughout his book that Saint-Exupéry places an existentialist emphasis upon "construction" rather than "consumption": "the subject must 'make' the object, since, by his activity, he becomes" (76). This manner of resemblance undoubtedly exists between Sartre and Saint-Exupéry, though Ouellet judiciously calls attention to several points of divergence (and cf. Chevrier 43–44).

Is deconstruction any different—any less quixotic—in seeking to wrest something *ex nihilo* after mercilessly exposing reality's ruthless void? What would be the point of demonstrating the self-contradictory nature of human philosophical systems if one could not walk away the wiser? Derrida has reiterated that his method does not aim at disparaging the truth of either pole in those binary oppositions which rule our thoughts like so many halls of mirrors. He even acknowledges grandly that deconstruction "always in a certain way falls prey to its own work" (*Of Grammatology* 24). If we take him at his word, then does the deconstructive project merely strive to "sensitize" us—to make us always avoid absolute terms? It clearly does not explain why we should be concerned about the rights of the weak, disenfranchised, and oppressed. In fact, inflexible ideologues have sometimes availed themselves of the method to pursue intellectual and social revolution in a rather despotic manner, since no such thing as "common decency" remains. If deconstruction does not license ferocious crusades with the same relativism that nourishes healthy self-deprecation, *why* does it not? A hall of mirrors reflects nothing if nothing has ever been placed before some unidentified mirror.

Saint-Exupéry's lifelong effort to create cosmos from chaos—to will into being an object of desire without considering *why* or *how* the will desires—is nothing less than a pleasantly simplified (and thoroughly unwitting) model of deconstruction's *aporia*. Let us recognize, in fact, that most of the twentieth century, modernism as well as postmodernism, has sensed in some degree the liability of forms. They are at best a trick of dreams conditioned by genetics or biology, at worst a heritage of shackles and whips: in the middle somewhere, they are a rallying point, a flag planted thoughtlessly in the earth. No school of thought during any of these troubled decades has stubbornly addressed the question, why *should* we act one way and not another? We are given only different accounts for why we happen to have acted as we did, or else liberated to act as we may.

Yet Saint-Exupéry forces the question. As much as any author in these generations, he seeks cause. He posits the human will, and deduces that virtually anything should be possible thereafter . . . but he also, over time, understands that such a will may not be simply posited—that the range of the real is much narrower than the possible, and that what the will wills must thus itself be rather narrow, for some reason. And what might that reason be? The ultimate failure of Saint-Exupéry's narratives, I contend, to propound an order with ethical validity helpfully dramatizes deconstruction's failure to acknowledge an unconditional reality behind, within, and beyond labyrinths of shifting, reflecting signifiers. I call the drama helpful because, after all, we are not really in a labyrinth unless we want out. In Saint-Exupéry is revived a kind of moral urgency which too many current theorists have misplaced.

That the unconditioned reality behind our prison walls deserves the name of God also belongs to my contention, since its influence seems scarcely (if at all) empirical. Instead, its magnetism is responsible for whatever thoughtful approbation or revulsion we still register in the new twenty-first century—whatever cause still makes us put our interests, and even our lives, at risk. It is felt from within, not from without. In a recent essay, Kevin Mills writes, "If Christian approaches to interpretation are to avoid charges of obscurantism, and if Christian readers are to develop a critical approach to the postmodern malaise, then we could do worse than allow deconstructionist models to inform our work" (135). The study of where fictive worlds contradict themselves is a most promising method of mapping out the real world—the *real* real world, the one whose intuited presence lures us from the penumbra we inhabit and into the sometimes dangerous guesses of art and philosophy. As we engage in this study, we must simply remember not to confuse the truth we seek with the method through which we seek it. We must not repudiate presence just because we only ever find its tracks and cold campfires.

II.

As well as I can make out, a dyed-in-the-wool Derridean deconstructionist is expected to believe that self-contradictions are inevitable in literary texts. Rejecting this proposition, however, enhances rather than compromises the method's utility: the method is no longer rendered bland by its own systematic rigidity (for a rule to which there are no exceptions must at some point become a tautology). Yet Saint-Exupéry's texts present us with self-contradiction at every level, from the fundamental on up. Some of the more superficially located tensions appear to have attracted his authorial eye and motivated him to reallocate the stresses of his next novel's cosmos. Instead of resolving the original contradictions in these cases, however, he always ended up reproducing them at a less visible point in the structure.

Less visible to himself, at any rate—for he would never have condoned the fraud of deliberately drawing the reader's eye away from textual inconsistencies. Delange acutely notes that the young Antoine's failing French composition on his baccalaureate exam was predictable in one "who only rarely employed the license of gratuitous imagination . . . [and] who never sought to dupe his readers with artifices and impostures" (14). Antoine once wrote to his mother, "I detest these people who write to amuse themselves, who strive for effect. One must have something to say" (*LM* 140);[3] and, a little later, he informed her with still greater earnestness, "You must look for me, such as I am, in what I write: it is the scrupulous and deliberate result of what I think and see" (*LM* 153).[4]

This is not a man who wishes to deceive us. He would probably have died first—and perhaps he did. Perhaps his jockeying for dangerous missions at the end of the war was somehow colored by a feeling that he could no longer write the truth. Unfortunately, the impasses in Saint-Exupéry's work are truly basic. The structure of every narrative he ever wrote rests upon them. Something about Saint-Exupéry's tireless ambition to interlace beauty and morality—to refine aesthetic order until it perfectly enunciated ethical goodness—was doomed from the start.

In this section, I shall anticipate two of the more specific, easily observable, and ostensibly amendable self-contradictions in Saint-Exupéry's novels. One seriously encumbers the earlier works: his choice of narrative voice, of that specially authoritative point of view from which to tell the tale. One would think that the doer would naturally be the teller in the writing of so committed an active-contemplative. Yet Saint-Exupéry seems to have decided upon this strategy only after much experimentation. Instead, the early books offer us protagonists viewed from a respectful distance, figures for whom we may prefer the morally elevating word "hero"—which is just the problem. Ethics is the science of how ordinary human beings ought to live, not the *res gestae* of supermen. If Saint-Exupéry's stories were to be true of life as well as pleasantly ordered, they were bound to present situations in which ordinary people might be expected to meet the crucial challenge. Yet the alienated Bernis of *Courrier Sud* (the first published novel), though he fails to perform any distinctly heroic feat or even to die an unequivocally heroic death, has already gone adrift from the rank and file. Saint-Exupéry's next work, the glorious *Vol de Nuit*, presents both a much more heroic pilot-hero and an arch-hero—the pilot's boss Rivière, who might as well be the *Aeneid*'s Jupiter. Such characters are much too big for you and me: we could never fill their shoes.

In all of his subsequent works, Saint-Exupéry would circumvent this difficulty by casting himself in the role of protagonist, or at least of narrator and occasional participant. If properly understood, his alteration was an act of humility, for his objective was precisely to put the narrated experience within reach of the ordinary man. "Though an aristocrat, he makes a case for the entire species," writes Pierre-Henri Simon, "which is to say for a superior type of human being realized only in certain heroes" (qtd. in Borgal 95).

A superior type of human being . . . well, morality ought to call us to great heights, as long as we need not sprout wings to get there. Saint-Exupéry never for an instant seeks to represent himself as Saint Antoine: to do so would have undermined the viability of his cosmos. Yet Borgal's phrase nonetheless hints at a contradiction waiting at the other pole, the humble, un-heroic (or unconsciously heroic) "I" of Dante. This "I" is able to beguile us with his humor and sincerity: he is "one of us." The confidence into which he lures us proves treacherous, however; for while his capacities are no greater than ours, he vaults to a higher state by a kind of grace not imparted to us. The physical circumstances of these transports are improbable enough. How many of us will have the chance to fly through an Andean snowstorm or through the deadly fireworks of an artillery barrage? The full revelation also calls for a poet's mind fertile with rare images.

Prophets are born, even though the real ones must still wait on the spirit to move them.

Major observes that, to many critics, Saint-Exupéry's protagonists mistakenly seem to discover a truth "reserved for a few initiates" and beyond the reach of the rest of us (81). He is surely correct that Saint-Exupéry did not intend such readings, yet their influence compromises the narrative's moral objective as unhappily as do the leaps and flexes of a superhero. The first-person point of view could not disguise the tendency of these later works to tap into ecstasy through a deeply introverted interpretation of experience. Avoid or understate this introversion as he might, Saint-Exupéry never quite managed to conceal that the path to spiritual transformation must lead away from cultural forms rather than into their midst. Access to it cannot be won by any particular etiquette, conditioning, or ritual.

Such an impasse in the search for an intimate yet potentially universal source of spiritual energy becomes more visible elsewhere as the later novels shrewdly feel their way around it in the choice of narrative voice. The advance of the plot becomes more studied, more allusive. Now that Saint-Exupéry, using his own voice, is able to concentrate on what he says rather than how he is saying it, the action of his works more clearly pits inner and outer revelation against each other. The duel between intimacy and universality (which need not be to the death, but whose reconciliation through some pre-experiential love or longing the author would never countenance) occupies the heart of the story. A second impasse looms.

Already in the transitional novels (first-person accounts of aviation adventures), the climax was failing to resolve the narrative's moral tensions—which, of course, also constitutes an aesthetic failure. These books confidently imply that the purgative act of braving cyclones, glaciers, and deserts could save one from the world's corruption if only one might turn such once-in-a-lifetime ordeals into a routine. But how *does* one create such a routine? The protagonist of Norman Mailer's *American Dream* goes for a walk along the ridge of his skyscraper whenever his soul becomes too tarnished to endure more stains. Is the rite of renewal as simple as a monthly or weekly game of Russian roulette?

There are two problems with this formula (neither of which is that the gun will eventually go off: death is the accepted, perhaps eagerly anticipated conclusion of such devotions). In the first place, the "high" may not last a month, or even a week, after a few repetitions. Like any other addictive drug, death-daring invites stronger and more frequent doses. "There is a kind of action," reflects Mounin aptly, "which is intoxication, and only intoxication; one sobers up from it, since one cannot always be drunk" (127). Are the sober periods, then, to be dedicated entirely to preparing for the next debauch? How seriously can one serve so obviously, painfully shrinking and ineffectual a god?

In the second place, even if the "high" were assured of lasting until the next sacrament, it is inherently unsuited to ritual, at least if that ritual is intended as a rehearsal for life. (A moralist who presents the ritual narratively has just such an intent.) The Exupérian ritual has certain basic requirements. One must serve something beyond oneself to find fulfillment, and the service of that something must demand such commitment that one's worldly self—one's body and narrowly programmed mind—is vigorously rattled, even threatened with demise. Now, a service which may be performed routinely, week after week, can scarcely supply a soul with the kind of epiphanic encounter necessary to ward off daily life's encroaching tedium; but the execution of a service which can never be repeated, while leaving the spirit exhilarated in a realm beyond its normal purview for a few hours or days, cannot pose a pattern for daily life.

One solution to the quandary is plainly to avoid completing the rite: or rather, since a deliberate avoidance would be cynical, to embark upon doing something which can never be completed. For an author, such a project would be the never-ending book—which *Citadelle* certainly is! Such an assessment of the unfinished manuscript would have to be facetious, of course: Saint-Exupéry was much too idealistic to have wittingly begun a work incapable of completion. What might have consoled him in the ongoing project, instead, are its closed chains of allegory. The pastoral monarch, the bluntly motivated guards and artisans, the invincible desert, the lost oasis—all are too weakly focused for the kind of political commentary which posterity has often tried to make of them; yet they gracefully convey another, less palpable presence. Indeed, Saint-Exupéry's narratives had grown increasingly abstract as his literary search for the perfect expression of truth matured. As Boisdeffre remarked in initial reference to *Vol de Nuit*, "Saint-Exupéry will soon abandon the support of deeds to rise to the level of images, then of symbols. At the end of his life, like an oriental story-teller, he will be speaking only in parables" (168). Even *Le Petit Prince*, so direct and naive on the surface, uses that very naiveté to draw us beneath the surface.

Saint-Exupéry, then, perpetually lifted his service to higher and higher levels, to an ever more exalted, less empirical god. No doubt, his activity as an author grew in importance to him as his various flying activities—mail routes, "raids," test-piloting, wartime reconnaissance—resisted the vector to a more spiritual objective. The awkward looping of his first novel, *Courrier Sud*, in quasi-allegorical fashion around the same places for new meaning—or for renewed meaning—was steadily refined. This tropological kind of narrative might have served his purpose. Sometimes it ends up working, both aesthetically and ethically: that is, an allegory may both impose an elegant order *and* present that order credibly as moral duty. Yet the strategy only works if the author knows when to stop—if he admits that he is indeed trapped in an allegory.

Saint-Exupéry fought against allegorical closure to the very end, even though all of his books had always been approaching it (and none more than the unfinished manuscript). He had been convinced from the start that the sublimated message of his narrative must be mythic, not allegorical. In allegory, human actors are "averaged out": the ordinary is caught in the shadow of an archetype. Myth celebrates the success of human action in creating new epochs: the unique casts its shadow over all that has yet to be. Saint-Exupéry's preference for the latter was entirely ethical, not aesthetic, but his continued insistence on a mythic code within the story's aesthetic exigencies disrupted his work in both dimensions. He had found the right service, but not the right god.

I shall argue that each novel reflects in its own way Saint-Exupéry's ingenious—and probably anguished—efforts to resolve the impasses described above so as to achieve a practical validity, to touch life directly. The author's principle concern that his books' tensions be *real*, that their order be *dutiful*, may explain why so much scholarly criticism of his labors is steeped in biographical data. The fundamental issue here, however, is not what Saint-Exupéry was doing as he wrote a particular book, but whether any literary sequence of events can validate a program for living life. We must now briefly consider this issue, lest we flaw Saint-Exupéry for failing to do what none of us could do—what no one has ever done. Is the literary medium, perhaps, dangerously inept as a test of truth? Do not all serious writers inevitably end up trying to live their books rather than recording their lives? Does authorship, as Saint-Exupéry practiced it, represent a responsible and successful integration of active and contemplative existence, or is it instead an artificial integration sought as a *pis aller* when the real thing cannot be achieved?

III.

Vast as these questions are, many authors rest safely beyond their scope. Not every writer cares that story-writing may well be divided from practical philosophy by unbridgeable schism. Saint-Exupéry plainly belongs to those who do care, both because his philosophy itself would preclude idle fantasizing and also because his narrative efforts are a persistent struggle to fuse art and life seamlessly. In this struggle, he measured the generic length and breadth of serious literature as few authors ever have. Novels, anecdotes, confessions, revelations, and even fairy tales seem loosely represented by his endeavors, not to mention the non-narrative prose genres of essay, sermon, and editorial (cf. François 189–94). He has been called a poet, besides, and rightly so. Since such virtuosity cannot be the result of an undisciplined passion for literary art in his case, we must assume that he was seeking something in these generic shifts—that his discomfort with each set of conventions resulted from having to work within strictures which would not let him touch life immediately. A realist novel does not package life as a fairy tale does. Saint-Exupéry seems progressively to have recognized the shortcomings of each genre without ever having given up on the possibility of melding life and art together perfectly.

Clearly the escapist/surrealist genres of narrative with which some aspects of Saint-Exupéry's style may be paradoxically identified do *not* reflect any concern for practical consequences. Is the only moral compromise available to the artist, then, that he or she resign any claim whatever to transmitting a valid moral message? This looks much more like complete surrender, as if artists were to be sent out to play harmlessly in a cloistered area otherwise preserved for children and non-violent lunatics. Yet if (as I said earlier, invoking the mighty Solon) a lived life cannot be a living life, what other conclusion may we possibly draw?

To take stock of story-telling's practical capabilities would be highly useful at this point. Aristotle says that every dramatic representation of life must have a beginning, middle, and end—a rather facile remark unless we consider the three qualities as one: coherence. Every good story should be, in some sense, self-contained, the record of a significant or poignant event which includes causes, complications, and the cathartic clash of all those pressures built up within the closed system. It is a kind of laboratory experiment, this story, allowing minimal contamination from the outside (no deus ex machina, please) and revealing something new—some "truth"about the chemicals of its brew which one would not have foreseen in pondering them separately. Yet a change *is* expected: otherwise there would be no experiment. In the same way, a story is expected to end up at a point quite different from where it began. A problem is essential—much more so than the resolution, in fact; for problems imply resolution, however disappointing or devastating, but no moral insight can emerge before a crisis has occurred. One does not throw water and sand into a test tube: one selects the rare red dust and the liquid that fumes and reeks.

Thus a major practical concern about stories arises immediately: the "problem of the problem." If stories vitally depend upon imbalance, volatility, incompatibility, and crisis, then they may hardly be expected to create a formula for the good life. Every major religion and "wisdom" tradition equates a virtuous existence with inner peace. Plato's Socrates has achieved such a level of beatitude that he can discuss philosophy over a cup of hemlock. The "story" of Socrates, though, draws our attention away from his teaching. It seduces us with the drama of his confronting the city's old guard so that we cease to contemplate the ideal city without drama—the utopia of the fully harmonized republic. Not surprisingly, poets are among those whom Socrates would banish from his perfect state (and the blacklisted poets are clearly Homeric crafters of fiction, not wholesome lyricists). He thus inaugurates two millennia (and counting) of literary critics worried by the effect of story-telling upon public morals. The list includes Dante, whose Paolo and Francesca are perusing the tale of

Lancelot and Guenivere when they begin to read themselves into the lead roles; Cervantes, whose immortal knight of La Mancha works his brains loose following the intricate weave of chivalric epic; and Walter Scott, whose Waverly attributes his flighty spirit to a misspent youth of poring over fictions. Even the unflappable Immanuel Kant warns us that "romance-reading . . . makes ill-focused attention habitual" (*Romanlesen . . . die Zerstreuung habituell macht* [208]).

Hence a story which has ambitions of having practical worth—of teaching good lessons—faces the paradox of luring readers into an artificially tense, imbalanced, unenlightened universe in order to warn them of that universe's corruption. The paradox may be resolved in only a very few ways. The emphasis of the story might rest upon the serene sage's ability to hold himself aloof from the slings and arrows of outrageous fortune. It might become the sort of anecdote in which oral traditions abound: e.g., a witless sadist twists the young (but already stoical) Epictetus's leg as the boy cries, "You're going to break it," does indeed shatter the limb, and is lectured by his victim, "You see? I told you so." Yet such exempla are more provocative or humorous than aesthetically pleasing. They certainly offer no very complicated plot (which is why they are so easily preserved by word of mouth). One might as well build the story of Socrates around his asking the executioner for a clean cup. The protagonist's refusal to register tension goes far toward releasing the reader from narrative pressures—and so, in effect, undermines the story.

A story may also simply decline to resolve its pressures, to bring its complications to an Aristotelian end: i.e., its moral lesson may be that the world is insolubly corrupt. It thus liberates itself from the contradiction of tacking a happy ending onto sad circumstances, as if complete and steady immersion in crises might purge one of misery through overdose (an attitude especially apparent in Hellenistic romance and TV soap operas). Yet the story thus liberated no longer satisfies Aristotle's formula, and it often frustrates readers on a massive scale—which says much for Aristotle's common sense, perhaps. Chekhov's "Lady with the Pet Dog" leaves two very vulnerable characters involved in an adulterous affair which they naively hope to render open and respectable as the curtain falls upon their latest clandestine rendezvous. Their final thoughts are entirely deluded: they will never attain a comfortable happiness in the society of their day.

Chekhov's conscience is clear. He has left his universe in crisis, even though his characters are convinced (like would-be authors) that their life's whole will eventually unite all of its most elementary motive forces.

Postmodern metafiction—the attempted story which becomes a labyrinthine corridor of possible beginnings, middles, and ends—might be said to seek a similar absolution. The author's ultimate failure to produce a story is proof of his or her moral earnestness and honesty. If these virtues sound like the very ones most prized and sought by Saint-Exupéry in his writing, perhaps one could do worse than to view his corpus collectively as an unintended work of metafiction. To a degree, such is my own position.

Obviously, the author need neither endorse the frenetic responses to living exhibited by his or her characters nor decline to impose a clear ending on their desperate struggles. The verdict might be, "Don't do this. Go, and sin no more." The story would become a negative example, a study in how *not* to live. Dante's *Inferno* is the preeminent illustration here: never have so many instances of doing things the wrong way been collected into a single work. With slight modification, though, the bad example might be transformed into a flawed but promising one (the idea behind Purgatory, at least for Dante). That is to say, the story might trace how a benighted but open-minded spiritual pilgrim ascends painfully to enlightenment by toiling in a fallen world. While we would not want to replicate the protagonist's agonies, his or her ability to profit from error would highly be commendable. Twentieth century novelist François Mauriac's characters spring to mind.

Yet if the kind of work described in the previous paragraph does not overtly contradict itself, its immunity to deconstruction must remain dubious. Both scenarios—"don't do this" and "behold how bad things may turn to good"—strongly imply that the wrong way serves as a supplement in defining the right way. They raise the question, could goodness be defined at all without the contrasting help of bad examples? But if the understanding of goodness is thus dependent upon badness, then badness is not really bad, since it assists in creating knowledge of goodness, and the dichotomy between the two is at best spurious, at worst hopelessly deceptive and confusing. . . . Of course, if the distinctive quality of goodness turns out to be spurious, then badness's claim to doing some good dissolves, and it reverts to its old smell and shape!

Playfulness aside (and, at the risk of seeming humorless, I must say that deconstruction's playfulness can become more self-anni-hilating than the antinomies of the texts it plays with), Dante and his inheritors really do have something of the schizoid about them. Dante's observations of sinners in Hell are far more interesting than Heaven's light-and-fireworks displays, nor does his implicit message that one must walk the straight-and-narrow looking only up and down entirely jibe with his own journey's many horizontal di-gressions. (What accommodating geometry a spiral turns out to have!) The Ulysses of Canto 26 actually reaches Purgatory by lateral travel, though he is quickly, permanently ejected; and his words so enthrall the listening Dante and Virgil that the canto ends when he stops speaking accorded to no other sinner's confidences.

Milton had much the same trouble with God and Satan. God and the Son need a formidable adversary to fight if they are to achieve epic stature; and Satan, like Virgil's Turnus, very nearly steals the show. Perhaps Milton's most vulnerable point, however, is Eve. She is *created* coy and hard-to-get: Adam has to chase her down. "Nature herself, though pure of sinful thought,/Wrought in her so, that seeing me, she turned" (8.506–507). The "though" reveals the poet's own discomfort with his vision of pristine humanity. What is Eve running from in a sinless world—or, in this sinless world, does Adam already require evasion in what he desires to keep the desire alive?

There remains the possibility of an "artificial tension": i.e., of a narrative suspense which would vanish as soon as the reader grasped the story's broader frame of reference. Anxiety is transformed into comedy by "springing" a broader framework upon the audience. This occurs most patently in genres involving physical humor, such as slapstick. When a keenly alert businessman impeccably dressed in a three-piece suit slips on a banana peel, the fictive universe changes. Even if this figure were to be kicked and robbed in the next sequence as he flounders on the sidewalk, the audience would not feel his bruises in the same way: from now on, no situation, however serious, will be taken quite seriously.

At a more ethically ambitious level—and this discussion is all about art and ethics—the broader framework is provided by allegory.

Dante's *Divine Comedy*, of course, is comic in just this way: it dispels tension by inviting us to consider not just that there is more to reality than the narrow vision of businessmen can detect, but that the broader reality—true reality—has an intricate and benign order. No problem is *really* a problem, at least if we are worried over how the world may abuse us once we have decided not to abuse the world. For the world is in God's hands: its messes will be cleaned up somehow, someday—they are indeed being cleaned up before our unseeing eyes. If the broader framework brings bad news for those who are Inferno-bound, it is precisely because they have made the mess and are destined for the bucket. They are the tension which the good story finally eliminates. They are not the audience for whom the morally conscious writer writes (except, of course, by way of exhorting them to begin the cleanup themselves).

In a significant sense, the allegorical worldview of Christian authors is a feature of literate-analytical thinking. It requires that the individual days and crises of our lives be considered as phenomena arranged categorically under types—i.e., through speciation. Despite the eloquent insistence of scholars like Northrop Frye that science has been the undoing of metaphorical thinking, the two are in fact opposite sides of the same coin (an insight highly accessible through deconstruction). Clearly Homer's oral-traditional audience would never have thought to interpret his adventures and gods as representations of forces within the human psyche. Yet Homer's fully literate imitator Virgil seems to understand the Olympians in precisely this manner. Small wonder if Christian literati found in the Roman author a prophet of their truths: they, too, were engaged in the delicate operation of refining *merely* historical sequences into prototypes for human behavior of all times. When Paul writes that Sarah and Hagar allegorize the believer's relationship to the old law and the new (*Galatians* 4:24–25), he is undertaking the same kind of literary endeavor as Virgil does when he has his hero reject Dido's torrid affection for Jupiter's appeal to duty.

Allegory is post-tragic, in the same way and for the same reasons that Christianity and literate culture generally are post-tragic. The broader framework of categories, species, and logical systems is now so thorough that the individual protagonist cannot possibly find himself braving the lonely chaos of the mythic hero. At the same time, the anagogical network which lifts this new protagonist's puny endeavors to a higher plateau allows for self-realization in a higher purpose. The system is not Big Brother: it is the Platonic sunlight from whose benign warmth one's soul had been temporarily obstructed.

As soon as Western civilization loses its confidence that the system is based in people's hearts, of course, we enter the post-allegorical age of postmodernism—which leads we know not where; but the literary labyrinths beloved of Borges and Robbe-Grillet bear more than a passing resemblance to caves of old. In the meantime, the pseudo-tension of such modern allegorists as Charles Williams, C. S. Lewis, and J. R. R. Tolkien seems to impress many readers as suitable fare for children, much as the Victorians relegated myths of bygone ages to the nursery. Allegory may escape deconstruction, at least if its abstract coordinates are adequately projected beyond the material realm (otherwise we chase our tails); but perhaps a genre which absolves us from tension is simply too good to be true in a time when the world has never been so tense.

One can at least understand why an author as dedicated as Saint-Exupéry was to expressing a credible, feasible spirituality would look elsewhere. Not surprisingly, the schema toward which he gravitated has attracted other modernists, from Camus to Garcia-Marquez: myth, that child of the pre-literate, pre-scientific mind—and now of the post-scientific world, wherein people are again adrift in chaos, only chained to a technology which makes their drift more incalculable than ever before. Mythic problem and tension are illusory inasmuch as the story's dénouement is never in any real doubt. This is so simply because the story has grown to be universally known throughout its culture, not because it enjoys any allegorical reference to patterns embedded in human nature. Freud would have disagreed, of course; but then, as has been said already, literate cultures have a habit of foisting allegorical meanings upon ancient myths. Certainly Sophocles's original listeners must have found neither much suspense nor many insights about family structure in *Oedipus the King*. Their catharsis flowed from their utter foreknowledge. The effect must have been similar to our watching old clips of the space shuttle *Challenger* about to lift off.

For the mythic hero is tragic: he or she sallies forth amid

appalling ignorance, confusion, and fear to suffer a fate which none of us can share and make lighter. We share it now in retrospect, too late, and vicariously, more convinced than ever that we would *not* accompany that valorous figure if given a second chance to do so. The hero helps us put life in order but has not survived to draw some sense of order, in return, from the gratitude paid to his sacrifice. And, in any case, mythic heroes do not dare the gods in a communal spirit of sacrifice: they do it to find out if they themselves are really less than gods.

Allegory leads upward, craning its neck at a paradigm: myth leads downward, its protagonists throwing their long shadows over subsequent generations of punier beings. In allegory, the sense of things rests in a pre-established, well-recognized system—almost necessarily an *a priori* system, since broad points of reference embedded in circumstance rather than essential human nature can hardly be very broad at all. The story's action gradually settles into the silent, amused creator's hands who awaits it patiently, all but invisibly, in the distant background. In myth, no clear sense of things pre-dates the story. The story itself—the trail-blazing example of the hero who flings his life into the void—becomes one of reality's parameters. Naturally, there are uncomprehended powers within the void which cause the hero's battle-scarred body to fall left instead of right; but, to the extent that these powers become slightly comprehended in the process, the hero has created their perceptible form in presenting them with an adversary, a target.

Derrida's deconstructing of Lévi-Strauss notwithstanding, the latter is sometimes quite close to the former in describing the vital role of contradiction in myth. Perhaps what so antagonizes deconstructionists about Lévi-Strauss, in fact, is that his account of myth as negotiated contradiction lifts mythic matter above the contradictory. That is to say, myth is a formal concession to the truth of logical nonsense—to the irrepressible corrosive forces constantly at work between nature and culture. If Lévi-Strauss tends to overdramatize the process's give-and-take (all of Derrida's favorite subjects have a tendency to romantic polarization) or to invoke rationalism with his formulas, he nevertheless ultimately grasps that the wrestling match is more dance than war: human beings would be fatally mutilated if deprived either of their natural spontaneity or of their cultural conditioning. The two sides must work together, even though their collaboration produces toxic waste on the fringes of society.

Such is *not* the mythic message which Saint-Exupéry wished to broadcast. For reasons which I shall explore in the next section, his message was indeed entirely incongruous with the mythic schema, being much more properly allegorical; yet he believed in no abstract system of values which might have anchored an allegory, and so—to "keep the faith"—sought out another approach. The contradiction here turns out to be real and profound. It succeeded in sabotaging every novel he ever wrote as a work of moral instruction, and was the originary cause of all those other, more observable contradictions that came and went.

IV.

With the reader's indulgence, I shall approach the subject of myth somewhat more circumspectly than I did above, where it was ushered in under the coattails of various genres as an all but suspenseless quasi-ritual. That vantage will remain useful; yet the reasons why Saint-Exupéry was drawn to myth and why, despite its attraction for him, it ultimately proved incompatible with his purpose cannot be appreciated without a broader critical foundation. Allow me, then, to discuss myth not just as a sequence of events, but also as metaphor.

Tropological language enjoyed an increasing importance in Saint-Exupéry's corpus as a means of transcending linear time and immediate reality: i.e., as a means of dispelling tension, or at least the explicit tension of the narrative. The term "metaphor" is broadly intended in this study as the juxtaposition of an objectively based image with a subjectively created image. While the juxtaposition is most often motivated by a single emphasized similarity between the two terms, the explicit common ground should never be regarded as precluding further, more implicit points of intersection. Otherwise, a metaphor would be a mere riddle, its established correspondence shocking or amusing its readers without enticing them to delve more deeply for obscurer meanings.

From this perspective, symbolism and allegory may be considered to elicit metaphorical thinking, though they make special use of it. The symbol, as its name declares literally, "throws together" several highly abstract concepts into a single concrete one. (The same word in ancient Greek denotes a legal contract, where numerous items are agreed upon.) Allegory projects metaphor through time, demanding that the reader view each event, not only as a more general truth beneath (or above) the particular narrative surface, but also as vitally linked at all levels to other events in the temporal chain. In metaphor, things are always more than they appear to be.

The three concepts above share what Ricardou calls polyvalence (and what I would prefer to call "multivalence" or "polysemy"): i.e., the original object or event in all three potentially signifies several objects or ideas at once, though some are more prominent and credible than others within the literary context. (Even when an allegory cannot sustain more than a single ulterior level of meaning, by the way, an indeterminacy surrounds the choice of exactly which events may properly be projected onto the deeper level.) Ricardou himself does not believe that all such tropes are polyvalent. In fact, he claims that "the metaphorical relationship is fundamentally triangular: it comprises the two elements brought into accord and the point where their rapport is effected" (200). This point of rapport occurs at a precise moment in the narrative, apparently, rendering the metaphor's single meaning dependent upon the narrative's pre-dominant mood at that moment. So structured a view of tropology leads Ricardou to find profound flaws in *Vol de Nuit*: these I shall discuss later on.

The study of tropes was once severely squeezed by structuralist cultivation of a mathematical rigor. A metaphor confined to a single sense based upon its context—which cannot, for instance, be uplifting if the narrative registers despair—would be unjustly subordinated to the narrative and would become, instead, the answer to a scholar's riddle. Later critics of the so-called reader-response school have noticed that the trope's purely structural properties, though not irrelevant, do not dictate its character. Writes Wolfgang Iser, referring to metaphorical language,

> The split signifier turns into play, swinging to and fro between its code-governed determinacy and a signified to be brought forth. . . . The signifier appears to coincide with what it generates, yet the product emerging from the free-floating implications also remains different from the signifier. (249)

Iser's own metaphor, which suggests a buoy (or perhaps a harbor mine) whose cable has become unmoored, implies some of the dangers of conceding full authority to subjective readings of a text. While not entirely unlicensed, either, extremely subjective interpretations must surely yield in priority to those which have more objective grounding in the text's imagery or in its author's culture. Yet the most distinctive trait of the indefinite aesthetic experience remains the complete range of reactions, gradually merging into subjectivity, which it calls forth. It may particularly justify one or two meanings, but it always slightly evades these meanings, as well.

The indefinite experience, then, which includes tropology, should not be considered infinite, in that it requires limitation precisely to create a domain of free imaginative play. Metaphor begins with clear forms between which various connections are sought. The audience only persists in finding resemblances as long as it senses a convergence upon the metaphor's totality, the heart of hearts—but that point of convergence is never reached, of course. Hence my choice of the word "indefinite": such art approaches its limits without ever quite meeting them. Verlaine was so confident of poetry's indefinite nature that, in his "Art Poétique," he incited poets everywhere to strive after "rien que la nuance!" A poet may well have one level of equation most prominently on his or her mind, but the poet's genius creates— perhaps unintentionally—a resonanting corridor instead of a bland doorway. Even Aristotle, the man who wrote the book on dramatic plot and who became the tutelary spirit of Russian formalism, knew that only a persuasive context can reduce the trope to a single meaning (cf. *Rhetoric* 1.1.14). To that extent, then, art *is* useless, just as open-ended speculation is useless to a candidate who wants the audience's vote.

Thus metaphor means more than we can ever say, but not whatever we may say. Poet Pierre Reverdy, a contemporary of Saint-Exupéry's, proposes the following formula, itself highly poetic: "the imagination [of the poet] is dilated to the infinite, and real motions reduced and compressed into the bordered indefinite" (255). Similarly, René Ménard, a poet of the years following World War II, concludes his chapter on poetic images by observing that metaphors are "almost always concrete. The correspondence is established between things created, and the more forceful to the extent that these things are of a natural order" (98)—natural because they will then be familiar to all of the audience. So dynamically structured are the images of a Baudelaire or a Rimbaud that they may even be translated from their original language with surprisingly little loss of power, a quality which Lévi-Strauss (that great adversary of deconstruction) attributes to folk narrative but perhaps too summarily denies to poetry (85–86).

Ménard borrowed a metaphor from Breton to emphasize the poetic image's playful, stimulating elusiveness within real limits: "I present to myself a secondary reality, where 'dew' and 'cat's head' enjoy a kinship, where my spirit wanders around this association and implicitly transposes its requirements into a world different from that which I have before my eyes" (95). In the ensuing discussion, Ménard anticipates the objection that he is describing an entirely subjective encounter with the text, and parries it with a rather abstruse belief in the universal presence of something like psychological archetypes. Ménard's remark does what deconstruction has always disdained to do: it underscores the relationship between the metaphor's terms, as opposed to regarding metaphor as the sum of its terms. Reverdy anticipated this emphasis when he wrote two decades earlier, "Words . . . when isolated, support objects; in a current of sentences they dematerialize and become conductors of ideas, [and] what they represent in their own right is effaced in favor of what coalesces from the movement of the combinations in which they are bound" (154). Tobin Siebers's "Case Against Linguistic Ethics" (chapter 3 of his recent book), with a polite bow to Schank and Abelson, specifically challenges deconstruction for slighting verbal collaboration, though he views verbal clusters as governed more by extrinsic (social) than intrinsic (archetypal) factors. "Both literary and ethical notions of character," he writes, "rely on a dense social context that is responsible for their applications and that is influenced in turn by those applications" (34).

Without dabbling in literary theory, Saint-Exupéry had apparently decided for himself that the trope cannot be restricted to any single purpose within its context. In a preface to Anne Morrow Lindbergh's *Le Vent Se Lève*, he muses,

Consider the poetic image. Its value. . . does not reside in either of the two elements which one is associating or comparing, but in the type of *liaison* which it specifies, in the particular internal attitude which a certain structure imposes upon us. The image is an act which constrains the reader without his knowledge. It does not touch the reader: it surrounds him in an arch.[5] (*SV* 249–50)

If what the poet specifies is a *liaison* (lit. "tie"), and if the particular is as general as an attitude, then the reader's imagination is presented with a dynamic model capable of achieving balance in innumerable living applications. Individual words ("the dry word outside of the poem" [*Citadelle* 709][6]) have little to do with such dynamism. Just as a bridge means little in an allegory unless it spans a dangerous chasm and someone wishes to cross it, so the relationship established between the words gives the poem its indefinite allure—a relationship capable of generating an entire universe, Saint-Exupéry would add in *Carnets* (150). "For if everyone has spoken of stars and springs and mountains, no one has told you to ascend the mountain to drink the pure milk of the stars from its springs" (*Citadelle* 705).[7] Even the tritest vocabulary, then, can stir the reader's imagination when it collaborates in a rare image. Saint-Exupéry precedes the remark cited above from the Lindbergh preface with a celebration of Baudelaire's "Chant d'automne" as a masterful imagistic network. "Say that I give you these words like so many pieces: courtyard, pavement, wood, and echo. Now go and make something of them. . . . Yet Baudelaire, using this same verbal material, will show you that he knows how to construct a beautiful image" (*SV* 248).[8]

The author may be seen practicing his art of poetry in chapter 203 of *Citadelle* (948—a passage reproduced by François, who sees a link with the doctrines of surrealism). The monarch narrator, conceiving of an epic adventure with Homeric echoes, observes, "And if I wish to convey to you a certain nocturnal carnage by which, pouncing upon him silently in the elastic sand, I drowned my enemy in his sleep, I will bind one word to another, saying, for example, 'sabre of snow' in order to take in my snare an informulable gentleness, and neither snow nor sabres alone can account for the image's effect."[9] The immediate narrative context of the deed—a scene of grim carnage—is obviously at odds with the evocation of a snow-like peace and purity, much as Fabien's predicament in *Vol de Nuit* has a mortal tension alien to the onlooking stars. Is the snow's discreet suppression of footfalls, then, its one relevant quality here? But the desert sand has the same quality to an even greater degree. Saint-Exupéry, through his philosopher-king, can only be trying to tease our minds into discovering some relevance, not just for the snow's peace (which the presence of death might explain ironically), but for its purity, as well.

So a distinction clearly exists between the definite art of problem, tension, and release and the indefinite art of nuanced evasion. The former may be deconstructed: its closure necessarily implies a judgment of how reality works, and that judgment would become invalid if it were shown to rest on contradictory assumptions. The latter, however, does not reach closure and, at most, insists only upon a range of judgments consistent with a created mood. Its ongoing quest of the asymptote is hardly a slight-of-hand postponement of the supplement, exactly because the whole endeavor is so evidently a quest. For the deconstructionist to highlight incoherencies in such metaphorical language, he or she must be reading that language in a perversely, restrictively structuralist sense.

No doubt, Saint-Exupéry sensed at some level that he could retreat into metaphor and find refuge from the impasses which frustrated his moral formulations. Unfortunately for him, the retreat demands a relinquishing precisely of those narrative moralizing powers which drive toward closure. Hence he would naturally, if subconsciously, have explored a sort of middle ground, a more "poetic" or indefinite narrative which nonetheless presents a clear central sequence of events.

Not that Saint-Exupéry's poetic side was only a cover-up of dimly perceived inconsistencies—not at all! The overt importance of multivalence to his practical philosophy can scarcely be overstated. Just as a star (to use that example so odious to Ricardou) can represent eternal serenity even in situations where it represents a hopeless distance from that serenity, as well, so life is composed of situations whose unique quality demands careful attention, yet whose general structure nevertheless conforms to a recurrent pattern. A coherent life is always partially—but never completely—ritual. It requires an imaginative transformation of routine, because the daily grind seldom brings one to meaningful closure. Yet to live only in closure is to miss life's poetry, subtlety, and poignancy: it is to refuse any sensitive response to the day's specific challenges, just as the falsely pious believer mumbles a liturgy without reflecting upon its words.

Of course, people tend to ignore one level of living and concentrate upon the other. To the existentialist, everything is unique: to the mystic, nothing is. In this regard, at least, Saint-Exupéry certainly belongs among the latter . . . somewhat. He was convinced that though the specific meaning of what we do changes daily, the general sense of our efforts *may* remain immutable, not only throughout our individual lives, but throughout our collective endeavor as a culture. The struggle to impose ritual, though, is indeed a battle, because the ritual (for Saint-Exupéry) has no basis in reality. Mysticism is not a door to higher reality, but a duty in a world whose only ultimate reality is chaotic. One must strive to recognize that change makes sense in the context of grand purpose—but one must keep changing to give that purpose its justifying sense of sameness.

There is a kind of faith in this circular reverence for order; there is at least a very reluctant faithlessness. Such was the faith, or faithlessness, which Saint-Exupéry possessed. His uncompromising engagement of life did not shy away from apparent incoherence. The pattern which had all but disappeared could be rediscovered with determined and imaginative thought, and would ever after be the more securely implanted in life for having been so painfully sought on critical occasions. Action would produce substance for meditation, and meditation would confirm the context for further action.

At this point, we find ourselves once again plunged into allegory and myth. Both schemata are narrative *and* tropological, definite *and* indefinite: they offer a sequence of related events, or plot, and also a powerful suggestion that these events refer to others at a very distant remove. Now, the indefinite operation of allegory is essentially comparative, while that of myth is counter-comparative—not contrasting (which implies comparison), but anti-analytic. The allegory invites us to see apparently isolated and quotidian events as participants in an inclusive archetype. It gives us a mold, a skeleton. The myth, if properly understood, sits beyond the limit of possible comparison. It convinces us to relinquish our puzzling over the universe in our vain hope of manipulating it. Frye hints at this distinction with his rather Arcadian metaphorical phase of culture, where "there is relatively little emphasis on a clear separation between subject and object: the emphasis falls rather on a feeling that subject and object are linked by a common power or energy" (6). To blend object and meaning together in sweeping synthesis not only reflects oral thinking, but also helps to explain why such thinking creates mysteries and "agonistically toned" polarities (cf. Ong 43–45). Only when objects may be separated from their meanings can we find sameness in difference and difference in sameness.

There will never be another Gilgamesh, Herakles, or Cú Chulainn—and these are all mere mortals! More often than not, mythic traditions concern gods, whose capricious yet highly consequential behavior is obviously beyond the scope of ordinary human beings. Our literate society can scarcely grasp why anyone would worship divines whose conduct not only cannot be replicated, but *should* not be. The oral-traditional universe is multiply schizophrenic, with humanity cast in the role of the weakest personality. Though synthetic thinking has brought a grand cyclicity to things, the cycles harmonize only because their parameters are enforced with inscrutable, uncompromising rigor. There are places one just does not go, names one just does not say, calamities one just does not question. Mythopoeic cultures accept their humble lot in the cosmos without analyzing it. If Lévi-Strauss has erred in finding their tales essentially polarized, it is only insofar as he sees in traditional narrative an attempt to tame contradiction, the story-tellers vainly striving to work out impasse through repeated telling. Just as probably, mythic stories are *enhancing* the gap between how the universe runs and how people must live within its running. Did the Greeks set their heroes in the stars in order to be close to them and "hold them up" as models—or, instead, to emphasize their awe-inspiring aloofness from mortal affairs?

Tropology draws the mythopoeic audience not more deeply into the mind of God, but more resignedly into their own loop of pain and death. The near end of the narrative strand is not twined into their heart-strings, but knotted around their necks. If you can hear about the labors of Herakles and say, "Yes, that's just what happened to me today," then you are either an arrogant fool or a demigod. The proper response is, "Not much labor in my day, after all. If I seem to bear a heavy burden, it's only because my shoulders are so weak."

Unlike René Ménard, Saint-Exupéry possessed no rational paradigm or metaphysical belief upon which to found anything like an archetype. Allegory, as a trope, was therefore closed to him: for if the only broader context for events is cultural—and hence circumstantial—then the context breaks down when culture breaks down. Such a decay was well under way in the West during his lifetime, and it severely afflicted him, sometimes plunging him into what we would now call severe depression. There remained, however, the heroic option of creating a new culture—of setting into motion a series of mythic acts that might define the limits of future endeavor. Saint-Exupéry's novels thus became an exercise in mythopoeia, as he himself recognized early on. "I do not admire men for serving the postal line," he wrote in defense of his pilot-heroes, "but I favor the myth of the postal line because it forms such men" (*Carnets* 51);[10] and the quasi-mysticism of all his work would probe for that "certain something, as informulable, elementary, and universal as a myth" (*Confluences* 196).[11]

A mythic act is not repeatable (though, in oral cultures, it is undeliberately and incessantly crossbred with other acts through myriad tellings). Nevertheless, it may invite a kind of emulation. It offers comfort in its very demonstration that the worst has been exposed, that the unknown has been robbed of terror. Those who come after, then, while they cannot achieve heroic stature, may certainly follow in the hero's footsteps. In this sense, myth may simulate allegory as the essential story of life, or of one of life's most crucial rites. The important thing is to convert infidels to the cult. The particular events of each day will reenact the mythic sequence allegorically only if particular performers are given the script and are sufficiently excited by it to learn their parts.

For Saint-Exupéry, myth represented an attractive compromise between the opposing realist and romantic tendencies of his work. Since the mythic sequence happens one time only at the beginning of a cosmos or culture, its lawgiving conquest of chaos can never again be equaled: it remains one of the original wonders of the world, and the mythic hero will forever be as remote from ordinary mortal imitators as the Byronic outcast. On the other hand, the myth endures as a cosmic limit. All who live after the hero will honor him and, in a weak sense, mimic him by dwelling where his huge arm cleared a space. If the hero is tragically alone, his audience is comically raised and united in his cult—and myth, we must remember, always implies a receptive posterity as well as a primeval burst of creation.

Of course, cults are viewed with suspicion in our free (and still not entirely post-rational) society. Myth fairly shares in that suspicion. Edward Slotkin chose the word "myth" to convey his thesis that the United States has thrived on artificial adversaries who can be vigorously, unconditionally combatted (a Lévi-Staussian proposal if there ever was one). Though he seldom wrote explicitly of myth except in his private notes, Saint-Exupéry was charged with encouraging this same variety of fanaticism and social hysteria in the fifties, when the brilliance of his apotheosis was beginning to wear off in France. His irrepressible belief in a reality waiting beyond science—his facility for finding wind, sand, and stars in the squalor of gears, grease, and exhaust—staggers most postmodern imaginations. Its naïveté seems a bit appalling. Yet as bigoted or fanatical as the myth-maker may potentially be, he or she can also be seen as the giver of life. Is such naïveté more appalling than our own bemused paralysis of belief? Saint-Exupéry's words, "One dies only for that by which one can live" (*PG* 380),[12] have been said by others, but they have not been said much lately.

What one can ultimately live by, though, is what gives breathing room to one's purest feelings while doing minimal violence to one's reason. A myth may do this for an oral-traditional culture whose members are still insulated both from the larger world around them and from the world of free will within them; but we postmoderns are too often bombarded with multicultural dissonance to place such hope in a purely circumstantial set of references. We expect the hero, if he or she is a true prophet, to show us how to live by example—to wade through our morass of circumstantially based customs with a step that all onlookers can conscientiously approve (the celebrated "role model"). This the mythic hero cannot do. "He conquers and brings order to a domain of nascent yet frail civilization," as Caillois naively says (xii); but he cannot be called *morally* admirable in doing so, since the law would have pre-existed him if he could be judged under its strictures, thus deflating his mythic stature. As an arbitrary lawgiver, he is necessarily anything but an exemplar of the law-abiding spirit. The act of imposing rule upon chaos reveals in him a certain whimsical, self-willed energy which he shares with chaos. Were he not part wild himself, he would never have conceived and executed the project of taming the wilderness: only a character who cannot ultimately be assimilated into culture can successfully vie with nature on culture's behalf.

James Redfield's formulation of the Homeric hero's fundamental inconsistencies is apt in this context. "The community is secured by combat, which is the negation of community; this generates a contradiction in the warrior's role . . . [since he] can protect the human world against force only because he himself is willing to use and suffer force. . . . The warrior stands on the frontier between culture and nature" (101). So with virtually any great mythic hero: he is both the champion and the victim of order. The Herakles and the Oedipus who rid the community of anti-social monsters are themselves driven from the community for anti-social behavior.

The Exupérian hero has something of Redfield's Achilles in him. A vanquisher of thunder-gods and wind-dragons, he cannot find contentment in his evening paper, pipe, and bedroom slippers. Of course, he must be given credit for a willingness to lay down his life in the selfless performance of a mission. One must wonder, however, whether the sacrifice is not an afterthought—whether the service of community and ideals is not simply a license to kill, in much the same way that Don Quixote needed a lady (any lady would do) at whose feet he might lay his conquests. Why does Saint-Exupéry not offer us so much as a single example of a pilot successfully reintegrated into one of those villages over which he flies so patronizingly? How may a healthy society be constructed of people who display an incorrigible need to run away from society and die saving it from the nearest enemy?

Perhaps, then, Saint-Exupéry's heroes are nothing more than romantic loners who do not know—or have not admitted—the full extent of their loneliness. Their ignorance is scarcely an answer to the genuinely opposing strains of their world. In fact, such ignorance may be little more than an artistic posture—a retreat from the third into the first person. Imagine Achilles telling his own story. He *does* frequently tell bits of it—to Thetis, to Agamemnon's envoys—so we know that his version would have cast him as a humble victim of circumstance and politics. He hugely underrates the mythic proportions of his role, so that, in a way which he never begins to suspect, his self-styled victimhood is quite real. As a half-god, he has no place in human government and polite society; and whereas he proves very useful in war to the community, his utility ends with the fighting. Yet he attributes his loneliness to a stolen concubine, a slain friend, a forsaken father . . . he hasn't added it all up.

In the same way, the pilot-hero, speaking in the "I," attributes his hardships to the terrain, the elements, the flawed technology. He fails to comprehend that, were he to master and perfect all of these by magic, he would still be a misfit, a wanderer perpetually shying away from cosmos and gravitating toward the fringe where it crumbles into chaos. A portrait of him painted from any vantage within the cosmos would reveal him balancing over the abyss, but his self-portrait always shows the cosmos at his back and to his side. Humanity sees in him a limit, but he is wholly incapable of perceiving the boundary he stands upon.

Thus the problems of narrative voice and self-induced ecstasy which I discussed in section two reappear when we approach Saint-Exupéry's work tropologically. From this approach, one may more easily discern that the problem lies in mythicizing that which cannot be myth. The isolation of Achilles is indeed tragic, is consistently tragic, and is intended by Homer to be tragic. The young warrior's misreading of his own tragedy is irrelevant, except to the extent that it enhances the effect.

The pilot-hero's isolation, though, is hopelessly vexed. It is certainly not intended to be tragic, and Saint-Exupéry struggled throughout his writing career to redeem it from tragedy. A "meta-myth" about a charismatic figure who seeks to guarantee humanity against its own nature by sacrificing himself would be another matter. Such a hero could be somewhat tragic in the sense of Shakespeare's Brutus or Conrad's Lord Jim, that "incurable romantic"—or even Mahatma Gandhi—but he could not be mythic, and so not classically tragic. François considers Saint-Exupéry's heroes non-mythic precisely because of their pseudo-tragic character. "They create their own destiny less than that of their species," he rightly observes. "And that again distances them from the tragic in myth"

(153-54). I would add that the destiny they "create for their species" is, in fact, nothing very new. The pilot-hero perishes, not in extending the boundaries of cosmos, but in attempting to extend boundaries which are immovably fixed. He falls victim not to an all-but-irresistible natural environment, but to the fully irresistible elements of our human heart. His example is closer to becoming an allegory of an ageless condition than a new wonder of the world.

Major aptly refers to Mircea Eliade in considering the symbolic elevation of Saint-Exupéry's final works, and then summarizes: "A myth such as that concerning God [in *Pilote de Guerre* and *Citadelle*] has no other purpose than to give a dynamic coherence to the totality of existence. It is a myth which is made true through daily experience, and the truth resides not in the myth itself but in what is accomplished through it in man" (187). It is this circularity of formulation—man accepting myth's circumstantial limits because he may create sense out of their arbitrary coherence, myth bestowing coherence because man chooses to accept its limits—which least withstands scrutiny. Saint-Exupéry would eventually find himself trapped in a quasi-mythic cycle without exit, a labyrinth built to wall out the void yet revolving aimlessly around an internal void.

V.

I am not suggesting that Saint-Exupéry lacked an altruistic spirit. The manifest presence of that spirit is exactly what renders his narratives disastrously insoluble. He was not alone among his generation in wanting to offer sacrifice but not being able to find a worthy altar. Major's remarks just above obviously embrace his circular service without criticism. Pierre Reverdy's aphoristic notebook eloquently celebrates the motive power of arbitrary ends: "And if it's necessary that illusion preside over this spiritual thrust which makes us live, who cares that it may be an illusion? Insofar as it favors life, this illusion is truth" (26). Emmanuel Mounier, whose "personalist" philosophy shows a spiritual kinship with (if not a direct influence upon) Saint-Exupéry's, believed that everyone everywhere must take a heroic stand in the unknown. "There is one way out, and only one," wrote Mounier in his manifesto. "That is to confront the event, to invent, and to go ahead—the way which, since the dawn of life, has alone enabled life to cope with crises" (100).

Mounier's terms praise the same active but often lonely dedication to idealism which we find in Saint-Exupéry's work. Moreover, they share a reluctance to identify idealism with tradition. When we reflect upon the unholy alliance between the Church and fascism in Western Europe, we need not be surprised to find Christian tradition suspect. Besides, if allegory works to release tension by dissolving it into universal, eternal patterns, it would scarcely seem to offer a conscientious author the most electrifying literary vehicle for awakening and mobilizing the public in a crisis; and just because human nature causes repetition in human affairs does not mean that people have a moral license to sit idly by while neighbors are murdered. Tension is real in this fallen world. In the fullness of God's truth, it vanishes—but we do not now live in that truth fully, and to pretend otherwise is to parody truth. Camus's Père Paneloux teeters on the edge of such indolent pseudo-mysticism in *La Peste* until he watches a child die. Doctor Rieux perhaps expresses greater piety when he opines, "Since the world's order is ruled by death, perhaps God is more impressed if we disbelieve in him and struggle against death with all our forces, not raising our eyes to the heaven where he sits silently" (1323).

We know from personal notes and private correspondence that Saint-Exupéry admired Christianity (he was quite reticent on religion in public) for its efficacy during the Middle Ages in creating a faithful, durable, energetic person. "Always the same myth . . . abandon, renounce, suffer, struggle, cross the deserts of thirst, resist the fountains, and I will conduct you to your self's florition" (*Carnets* 44).[13] This is a noble sentiment, and—especially at the present time—a crucial one for preserving the flagging health of Christendom. The modern believer often seems more interested in faith than personal sacrifice. Anyone who had toiled as Saint-Exupéry did to blend thought and act into a single expression would indignantly reject the notion that, although you lied and cheated yesterday and intend to do so tomorrow, you are spiritually saved beyond the possibility of repeal (cf. Major's distinction, borrowed from Francis Jeanson, between *foi-croyance* and *foi-action* [187–88]). The doctrine of grace is too often distorted to shelter half-heartedness, lethargy, and insincerity, if not outright hypocrisy.

It is not my intention to present Saint-Exupéry as a Christian *malgré lui*, as so many of his apologists have done, or to mitigate the weaknesses of an ethical system based on the life of the spirit yet rejecting any spiritual reality. Devaux and Borgal have taken Saint-Exupéry's measure quite well in this regard. Nevertheless, I would contend that he remains an author of the utmost importance for those who believe in a reality beyond the material world. Saint-Exupéry's impasses are extraordinarily instructive. Both his moral and his aesthetic experiment—or, better still, his mythopoeic experiment in which the two realms are uneasily fused—demanded a terminus more rewarding and unifying than he could find in his cultural heritage, search as he might. Surely a man of his ardor and imagination would have found the wholly worthy end of human action in this world if such an end were to be found. The world of spirit owes Saint-Exupéry a great debt of thanks for having struggled in such agonizing futility to dispense with it. In the words of his close friend Georges Pélissier, "Saint-Exupéry himself, though he aspired to serene contemplation throughout his life, always preserved a certain spiritual discomfort" (110).

Thus each of the subsequent chapters addresses a certain aesthetic objective in pursuit of which Saint-Exupéry garbled or canceled out his desired moral message. Impasse is indeed the key to his literary career, just as it is the key to any successful experiment or genuine growth. In Reverdy's poetic prose, "Extending a destiny whose mediocre limits one does not accept is reflected, not in success, but in the much greater number of abortive attempts" (227). For other authors, perhaps, success is as simple as pleasing the public. A fictional work need aspire to do no more than give the reader pleasure—the aesthetic pleasure of an original disarray gradually subsumed under a single purpose. There is nothing particularly cheap about such an accomplishment. Yet Saint-Exupéry was seeking an order of orders. His story would be elevating as well as pleasing: it would be The Story, the grand cycle of life. In aspiring to reach nothing less than perfect enlightenment, he probed farther into the labyrinth by eliminating certain corridors than those whose only ambition has been to walk a dozen steps in darkness. He always accepted defeat as the necessary pre-condition of victory; and he would, I hope, understand my nomination of chapters as the compliment which it is intended to be. To use one of his favorite images, the decaying seed climbs to the sun. Life without setback and failure is not life at all, but the torpor of a sterile seed which will never produce a tree because it can never decay. To make mistakes, on the other hand, is to learn, and to love. Says the philosopher-king of the last, never-completed novel, "There is no love except where choices are irrevocable, for becoming entails being limited" (*Citadelle* 910).[14]

Irrevocable choices and love . . . is this not a true saying? Grace forgives, but it does not forget. What passes for forgiveness among us mortals is often nothing *but* forgetting. Ouellet has suggested that Saint-Exupéry neglects or misunderstands grace more than any other Christian doctrine: "If his philosophy postulates the existence of a spiritual principle in life, it teaches at the same time that man, the sole motive force behind his own ascent, must not count on any supernatural aid in his climb toward God" (22). Indeed, even when his works present Christianity most favorably, they make of it a network of morally indispensable concepts rather than metaphysical truth (cf. Major 176–88). "The truth is inside rather than outside of us," Saint-Exupéry once ruminated in his notes; "God is true, but perhaps created by us" (*Carnets* 34).[15] The vaguely Islamic creed of *Citadelle* which supplants the Christianity of *Pilote de Guerre* is likewise no more than a set of morally convenient concepts.

Yet perhaps we interpret grace too narrowly, as well, in so banishing it from Saint-Exupéry's system; for, as we have seen, he was acutely conscious of the imperfection inherent in all human acts. What he could not countenance was the notion of a faith without practical consequences. Throughout his life, he remained somewhat suspicious of Christianity on this basis—a basis in the frivolity of certain believers, properly speaking, rather than in doctrine. To the religious community, then, Saint-Exupéry's work should be accepted as challenge rather than antagonism. He was quite right, after all: we should expect conviction to inspire acts, just as we should expect a truly thorough act to originate in conviction. In the words of James's epistle, "As the body without the spirit is dead, so faith without works is dead also" (3.26); or in the no less powerful words of *Citadelle*'s philosopher-monarch, "Word and deed are not alternatives, but two aspects of the same God. This is why I call prayer a labor, and why I call labor a meditation" (700).[16]

NOTES

[1] L'arbre n'est point semence, puis tige, puis tronc flexible, puis bois mort. Il ne faut point le diviser pour le connaître. L'arbre, c'est cette puissance qui lentement épouse le ciel.

[2] Si je veux étonner, si je suis vaniteux, si, faute de vie intérieure et d'orgueil, je me juge selon l'effet que je produis, alors j'invente un laborieux petit rébus et je le montre.

[3] Je déteste ces gens qui écrivent pour s'amuser, qui cherchent des effets. Il faut avoir quelque chose à dire.

[4] Il faut me chercher tel que je suis dans ce que j'écris et qui est le résultat scrupuleux et réfléchi de ce que je pense et vois.

[5] Considérez l'image poétique. Sa valeur . . . ne réside dans aucun des deux éléments que l'on associe ou compare, mais dans le type de liaison qu'elle spécifie, dans l'attitude interne particulière qu'une telle structure nous impose. L'image est un acte qui, à son insu, noue le lecteur. On ne touche pas le lecteur: on l'envoûte.

[6] Le mot sec hors du poème.

[7] Car si tous ont parlé des étoiles et de la fontaine et de la montagne, nul ne t'a dit de gravir la montagne pour boire aux fontaines d'étoiles leur lait pur.

[8] Je vous livre en vrac les mots: cour, pavé, bois, et retentir. Faites-moi quelque chose de ça. . . . Cependant Baudelaire, s'il use de cette matière verbale, vous montrera qu'il sait édifier une grande image.

[9] Et si je veux transporter en toi tel carnage nocturne par lequel, fondant sur lui dans le silence, sur un sable élastique, j'ai noyé l'ennemi dans son propre sommeil, je nouerai tel mot à tel autre disant par exemple *sabre de neige* afin de prendre au piège une douceur informulable, et il ne s'agira ni de la neige, ni des sabres.

[10] Je n'admire point les hommes de servir le courrier, mais je tiens au mythe du courrier parce qu'il forme de tels hommes.

[11] Quelque chose d'informulable, d'élémentaire et d'universel comme un mythe.

[12] On meurt pour cela seul dont on peut vivre.

[13] Toujours même mythe . . . Abandonne, renonce, souffre, lutte, franchis les déserts de la soif, refuse les fontaines, et je te conduirai à l'épanouissement de toi-même.

[14] Il n'est d'amour que là où le choix est irrévocable car il importe être limité pour devenir.

[15] [La] vérité [est] en dedans et non en dehors de nous. Dieu est vrai, mais créé peut-être par nous.

[16] Il n'est point langage ou acte mais deux aspects du même Dieu. C'est pourquoi je dis prière le labeur, et labeur, la méditation.

WORKS CITED

Beucler, André. "Situation de Saint-Exupéry." See Tavernier: 139–47.

Boisdeffre, Pierre de. "Notre Jean-Jacques." See Tavernier: 161–82.

Borgal, Clément. *Saint-Exupéry: Mystique sans la Foi.* Centurion: Paris, 1964.

Caillois, Roger. Preface to *Oeuvres.* Antoine de Saint-Exupéry. Paris: Gallimard, 1959: ix–xxv.

Camus, Albert. *Théâtre, Récits, Nouvelles.* Bibliothèque de la Pléiade. Paris: Gallimard, 1962.

Chevrier, Pierre. *Saint-Exupéry*. Paris: Gallimard, 1958.

Confluences: Saint-Exupéry. New Series, 7:12–14. Paris: 1947.

Delange, René. *La Vie de Saint-Exupéry*. Paris: Seuil, 1948.

Derrida, Jacques. *Of Grammatology*. Trans. Gayatri Chakravorty Spivak. Baltimore: Johns Hopkins UP, 1977.

— . *Writing and Difference*. Trans. Alan Bass. Chicago: Chicago UP, 1978.

Devaux, André-A. *Saint-Exupéry*. Paris: Desclée de Brouwer, 1965.

François, Carlo R. *L'Esthétique de Saint-Exupéry*. Neuchâtel: Delachaux and Niestlé, 1957.

Frye, Northrop. *The Great Code: The Bible and Literature*. San Diego, New York, and London: Harcourt Brace Jovanovich, 1982.

Gallant, Mavis. "No Place for Innocence." *Times Literary Supplement* 27 January (1995): 3-4.

Iser, Wolfgang. *The Fictive and the Imaginary: Charting Literary Anthropology*. Baltimore and London: Johns Hopkins UP, 1993.

Kant, Immanuel. *Anthropologie in Pragmatischer Hinsicht*. *Kants Werke*, Vol. 7. Berlin: Walter de Gruyter, 1968: 117–333.

Kermode, Frank. *The Sense of an Ending: Studies in the Theory of Fiction*. London, Oxford, and New York: Oxford UP, 1968.

Lévi-Strauss, Claude. "The Structural Study of Myth." *Myth: A Symposium*. Ed. Thomas A. Sebeok. Bloomington and London: Indiana UP, 1974: 81–106.

Major, Jean-Louis. *Saint-Exupéry: L'Écriture et la Pensée*. Ottawa: U of Ottawa P, 1968.

Ménard, René. *La Condition Poétique*. Paris: Gallimard, 1959.

Mounier, Emmanuel. *Personalism*. Trans. Philip Mairet. Notre Dame and London: U of Notre Dame P, 1970.

Mills, Kevin. "Words and Presences: The Spiritual Imperative." *The Discerning Reader: Christian Perspectives on Literature and Theory*. Ed. David Barratt, Roger Pooley, and Leland Ryken. Grand Rapids: Baker, 1995: 121–136.

Mounin, Georges. "L'Espérance de l'Homme." See Tavernier: 125–35.

Ong, Walter J. *Orality and Literacy: The Technologizing of the Word*. London and New York: Routledge, 1989.

Ouellet, Réal. *Les Relations Humaines dans l'Oeuvre de Saint-Exupéry*. Paris: Minard, 1971.

Pélissier, Georges. *Les Cinq Visages de Saint-Exupéry*. Paris: Flammarion, 1951.

Redfield, James M. *Nature and Culture in the Iliad: The Tragedy of Hector*. Chicago: U of Chicago P, 1975.

Reverdy, Pierre. *Le Livre de Mon Bord: 1930–36*. Paris: Mercure de France, 1948.

Ricardou, Jean. "Une Prose et Ses Implications." See Tavernier: 187–95.

Robinson, Joy D. Marie. *Antoine de Saint-Exupéry*. Boston: Twayne, 1984.

Saint-Exuéry, Antoine de. *Oeuvres*. Ed. Roger Caillois. Bibliothèque de la Pléiade. Paris: Gallimard, 1959. Volume contains *Courrier Sud*, *Vol de Nuit*, *Terre des Hommes*, *Lettre à un Otage*, *Pilote de Guerre*, *Le Petie Prince*, and *Citadelle*.

—. *Carnets*. Paris: Gallimard, 1953.

—. *Lettres de Jeunesse (1923–1931)*. Paris: Gallimard, 1953.

—. *Lettres à sa Mère*. Paris: Gallimard, 1955.

—. *Un Sens à la Vie*. Paris: Gallimard, 1956.

Sartre, Jean-Paul. *Situations II*. Paris: Gallimard, 1948.

Schiff, Stacy. *Saint-Exupéry: A Biography*. New York: Knopf, 1994.

Siebers, Tobin. *Morals and Stories*. New York and Oxford: Columbia UP, 1992.

Slotkin, Edward. *Regeneration Through Violence: The Mythology of the American Frontier, 1600–1800*. Middletown, Conn.: Wesleyan UP, 1973.

Tavernier, René, ed. *Saint-Exupéry en Procès*. Paris: Pierre Belfond, 1967.

CHAPTER 2

COURRIER SUD AND THE IMPASSE
OF MULTIPLE VOICES

I.

C *ourrier Sud* appeared in 1928, the result of a painfully reworked short story entitled "L'Aviateur." Delange relates
how Antoine composed it hunched "over a wooden door
placed upon two gasoline barrels" during his lonely nights of service
in the Sahara (37). As the young author's first book-length publication, it possesses the merits and the flaws of inexperience, no doubt.
Any such *coup d'essai* is generally excused a certain ignorance of or
clumsiness with literary convention, especially when its freshness of
vision exceeds that of more mature novels. In Saint-Exupéry's case, the
first novel has often been said to reflect the chagrin of having to
dissolve his engagement to Louise de Vilmorin, whose family desired
a more prosperous and secure match, in order to pursue a career in
aviation (cf. Cate 159). That *Courrier Sud* launched his writing career
somehow attracts readings of it as thinly veiled autobiography, even
though the author's later work would speak much more directly of his
life. Hence Ouellet writes with typical confidence, "The personal and
wholly interior adventure of Bernis [the book's hero] translates a profound disarray, the same which was no doubt torturing Saint-Exupéry
at that time" (39). Schiff insists that the book "is as neatly biographical
as a novel can be" (16), though she also attributes the engagement's
dissolution less to Antoine's flying than to Louise's flightiness (cf.
104).

The story itself is supremely simple. A young pilot for a commercial mail service named Jacques Bernis is traced in his friend's imagination (another youth working for the same line at a Sahara outpost) as he flies his way south into Africa. Bernis is returning to his duties after a disastrous furlough in Paris. During this time, as his letters to the narrator tell us, he had acted upon his resolve to pursue a woman with whom he had been in love since childhood. Although now married, Geneviève is pleased to see Jacques. Her marriage to the mean-spirited, possessive Herlin weighs heavily upon her. When their only child suddenly falls ill and dies, Geneviève is left with nothing to hold onto. She elopes with Bernis in hopes of escaping her agony, but discovers that she has only created for herself the greater agony of leaving behind everything she has ever known. Bernis chivalrously returns her home, having passed but one night with her—a night of disillusion in which he anxiously nurses her through a grave fever. He wanders aimlessly through Paris for the remainder of his leave, then impulsively stops by to visit Geneviève on his way back south. For his troubles, he finds her on the verge of death, beyond the point of recognizing him.

The flashback is now reabsorbed into "live" action, as Bernis continues his dangerous flight across the Sahara. He lands at the narrator's outpost and supplies some of the details just mentioned. Then he takes off again, and makes one more human contact—a lonely sergeant at a minute outpost farther down the line. Shortly thereafter, his body is recovered. For some unspecified reason, his plane has crashed in the open desert.

As one can tell even from a plot summary, *Courrier Sud* is full of the romantic tendencies characteristic of young authors. It has more than a trace of the *Wertherroman*: the anguished young hero who pours out his soul in letters and conversations, the more stable friend who receives these confessions and passes them along posthumously to a world that may never understand, the exquisite soulmate who cannot escape the doll's house to which she was raised, and the unfeeling but socially respectable husband who commands the heroine's obedience; the hero's far-and-wide rambling in search of some release, his heightened sensitivity to exiles everywhere, and the despair which produces a distinctly suicidal ending . . . from a structural standpoint, Goethe's ghost might have charged Saint-Exupéry with plagiarism!

Yet structure, in many respects, is the novel's least successful dimension (and perhaps the most important, therefore, for locating unresolved tension). Cate endorses Edmund Jaloux's criticism that the novel tends to "explain psychological moods with poplars" (qtd. in Cate 157). Such obfuscations are all too common. The point of view is not clearly Bernis's at certain moments of would-be intimacy, but can logically be none other than his at several moments in the narrator's testimony; the motivation for crucial actions often remains deeply obscured, precisely because Bernis has not bared his soul to us in Wertheresque fashion; and the meaning of the whole ordeal to us as readers is vague, not only because of shifts in perspective and obscurity of motivation, but also because Saint-Exupéry's eye for realistic detail gravitates against any romantic interpretation. The author might have drawn our attention a little less to control panels and telegrams if he had wished for us to recognize behind it all the sacrifice of a unique, sensitive young man to a heartless social order. His insistence on the curiously crucial role of neutral technology, in fact, implies yet another voice. More poplars might have been more appropriate. Which voice is the reader to consider authoritative?

These confessions of a young outcast may look like an inexperienced author's attempt to proclaim his truth—an excessive compromise, perhaps, with literary convention rather than a resonant expression of personal judgment. No later work would end in such bemused, directionless melancholy. Indeed, the invincibly energetic ecstasy wrung from the darkness of some overwhelming ordeal would become the signature of Saint-Exupéry's writing. It may be that his disappointments in love and his puzzlement over life's options turned *Courrier Sud* into a lament, even though the spectacle of outright war could not suppress his optimism in *Pilote de Guerre*. Perhaps he matured artistically *and* emotionally in the intervening years.

Yet the first novel's failure to find and sustain an authoritative point of view reflects much more, I think, than youthful awkwardness of any kind. It mirrors and magnifies an epistemological impasse between objective time and subjective experience. The narrative representation of a forward-moving, causally related sequence of events demands a good eye-witness, or at least a group of witnesses whose testimony is consistent and plausible. For Saint-Exupéry, however (as for modern and postmodern authors generally), the meaning of events resides in the perceptions of the agent involved in them. Truth is colored, if not entirely determined, by one's long-standing prejudices, momentary state of mind, intelligence, temperament, etc. What distinguishes Saint-Exupéry from most authors of this century is his confidence that a powerful metaphor can ignite the same enthusiasm in several different participants (in a whole society, perhaps). In other words, circumstances and conditioning have far less influence over human behavior than the will—than what Saint-Exupéry would call spirit.

This is a dissonantly evangelical note in one who can only explain the terms of metaphor materialistically. Nonetheless, from the first work on, Saint-Exupéry constantly maintains that truth is a) created in comprehensible, earthly images, b) approached only inwardly, and c) more or less equally approachable by everyone. The formula does not work, but *Courrier Sud* adheres to it as faithfully as possible. Hence Bernis, the narrator, the author, and even Geneviève are stunningly sympathetic with a certain whimsical, almost mystical view of life. While the novel's critics mostly reiterate that it lacks any spiritually elevating idiom, its real failure is that all of its many voices share the same idiom, quite unaccountably. Whether this parlance is elevating or not, it remains based on such subjective responses to life that its invasion of several minds at once merely begs the crucial question: How do different minds come to place a common valuation on actions past, present, and future? How is morality (as opposed to behavioral programming) possible?

Of course, Saint-Exupéry will never answer this question satisfactorily in his fiction. In *Courrier Sud*, though, he at least becomes acutely aware that the psychic unity of the narrative's voices is insufficiently grounded in their shared experiences. His next step will be to adumbrate a more exhilarating and infectious experience: *Vol de Nuit*.

II.

The novel opens—and, for that matter, concludes—with a terse transmission from one station to another communicating the status of the south-bound mail. So workaday, realistic a beginning would seem to suggest an omniscient, behind-the-scenes narrator in the tradition of Flaubert. That impression is soon canceled, however: a textual space isolates the message from the rest of the chapter, which resumes and continues in an expansive, wistful, and poetic tone. "The lamp-like glow upon our faces . . ." betrays the presence of a speaker, some-one who may be presumed to have just read the radio signal.[1] But who are "we"? "Two pylons planted in the sand connected us to this world once a week" (4):[2] the speaker and his comrades are apparently land-bound drudges fulfilling their tour of duty in a remote desert outpost. Saint-Exupéry actually suffered through just such a lackluster posting (a generous promotion for him at the time) early in his career. He would write about it in *Terre des Hommes* more candidly, though the particular words would scarcely need changing. The beguiling tone of intimacy and the charming facility for metaphor are already present.

But the protagonist does not belong to this company of exiles. He emerges gradually from the mist of telegrams, assuming a shape in chapter 2 but not a name—or not for several paragraphs. Instead, he is "the pilot," and we watch him suit up awkwardly (with the same touch of Baudelaire's albatross which Saint-Exupéry would reinvoke in *Pilote de Guerre*) without ever seeing any distinctive facial characteristics. At last, "someone passes a paper to the pilot Bernis" (5),[3] and our newly introduced protagonist boards his craft and takes off.

A photographically precise description of this moment is soon followed by a poetic reflection remarkably similar in its wistful simplicity to earlier ones registered by the Sahara-bound narrator: "At two hundred meters you are still leaning over a toy sheepfold, with trees standing straight up and houses brightly painted, and the woods preserve their fur-like thickness: an inhabited land . . ." (6).[4] The naive vision of order induces Bernis to reflect upon his own chaotic existence. "I've put things in order,"[5] he ruminates throughout the chapter, referring to his physical act of departure from Europe. As he continues to admire the tidiness of human settlement beneath him ("Humble, well-groomed happinesses. Adult toys neatly arranged in their display window"),[6] the reader must wonder if the sheer poignancy of this privileged mile-high perspective has not tricked Bernis. Has he indeed put things in order, or rather has his machine-powered ascent inspired, by imaginative association, an illusion of personally created order?

Fair as such a question might seem, and crucial as it is for establishing the protagonist's character, it cannot be answered within the narrative context which Saint-Exupéry has posed us. For the narrator is predisposed to recasting objective reality in the same child-like images as Bernis uses; and, because the feelings of other participants can reach us only through this narrator, he himself—not Bernis—may even be responsible for the naiveté of the quaint *mise en ordre* at take-off. Yet there has been no indication, and will be none, that the speaker of chapter 1 is any more than a conventional narrative strategy—a patient Wilhelm to whom Werther may open his heart. If the narrator carries Wilhelm's voice of authority and impartiality, then, we must redirect our doubts about Bernis's trick for putting things in perspective back to Bernis himself . . . except that the narrator, once again, not only allows the pilot's poetic flights of fancy to pass without criticism, but practices them himself to mitigate his physical isolation. We have come full circle.

At most, we may say that Saint-Exupéry, the author, is the ultimate source of any naiveté, since all of his characters display it in equal measure. The belief that a coherent image, no matter how far removed from practical cause-and-effect relationships, can somehow resolve controversy—that a soothing poem read after a quarrel somehow constitutes a solution to the quarrel—is stunningly idealistic, yet bears the germ of Saint-Exupéry's more mature philosophy. In Mounin's words, "Like most surrealists, and poets in general, Saint-Exupéry also believed that changing the angle from which he viewed the world sufficed to change the world" (126). In subsequent works, we shall still find that whatever metaphor of experience gives one the strength to go on is a true metaphor; for all metaphors are equally true and equally false, and the only real truth is in struggling onward. In chapter 31 of *Citadelle*, for instance, the philosopher-king describes a lone mountain climber scaling to the peak and then enjoying the panorama below. "For if the countryside . . . is a blend of breathtaking labor and of resting muscles after their effort, and of the evening's blue tint," he concludes, "it is also the contentment of an order established, for each of his [the climber's] steps has slightly organized these streams, arranged those summits, and brought the village's pile of stones into perspective" (603-604).[7]

Has Bernis not created the order below him in exactly the same way: i.e., by risking his neck in a steep ascent and then pausing to look down? If the toy store display-window beneath him is not his own life put into perspective, he is wholly unaware of the fact—but so is the narrator, and so is the author.

The third chapter, far from clarifying any radical difference between the personalities of narrator and protagonist, transports both of them back into a shared childhood where their shared attitudes are rooted. The narrator leaves Bernis the Pilot en route to Spain in real time and recalls the briefing he gave his friend, then a young cadet, before his first flight. This scene, again, is related more straightforwardly at the beginning of *Terre des Hommes*: it encapsulates the young Saint-Exupéry's informal briefing by his mentor Guillaumet (143–45), even down to the detail of the lamplight glaring over the unfurled maps. We may infer from this flashback that the narrator is older, or at least a more experienced flier, than his friend. Any hint that he may therefore have a more mature or more moderate or more jaundiced view of life, however, is quickly dispelled when the reminiscence proceeds back to their common schooldays. The narrator recollects their return visit to the village schoolmasters (the author's teachers at Fribourg, according to Robinson [46]) who taught them literature, history, and other subjects irrelevant to the aviator's trade of braving death and the elements. The old men are duly impressed that their pupils are now taming the universe: "They spoke of Julius Caesar's childhood" (11) after Bernis had recounted his adventures to them.[8] The narrator, though the more practiced pilot, is strangely silent during this part of the conversation. The old pedants' erudition turns out not to be as irrelevant as the young men had imagined. Through human history, they have learned of "the bitter taste of repose after useless action" which their former pupils describe to them.[9]

These old men obviously understand the disillusion of returning home triumphant only to find oneself treated as a stranger—but *how* do they understand? An anguished, bittersweet nostalgia is sustained from now on, and the story never offers to justify its presence. Bernis's voice, the narrator's, and anyone else's along the way sing the same sad tune in harmony. We are forced, as a result, to consider it an objective fact of life, not a temperamental refrain borrowed from any particular character. So far are the characters from being thus distinguished, in fact, that the narrator seems virtually fused into Jacques Bernis during the flashback. It is Bernis, too, as we shall soon see, who undertakes to win the love of Geneviève, though both men have been enamored of her since childhood.

The abortive affair with Geneviève, which begins in Part Two and forms the main strand of the story's plot, is preceded by one more chapter. The narrator takes us back into Bernis's cockpit as he flies over Spain. The weather is bad and the mountainous terrain treacherous, even at high altitudes. As Bernis reads his gauges and scribbles in his logbook, the machine registers a sudden impact. Terrified, he sees ruin in a thousand forms hurtling toward him . . . but he quickly brings the craft, apparently unscathed by whatever disturbed its flight, back under control.

Does this minor incident foreshadow a problem in the plane's engine that will account for Bernis's mysterious crash at the end? If so, the hint is too subtle. Bernis quickly masters the situation—which leaves us wondering how the narrator could even have learned of it, since it would not have justified reporting. At most, the text seems to be reforging the ties between Bernis's somnolent reflections and the world of active menace, for Saint-Exupéry "refuses to separate action from thought and thought from dreaming" (Chevrier 49). With this vital connection thus established, Bernis returns to his recollections (conveyed, as always, by a narrator in the Sahara), and we begin Part Two . . . yet the bump remains oddly strident in retrospect, precisely because it seems to want a part of the daydream. Is this still another voice trying to nudge its way into the cockpit's time-traveling? Does it interrupt Bernis's musings or echo them?

Now the narrator again intrudes. In a brief paragraph, he identifies a vague need to go on, to tell the story of the last two months—not for therapy, but precisely because the pain of his memories is already abating. "Can I not already poke about where the memory of Geneviève and Bernis should be painful to me and find myself scarcely touched by regret?" (15).[10] It is as if the recollection of the event must preserve the event's pain in order to be faithful: an anguish subdued and "recollected in tranquillity," with pardons to Wordsworth, is *not* truth, to Saint-Exupéry, apparently. We gather from these words that both Bernis and Geneviève are now dead and gone. The prologue to Part Two, therefore, must be considered more advanced in linear time than any remark which we have yet read, since the novel's opening lines had Bernis in transit from Europe to Africa.

Immediately after this small step into a "nearer present," the narrator strides back into the past: two months ago, we must presume. Bernis is in Paris. He telephones Geneviève, and they meet for the first time in several years. He describes to the narrator in a letter (quoted to us) his sensation of an approaching fulfillment. "What is this obscure promise which has been made to me and which an obscure god does not keep?" he ponders, and counters triumphantly, "I've discovered the source. . . . It's Geneviève" (18).[11] These words plunge the narrator into his own reverie. He recalls a girl of fifteen when they were thirteen (the two men are the same age, after all!) who was the princess of their fairy tale, the center of every metaphor which animated their childhood domain (cf. "You had concluded so many pacts with the lindens, the oaks, and the flocks that we used to call you their princess" [19][12]).

So close is Bernis's nostalgic idolization of Geneviève to the narrator's own feelings that the former's letters fade into and out of the latter's fond images almost indistinguishably. The delicate fantasy differs for the two only in that one has dared to seek reality within it while the other looks on. A puzzling triangle not unlike that in Alain-Fourrier's *Le Grand Meaulnes* emerges, in which the self-doubting narrator strives to worship his love vicariously through his intimate friend's successes: but then, Saint-Exupéry does not give us *Le Grand Bernis* so much as a *grande illusion*. Bernis will have no success, and his unquenched yearning is shared by all around him. "I've discovered the source. . . ," he repeats. "I've discovered it the way one discovers the sense of things" (21–22).[13] The sense of things . . . the promise of some god made good . . . these are not naive phrases in Saint-Exupéry's parlance. The author, no less than his two male characters, believes in the palpable capture of the utterly desirable—in beatitude.

Geneviève's true personality seems irrelevant to attaining this fulfillment. She is the princess in the metaphor, and if she may be attained in some real sense, then so may the rest of the metaphor. The ultimate test of a metaphor's truth is simply its durability. "You wish to sit in your gondola and become a gondolier's song for life," warns

Saint-Exupéry in *Citadelle*. "And you are deceiving yourself. For that which is not ascent or passage is without signification" (611).[14] Though destined to be used as this sort of conduit-turned-Jacob's ladder, Geneviève nevertheless has more personality than any of Saint-Exupéry's few other female creations. Should we be surprised by now that most of her depth is revealed in an unsatisfied yearning for fulfillment?

Unhappily for the novel's coherence, the narrator could not possibly possess the knowledge of Geneviève's most secret motives and subconscious inclinations which is displayed in chapters 2–7. There is no indication that she posts letters to the Sahara, as Bernis seems to do faithfully; and we have already been alerted that she is no longer alive during the narrative's present, which precludes any sort of recent meeting between her and Bernis's friend. Furthermore, chapter 4 is at least partly told through the consciousness of Herlin, Geneviève's oafish, unintentionally brutal husband: our narrator is most certainly not privy to *his* thoughts. So close is the perspective of these crucial chapters to omniscient narration, in fact, that the narrator's judgments are reinserted rather self-consciously into chapter 6 as a formal letter addressed to Bernis.

After the hero's attempt to snatch his lady chivalrously away from her boorish husband ends miserably in his transporting her back to Paris, the final chapters of Part Two again wander well beyond what the narrator might plausibly have learned. In particular, Saint-Exupéry records word for word the exhilarating homily of a priest at Notre-Dame—an exhortation whose style and sentiment anticipate *Citadelle*, but which nonetheless fails to move Bernis. So powerful is the priest's rhetoric—so sincere is his effort to create order from chaos—that the narrative point of view is shockingly ceded to him for an instant as he grips the pulpit. "Images of an extraordinarily clear character came to him," writes Saint-Exupéry, apparently having entirely forgotten about his speaker in the Sahara. "He thought of fish caught in a net . . ." (44).[15] Bernis is momentarily captivated by the priest's search for "the formula which will hold sway over this mass of people" (45):[16] after all, he is searching for metaphors himself, like all of Saint-Exupéry's heroes and self-portraits. The net fails to hold him, however. He claims to hear only idle creativity, only despair; and if the priest is deluding himself, of course, then the story's receivers have picked up the plaintive voice of yet another homesick castaway. No wonder the narrator can put words in his mouth!

The young pilot then proceeds to a nightclub, which he leaves in the company of an unknown woman. Half of chapter thirteen is actually related through her consciousness as she longingly admires the taciturn, mysterious, strangely driven man asleep in her bed (a scene which mildly suggests the conjugal relationship in chapter 10 of *Vol De Nuit*). Once again, Saint-Exupéry has side-stepped the first-person narrative strategy with more determination than subtlety, lured away by the prospect of an empty but searching human being.

Part Three begins in much the same manner as did Part One. Having consumed an idle hour in retrospection (i.e., Part Two), Bernis reoccupies himself with the exigencies of flying. He lands in Casablanca and takes off again after wringing from the *chef d'aéroplace* a concession that he cannot be required to continue in such foggy weather. The otherwise amusing dispute perhaps foreshadows a navigational problem which will lead to the fatal wreck ... or perhaps not. Cape Juby (the narrator's post) and other stations along the line are already alarmed at the courier's disrupted schedule. The air waves are full of anxious questions. The narrator awakens the next morning with vague misgivings; and indeed, Bernis is again behind schedule, lost over the immense Sahara. Finally a garbled radio message is intercepted which announces the courier's delayed departure from Agadir.

Why the teasing sense of doom? The plane is apparently functioning, and the meteorological menaces come and go. Is it just that no one ever makes his ultimate destination in this book?

Chapter 3 is almost entirely devoted to a eulogy of childhood—or, more precisely, to a testimonial of the child-like mind's prophetic powers, its grasp of truths from which adults have insulated themselves. "And up there, we would watch the blue night filter through the chinks in the roof tiles," recalls the narrator of himself and the Bernis who shared his youth. "This minuscule hole: a single star would barely fall upon us, decanted for us from all the heavens. And it was the star which visits illness upon creation" (62).[17] In that attic back home so many years ago, they divined together the fragility of culture, the constant vulnerability of a tiny domain transfixed by the beams of innumerable stars and hurtling through a galaxy. To adults, it was the stars which suffered from the fragility of distance . . . but *they* knew better, and they lived their subsequent lives in fidelity to that knowledge. "Even a house is not protected against a vast cosmic movement," stresses Major. "This is what the narrator discovers in his childhood home" (251). Comfort is illusory. Home is precious, but ever so much more precious than most people understand, because it is perched on the brink of infinity.

Into this meditation—one of the most sustained "prose poems" which the narrator delivers in the book—Jacques Bernis enters with a dream-like ease. His arrival at Cape Juby is not even announced. "Assieds-toi," begins the new section: "Sit down." But Bernis is already eager to take off again. The narrator finally prevails upon him to recount the dénouement of his adventure with Geneviève (chapter 4). The weather is not a pressing concern after all, it appears. Bernis's ominous tardiness at each stop along the line begins instead to assume the character of a death wish, or at least a recklessness born of despondency.

For Geneviève is dead: this is the chaos upon which Bernis has been imposing order, and not simply the failure of their elopement. The lyrical account of his debarking from the train to Toulouse and visiting Geneviève's ancestral home scarcely resembles what we would expect from a man who, a moment earlier, had wanted to retreat silently back into his work. Nor does it become entirely clear how Geneviève happens to be here rather than in Paris with Herlin, or why Bernis should wish to drop in on her after having just returned her from so humiliating an adventure. Nevertheless, through his eyes we receive the impression of the magnificent old house's voyage into time—what we might call its cosmos. "The evening would fall here as an entire year would elsewhere," Bernis muses, evidently recalling still more childhood experiences, "it was a cycle brought to completion. The next day . . . that was when life began all over again" (65).[18] Like a well-caulked ship upon a vast ocean, the house bears its precious cargo of lives safely through a chaotic universe, its ritual adjustments to the flow of each new day offering a paradox of immutable references. It is the answer to that other childhood house through whose tiles a star once peeked: it is the closed system of a domestic economy whose ability to ride out the galaxy's vertiginous turns is nothing less than awe-inspiring to Bernis.

Major seems to attribute this stability to Geneviève herself in noting that her character "here exacts of material realities that they play a role other than that of simple objects of possession or of rational knowledge. They must in some manner compose a presence" (66). Yet the same "presence" imposed itself upon her ancestors: it has created her in the act of being re-created by her. Even death is comfortably absorbed into its substance. "How simple everything is . . ." he thinks while eavesdropping upon the nurses, "living, arranging bric-a-brac, dying. . . ."[19] Still undetected, he picks his way upstairs to Geneviève's room, finds her indeed in a moribund state wherein she can hardly recognize him, and slips back downstairs and out of the house. The eerily dream-like quality of the visit, allowing harsh reality to melt into Bernis's meditations just as he himself had crystallized amid the narrator's childhood memories a chapter earlier, implies a certain triumph for the house. Bernis did not belong in it, and he could not have passed more unnoticed if he had been a ghost. He admits as much before taking off (chapter 5): "I attempted, you see, to carry Geneviève off into my world. . . . I ought to have yielded her house, her life, her soul to her" (67).[20]

Is the house, then, that Eden from which all of us have been ejected, that place which is fully desirable (like childhood) because we can never return there? Does it belong to other dimensions because its order is inviolable, or because it has become Geneviève's gateway to death, the truly forbidden garden? And does Bernis's own approach to that garden now account for why the narrator cannot quite keep up with his ethereal steps?

In chapter 6, we are inscrutably at Bernis's shoulder as he crosses the vast Sahara. Whatever details of the past he might have supplied the narrator during his brief touch-down in Cape Juby, he is now embarked upon that portion of his journey which he will never be able to recount to his friend. Yet the narrator even shares his ruminations ("All of us at some point have fallen into this unknown planet. Time became too vast there for the rhythm of our lives" [69][21]). As always, he can read Bernis's mind.

An east wind flares up, threatening to choke the engine with sand. At this point, the perspective strangely shifts to the third-person impersonal: "On décolle de Port-Étienne . . . On est aveugle . . . On laisse pendre un bras hors de la carlingue" (70). The French here is virtually untranslatable. An English speaker might say, "Take-off from Port-Étienne . . . It's blinding . . . You leave your arm dangling out of the cockpit." It is as if Bernis himself were now narrating the story of his own body observed at a comfortable remove. If such impassivity insinuates a touch of bravado, it certainly does not imply any despair. Fully immersed in his struggles to reach the next outpost, Bernis has no leisure to think about Geneviève. As for the knocks and bumps, they have become familiar minor characters already. If they are not now a specific cause of crash any more than before, why are they here? Do they cancel Bernis's inner voice, or confirm it?

Bernis makes Saint-Louis du Sénégal. A company-starved sergeant celebrates his arrival (an amusing and true incident which really occurred at the outpost of Nouakchott [cf. Cate 124–26] and which will be related thoroughly in *Terre des Hommes*). The sergeant is such a bundle of frustrated longing that his effusions pass from pathetic to comic. No doubt, he will repeat this conversation later to the narrator, but Bernis appears enveloped in his usual mysterious reserve during the dialogue related in chapter 6.

In chapter 7, the radios begin to crackle once more, for Bernis is late again. There are no gremlins this time going bump in the narrative: just a lacuna. The narrator closes the story from his own perspective as he participates in a rescue mission, to no avail. "Pilot killed plane wrecked mail intact," reads Bernis's epitaph over the radio waves.[22]

III.

A wag might generalize that the narrative point of view in *Courrier Sud* features the first-person commentary of a minor participant isolated in an immense desert who has flashes of complete omniscience. On the other hand, the novel's awkward shifts of perspective do not simply result from a young author's inexperience. Instead, they consistently reveal Saint-Exupéry's irrepressible desire to relate the "truth" of each event—which means, for him, to capture the inner reality of the characters as well as the outer reality of the facts. Already, in his first book-length work, he insists on the fusion of act and thought. What sense would Geneviève's response to her son's death make without an intimate report of her spiritual condition? Why try to recount Bernis's homecoming, or any homecoming, if one cannot provide the reader a window upon the childhood passed at home—upon the minute kingdom that will forever be bigger than all the adult universe?

Saint-Exupéry's determined translation of such events into the human quest for meaning is more properly what makes his narrator ubiquitous and psychic. After all, every inconsistency mentioned above could be resolved with artifices well known even to fledgling writers. The narrator could have run into Herlin later, or Geneviève could have been his correspondent as well as Bernis. He could have claimed, "Bernis's end, as reconstructed from his logbook and my speculations, was as follows." The novelist's craft is full of such artifice. For that matter, Saint-Exupéry could simply have abandoned the first-person vantage altogether for third-person omniscience (as he would in his next novel). Such a strategy would have permitted him to read the minds and hearts of all characters at any moment, though it would not have licensed his subjective descriptions of sky, weather, and terrain (a major sacrifice, for we must remember that, to Saint-Exupéry, the physical universe has no genuine objectivity, but is always stamped by the perceiver's personal and cultural presumptions).

Yet Saint-Exupéry shied away from any such simpifying of reality's subjective-objective riddle to suit literary decorum. Even an unabashed fantasy, as we see so plainly in *Le Petit Prince*, had in his judgment a proximity to life which the classical novel's flawless causal chain of events fecklessly surrendered. *Courrier Sud* is not the story of a happening—the distillation of a climactic incident from a complicated problem. It is not even an unanswered question, for a question would still represent a problem. It is an unposed question—a silence awaiting some important question which does not come. It is a mythic world without a myth, a cosmos whose every shape is darkened and breeze cooled by the shadow of a Colossus . . . but without the Colossus.

Someone in this world should have cast the shadow—should have died slaying the dragon or fallen while scaling Olympus—whose remembered ordeal might explain the characters' shared grief at their limitations. Or if Bernis is a mythic hero in the making, then his battle with chaos should anticipate and dwarf both Geneviève's and the narrator's. Instead, the cause of the young pilot's death is so obscure that the air of fatality wrapped about it by the narration only suggests a yearning for myth. The narrator even confesses early on that he needs to write down this oddly circular sequence of events lest he forget it, as if he admired its susceptibility to myth yet also realized that the cycle's first grand loop—the distinctly mythic thrust against fate—had not, after all, been Bernis's work.

The narrator certainly acknowledges his own circumscription by the cycle, whatever it is and wherever it came from. He is so clearly, even awkwardly, talking about himself throughout that, at times, his and Bernis's biographical details merge most suspiciously. He too senses an absence of eagerly awaited meaning in his adulthood and his culture, he too loves Geneviève, and he too braves death to find life. Hence a linear succession of causes and effects would not express the essential truth in this essay on coming home, looking down from far above, and wandering blindly through mist and sand. This story is no road leading us where we were not before: it returns, over and over, to the same enigma, seeking a new perspective, hoping for a revelation. Naturally, a revelation would turn the narrated events into allegory, a metamorphosis which would deflate all the careful magnifying of Bernis's movements as heroically original and final. There would be some sense made of these human beings who expect more than life has to offer; and that sense would always have been awaiting discovery, for it would be grounded in the nature of things . . . but it would leave no room for heroism.

If Saint-Exupéry himself is but slightly hidden behind the narrator, and if the narrator is also Jacques Bernis reflecting upon Jacques Bernis, then Geneviève is scarcely less a direct extension of the author's psychology. She appears remarkably three-dimensional, not because the author successfully placed himself in the skin of a completely alien being—a domesticated female—but rather because her domestication is itself a frail outpost in a galactic Sahara. Likewise, her devoted activity in that outpost serves a synthetic vision of life—a vibrant, creative faith—at least as much as do the ethereal, order-imposing panoramas which Bernis's daring wins from the planet. Her death is also as abrupt, ill-explained, and disconnected from any causality generated by the narrative. At most, both deaths merely emphasize that these characters are fully trapped within the cycle (whatever it is, wherever it comes from). They might have died later, much later: but they would have died standing in the prow of their ship as it plowed the universe's chaos. Their death in action is the proof of their life's fervor, if they are mythic heroes—and proof of their life's unrecognized futility, if they are references in an allegory.

"In Geneviève," writes François of Saint-Exupéry in the act of creating his fullest female character, "he shows one side of life and one aspect of the truth: the possibility offered to Bernis of settling down and living within a framework which endures" (177). This strained interpretation of Geneviève's function in *Courrier Sud* is not uncommon, and probably results from an excessive attention to the author's personal life. It is quite true that Saint-Exupéry had himself decided with much anguish to sever a strong romantic tie when confronted with a choice between flying and domestic tranquillity. Bernis has no such choice, however. He fails to win Geneviève despite his best efforts to do so. In a passage already quoted, he informs the narrator that his efforts were doomed from the start: he had been wrong to think that he might simply transplant her from her world to his. He had tried, nonetheless, and she had wilted. Their miserable elopement during a rainy night (37–41) is a voyage through the classical chaos of utter disorder. "An army without faith cannot conquer," he reflects fearfully in a metaphor which will grow into the central myth of *Citadelle*.[23] After these dreadful hours, while he is taking her back to Paris and watching her revive more with every mile retraced, he is most definitely not concluding that a quiet house and a warm hearth are not for him. Rather, the lesson has been that each person's soul belongs to his or her own vision of cosmos, and that a being snatched from one order and forcibly transported into another dies for want of structure, as surely as a body without a skeleton.

As the narrator had warned in a letter to his friend, "Customs, conventions, laws—everything whose necessity you do not recognize, everything that you've evaded . . . that's just what provides a frame-work for her . . . and Geneviève, once you carry her away, will be deprived of Geneviève" (33).[24] Bernis has not rejected Geneviève's cosmos: he has discovered that she cannot live in his. He has not chosen his *métier* over an idle existence: he has stumbled at the edge of a gap immense beyond any ever disclosed from his cockpit—the space between two cultures.

Quite possibly, Bernis had sensed this chasmic space from

childhood yet mistaken it for a profundity belonging to Geneviève herself. The unfulfilled promise of some god, the source of everything's meaning—he had pictured her not as a slave to be led into his own life's constraints, but as a benign mystery into which he might venture, a utopia somewhere beyond even the deserts and oceans barely accessible by plane. In the childhood memories communicated by the narrator, she appears dimly associated with the forbidden cistern behind the locked gate: "Tourne la clef," the boy Jacques urges his friend ("Turn the key!"), and they discover the cool, impassive pond rumored to hold a drowned child within its unplumbed depths. "We were lost to the confines of the world for we knew already that to travel is, above all, to change bodies. 'Here, everything is its opposite'" (61).[25] For Bernis, Geneviève is also an opportunity to *changer de chair*. He does not seek to possess her, like the coarse Herlin, but to be possessed by her as by a fabled but forbidden Arcadia. She will be the ultimate, unending adventure in his life of adventure. She will not annihilate the principles of his order, as the chaos of a sandstorm obliterates all sense of things: she will counter them with inverse principles—she will complete them, making them whole, thereby bestowing that rest from activity which resembles death (cf. "that peace which is offered only by death, when what you have stored away finally serves you" [*Citadelle* 638][26]). In her ends the quest.

Under the circumstances, might Geneviève actually be the missing hero of the missing myth? Of course, precisely because the full myth is missing, we cannot determine its hero. Still, Geneviève's cosmos precedes Bernis's and, in a sense, governs his. It is the promised land toward which all his flying forms a vector. It preexists the various male struggles for order in the book; and, inasmuch as these struggles constantly seem to lead back home and into childhood, it preexists them in much more than narrative time. It is the domestic order—even the womb's security—which surely imprints all of our minds before they are capable of thoughts. As such, it is a possible source of archetype, and its mythic representations date back to Gaia, the Fertile Earth, and beyond.

But no . . . Geneviève is no fertility goddess, at least as far as she knows—and the mythic hero's actions must spectacularly reflect his or her will. Geneviève is buffeted around by forces which she only vaguely comprehends. She feels bullied into serving as the princess of paradise for admiring males, and it is *not* a role of her making. Those who imagine Saint-Exupéry incapable of understanding a woman's discomfort upon a pedestal should take note. He did his share of deifying the female, no doubt. Writes Schiff of the young Antoine's love for Louise de Vilmorin, she was "what he would most have liked to find ensconced at the top of a tower: a fairy princess" (96); and she proceeds to argue that Geneviève was indeed patterned after Louise, to whom Saint-Exupéry wished to dedicate his novel (104–106). Yet his commiseration here with the created princess is quite genuine. During a section which offers no pretense of arriving to us through the narrator and which could originate nowhere but in Geneviève's most private thoughts, she betrays her frustration with her husband, and with men generally.

> Why does no one ever love her utterly? Men always love one part of her, but they leave the other part in shadow. They love her as they love music, or luxury. She is full of spirit or fine sentiment, and they desire her. But what she believes, what she feels, what she carries within herself . . . they couldn't care less. Her tenderness for her child, her thoroughly reasoned concerns, all of the part in shadow: they neglect it.[27] (*Courrier Sud* 23)

Geneviève is a certain kind of woman doomed to repeat a certain kind of experience because she has failed to grasp its nature. She has the misfortune of appearing mysterious to men like Bernis—to all the men who desire her. Everything they have always sought for and missed may just possibly be waiting for them patiently behind her frail, reserved exterior. We know that both the narrator and Bernis, as children, had wished "to know if it was possible to make you suffer,"[28] and that Jacques would even catch her up in his arms and squeeze tears from her eyes (20). "First he pulled gently, then heavily on the fragile arm . . . He sensed that he was hurting her. He thought of children who get hold of a wild cat and, in order to force tameness upon it, almost strangle it so as to force caresses upon it" (29).[29] Already in such games is a trace of Herlin's genuine brutality—but his tortures, in turn, preserve a disturbing similarity to the children's games. Even this dull, inarticulate block of a man has a tinge of the questing knight!

A mystery to be solved, an animal to be tamed, a strange land to be explored . . . such is Geneviève's fate in a world of men all looking for something which they cannot find. A reluctant goddess seemingly might be wise to remain as impassive as the forbidden cistern, or as the stone which *Citadelle*'s philosopher-king dreams to be the face of God (683–85), and such is Geneviève's response by nature. Yet, in a sad irony, it is precisely this response which invites the suffocating male attitude—for silence might conceal anything, and silence under duress might well conceal the sense of things. "Omne ignotum pro magnifico est," say Tacitus's embattled Britons of the Roman imperialist mind— "Everything unknown is taken for something grand."

So Geneviève, though she represents utter fulfillment to Bernis for most of the novel, is plainly portrayed by Saint-Exupéry as herself just another traveler in search of the ultimate haven. Bernis is mistaken in imagining that she can fully supplement his life's deficient meaning, just as she is mistaken in supposing that her matronly duties can absorb her being. Bernis finds her too much like himself, another unfulfilled seeker, even if the magnetism of the cosmos where she wanders has reversed the polarities familiar to him. He was once warned against trying to sweep her off her feet, and too late he realizes the wisdom of the warning. "Her house was a ship," he says to himself. "She was transporting generations from one shore to another. The voyage has no meaning, neither here nor elsewhere—but what a sense of security you draw from having your ticket, your cabin, and your yellow-leather suitcases" (41).[30] He had thought her an immeasurable depth of sympathy and inspiration: a charmed depth of consummate order and ultimate destination. Now he finds that she, like him, is embarked upon a tightly circumscribed, streamlined craft. A co-pilot or passenger was not what he had in mind. Major might have been speaking of either character—or of any character—when he concludes, "All of *Courrier Sud* could . . . be encapsulated in the drama of an unrest in quest of a sense of fulfillment. Bernis . . . intensely lives each of the experiences wherein he believes he will discover the final stage, then with the same intensity senses the limits of each encounter" (20).

Chevrier has written in reference both to Geneviève and

Citadelle's images, "The house that situates man in space makes of him a tributary to a place. And that house becomes an enriching constraint because it gives a sense to his steps" (103). When the infant son falls gravely ill, however, this *piccolo mondo antico* is shaken at its foundations. Geneviève fights the threat by busying herself with housekeeping around the sickbed: "She smoothed the bedsheets, arranged the flasks, wiped the window. She created an invisible and mysterious order" (25).[31] Such frail order does not suffice to keep the forces of disorder at bay. The boy dies, and Geneviève suddenly finds herself in free fall through a vacuum, her entire frame of reference annihilated. It is in this state that she seeks out Bernis. She tells him, "The things around me used to outlast me. I would be received, accompanied, assured of growing old one day—and now I'm going to outlast those things" (55).[32] Like a pilot who has lost all his beacons and all his stars in a mist, she is utterly lost somewhere between earth and heaven, neither dead nor alive.

Saint-Exupéry, then, seems to be showing us that such dependency on others for completion of oneself is hollow and futile. If he replicated this kind of futility in his personal life, he would not have been the first moralist who failed to take his own good advice. He seems to recognize that here, at last, is The Cycle, the sad orbit from which none of us has any escape unless, perhaps, through acknowledging gravity's invisible strength. He seems to deconstruct human ambitions and find only a nameless, ever-unsatisfied yearning at their base. He seems within a few well-chosen words of standing above the cycle like an allegorist who has discovered life's operative archetypes.

Yet this "seeming" mysteriously evaporates under scrutiny. Not only in his personal life, but also in his characters' lives, Saint-Exupéry cannot quite call the chase a delusion just because he has glimpsed the goal's unworthiness; or, at least, he cannot pronounce it any more deluded than other chases—and life requires a chase. Bernis says it above: the voyage has no meaning, but what a sense of security you derive from going through the motions!

Thus Saint-Exupéry will continue to use the patently vulnerable ideals of woman and home as viable gods, though his first novel has already taken their very finite measure. The crime of *Citadelle*'s *femme adultère* is not merely that she has betrayed her husband, but also that she has betrayed her own realm, whose delicate ritual might have beguiled away her emptiness. "I spread about her, like so many frontiers, the stove, the kettle, and the plate of gilded copper," says the philosopher-king about his typical female subject, "so that little by little, through these assembled objects, she may discover a recognizable, familiar face and a smile which is not of the here-and-now. And this will be for her the slow appearance of God" (516).[33] The king later makes his relativism explicit: "Since ends have no significance . . . to prepare the future is only to found the present" (649).[34] If there is no terminal objective to life, then the living of it—the passing from one present into another—becomes an exercise in aesthetics, in creating order for order's sake. Any order will do as well as another.

But who, then, will play the hero in the myth? What character's motion will generate the curves of the dominant arabesque? If only *Courrier Sud* did not offer so many voices calling us to the same Siren-shoals at once! Woman, childhood, home, babies, death—for death, too, might as well be an ideal end: it is certainly no logical consequence. Geneviève is quickly recovering from her fever as Bernis drives her back to Paris, and Bernis himself is neither tormented by Geneviève's loss nor beset by particularly bad weather when his plane goes down. Both events are absurd, in that they do not represent an effect of any of the novel's moral dilemmas. They imply, perhaps, the narrator's own suppressed Shangri-La, since he has no family and misses out on the girl but may still look forward to the rapture of leaving life.

Are we truly to believe that so much anguished emptiness can occur in so many ways within so many people yet not reflect an essential condition of life? If such longing is essential and hence inevitable, though, of what use is action against it? Why do critics rightly sense the pilot-myth in the making—why are Bernis's aeronautic closeshaves at all relevant to his disillusionment? Why are we left feeling that he might yet snatch Geneviève's soul from the clouds, or that he does, perhaps, and discards his body in the process?

A myth is an unrepeatable, unforgettable deed within whose parameters all future deeds are performed. Why does Saint-Exupéry insinuate that all of the deeds in *Courrier Sud* are reverent, ritual imitations of some grand quest just over the narrative's horizon—perhaps the metaphor of the ship at sea evoked so often, perhaps the memory of Julius Caesar invoked one time? What has an epoch-making accident to do with a recurrent delusion?

The same Saint-Exupéry would remark in his notebook, "God is the perfect symbolic underpinning for what is at once inaccessible and absolute" (40).[35] Teilhard de Chardin's "omega point" is similarly symbolic. "If we are to be fully ourselves we must advance in the opposite direction," writes Teilhard, "towards a convergence with all other beings, towards a union with what is *other* than ourselves" (122). For Saint-Exupéry, men and women alike can only progress toward completion by working within and working against (as opposed to working outside of) the limits which time and place have imposed upon them. One must simply be before one may become—or perhaps we should say, one must be becoming before one may occupy any state of being. Teilhard places the same emphasis on becoming, on growing. Where is the difference? Why can Saint-Exupéry's god also be a woman, or a house, or death?

Significantly, the framework of orthodox faith—or even of a Teilhard's unorthodox orthodoxy—is overtly rejected by Bernis during the mass at Notre Dame. The priest who delivers the homily shares most of the author's *bêtes noires*. Scientific determinism, the infrangible laws of logic, the pretentious vacuity of adult wisdom—all of these are favorite themes of *Citadelle*'s monarch. Even the images chosen by the priest—the ocean tide, the prisoner in his cell, the uncorrupted young girl, the inscrutable yet ever-enticing stars—recur throughout each of Saint-Exupéry's works. In fact, here we have yet another voice speaking in the idiom which mysteriously invades the major characters' thoughts.

Why, then, does the sermon fail to inspire Bernis, and why would it have chafed upon Saint-Exupéry himself, as Devaux claims (25–26)? The point of disillusion for our hero comes exactly where Christ is offered as the bearer of all burdens. The phrase, "I shall make of them something human," sickens him as it is repeated over and over.[36] Obviously, the message that he might surrender the onus of his grief and bitterness to a savior and otherwise continue as he had been going was not what he had hoped to hear. Rather, he had sought true inspiration: a program for action, a metaphor which would animate new movement. "Something human" is just what the offered redemption does not produce, in his (and Saint-Exupéry's) opinion; for it allows people to remain as they are instead of demanding that they outgrow themselves constantly. To put it another, more tropological way, the priest's "something human" is allegorical, whereas Bernis's is mythic. The priest's god receives flawed, failed human beings with open and forgiving arms. All has been foreseen, and all is pardoned to those who break the cycle by confessing its presence. This god's word existed before his act and has freed his creatures from the deficiencies of their acts. Bernis wants to see the act before the god—he wants to hear of an act that has created a god, and may, through its inspiration, elevate others to celestial heights.

Teilhard's becoming lies in confession and surrender, Saint-Exupéry's in loyalty to unworthy causes and fighting to the finish. Teilhard believes that the truth stands fully accomplished outside linear time and merely waits, within that time, for us to discover. It was, is, and will be "always already" (*pace* Derrida). Our discovery of it, precisely, is our becoming, just as the cause-and-effect articulation of it in natural history is science. Saint-Exupéry believes that the only truth is what we create and sustain. Our ability to remain firm in its service even as we discover its treacherously shifting basis in circumstance is the measure of our faith's maturity.

When Simone Weil (who, like Teilhard, has often been juxtaposed with Saint-Exupéry) writes, "The grandeur of man is to be ever recreating his life—to recreate what has been given to him" (203), she too departs in a subtle yet essential way from Saint-Exupéry's philosophy. For her, life would indeed be a bestializing routine without the belief in some transcendent purpose. To recognize this purpose is immediately to transform routine into worship. For Saint-Exupéry, the routine and the purpose are indissoluble. Imagination is required not to connect an apparently dull act to a spiritual reality, but to expunge the act's dullness. One's daily steps along a daily path must tingle in the bodily warmth of the hero who recently passed this way. The value of viewing life tropologically lies not in the depth of unconditional truth revealed (for, to Saint-Exupéry, no such truth exists), but rather at the surface, where freshly created muscles—lines of force—are exposed in quotidian affairs. The ritual is itself the religion.

Hence Bernis cryptically accuses the priest of answering himself and becoming his own god when the homily merely calls for introverted action—i.e., for meditation. To him, the crime is not in becoming a god—every mythic hero does that—but in *pretending* to do so, in putting the word before the act. Gods are created by service: they are not served because they create. *Citadelle*'s monarch will persist in condemning this sin of feigned heroism vehemently while overlooking the possibility of an immaterial, internal event—a pre-event: "And as for those who hope for a sign from God, they are making of him a reflection in the mirror and would discover nothing there but themselves" (708).[37] If you wish to find God in the mirror, do something godly.

Of course, it is Bernis who seeks a sign in *Courrier Sud*, and the monarch emerges (as we shall see) with a great stone as the perfect image of God; but Saint-Exupéry's fundamental meaning has not changed. Bernis seeks a program for action rather than a meaning beyond the futility of action, and the monarch's impervious image demands that the beholder continue to make overtures before it—a program whose self-contradiction he fails to remark, satisfied just to have new and more rituals. Neither persona is comforted by the thought of being allowed, through forgiveness, to act ineffectually. Though all gods are equally unverifiable to Saint-Exupéry, one may at least posit a god who requires arduous labor, and the spiritual progress entailed by such labor (so he believed) would itself be real. "If I have lost the blessing of the religious explanation, I must at least transpose its values, for they are necessary and fertile" (*Carnets* 40).[38]

Why, then, does Bernis not undertake something modestly heroic himself if the imperative to act must override any assessment of action's worth? There is always his flying, of course, and his death . . . why did Saint-Exupéry only think of weaving these elements into an epic later on? Subsequent works would make the pilot's cause more "worth dying for": critics readily identify this (and not its multiple voices) as the first novel's ground of inferiority. "The drama of Bernis," asserts Ouellet, "is that of a person who has not yet realized the synthesis between the external world and his internal universe" (58), as if orders to fly across the Atlantic without a compass might have been the young man's making; and Major concurs that "the *métier* has no other sense here than that of an empty routine, of gestures which are completed only through force of habit and surroundings" (109). The later Exupérian hero, committed to the development of aviation, then to the defense of Western civilization, will have no such identity crisis . . . or so the argument goes.

But Bernis's real problem is that he has already sailed off the edge of the earth while questing after Geneviève. To seek two paradises and fight two kinds of chaos in a single novel begins to look flippant. A Bernis who went down crossing the Antarctic after his abortive affair would appear just another disconsolate romantic. His death in the line of duty is already suspect: a sense that he is pining away behind the stick, perhaps suicidally, compromises his quasi-heroic vanquishing by the elements. Indeed, romantic qualities cling to him throughout the narrative. As he haunts the giddy nightlife of Paris dance halls, he muses, "This same dance, which collected gestures so as to compose a language from them, could only speak to a stranger" (48).[39] Such scenes move Major to declare that the novel "is made at once from a sentiment of internal alienation and of the difficulty of reaching another" (108).

A mythic act must arise from greater resolve than this—from greater arrogance, if you will. Alienation from the crowd must become contempt for the crowd: only then may the hero truly assert his will in the void and—paradoxically—be reunited with an admiring humanity. One might just as well say that Bernis is also too much a realist creation in this regard. His alienation is that of every man, not that of Prometheus. He is too isolated to set the world on fire, and too much of the world to think of setting it on fire. His lonely voice is heard in too many places: it is too often not his voice alone.

NOTES

[1] . . . sur nos fronts cette lumière de lampe.

[2] Deux pylônes, plantées dans le sable, nous reliaient une fois par semaine à ce monde.

[3] On passe un papier au pilote Bernis.

[4] A deux cent mètres on se penche encore sur une bergerie d'enfant, aux arbres posées droits, aux maisons peintes, et les forêts gardent leur épaisseur de fourrure: terre habitée.

[5] J'ai mis de l'ordre.

[6] Humbles bonheurs parqués. Jouets des hommes bien rangées dans leur vitrine.

[7] Car le paysage . . . est mélange de souffle et de repos des muscles après l'effort, et du bleuissement du soir, il est aussi contentement de l'ordre fait, car chacun de ses pas a un peu ordonné ces fleuves, rangés ces sommets, reculé ce gravier du village.

[8] Ils parlèrent de Jules César, enfant.

[9] . . . le goût amer du repos après l'action inutile.

[10] Ne puis-je pas me promener déjà, là où devrait m'être cruel le souvenir de Geneviève et de Bernis, sans qu'à peine le regret me touche?

[11] Quelle est cette promesse obscure qu'on m'a faite et qu'un dieu obscur ne tient pas? J'ai retrouvé la source. . . . C'est Geneviève.

[12] Vous aviez conclu tant de pactes avec les tilleuls, avec les chênes, avec les troupeaux que nous vous nommions leur princesse.

[13] J'ai retrouvé la source . . . Je l'ai retrouvé comme on retrouve le sens des choses.

[14] Tu veux t'asseoir dans ta gondole et devenir chant de gondolier pour la vie. Et tu te trompes. Car est sans signification ce qui n'est point ascension ou passage.

[15] Des images lui venaient avec un caractère d'évidence extraordinaire. Il pensait aux poissons pris dans la nasse.

[16] . . . la formule qui l'emporterait dans ce peuple.

[17] Et nous, là-haut, regardions filtrer la nuit bleue par les failles de la toiture. Ce trou minuscule: juste une seule étoile tombait sur nous. Décantée pour nous d'un ciel entier. Et c'était l'étoile qui rend malade.

[18] Le soir tombait ici comme ailleurs une année entière, c'était un cycle révolu. Le lendemain . . . c'était recommencer la vie.

[19] Comme tout est simple . . . vivre, ranger les bibelots, mourir. . . .

[20] J'ai essayé, vois-tu, entraîner Geneviève dans un monde à moi. . . . J'ai dû lui rendre sa maison, sa vie, son âme.

[21] Nous sommes tous tombés un jour dans cette planète inconnue. Le temps y devenait trop large pour le rythme de notre vie.

[22] Pilote tué avion brisé courrier intact.

[23] Une armée sans foi ne peut conquérir.

[24] Ces coutumes, ces conventions, ces lois, tout ce dont tu ne sens pas la nécessité, tout ce dont tu t'es évadé . . . C'est cela qui lui donne un cadre . . . Et Geneviève, emportée par toi, sera privée de Geneviève.

[25] Nous étions perdus aux confins du monde car nous savions déjà que voyager c'est avant tout changer de chair. "Ici, c'est l'envers des choses."

[26] Cette paix qui n'est offerte que par la mort quand tes provisions te servent enfin.

[27] Pourquoi ne l'aime-t-on jamais tout entière? On aime une part d'elle même, mais on laisse l'autre dans l'ombre. On l'aime comme on aime la musique, le luxe. Elle est spirituelle ou sentimentale et on la désire. Mais ce qu'elle croit, ce qu'elle sent, ce qu'elle porte en elle . . . on s'en moque. Sa tendresse pour son enfant, ses soucis les plus raisonnables, toute cette part d'ombre: on la néglige.

[28] . . . savoir s'il était possible de te faire souffrir.

[29] Il tira d'abord doucement, puis durement sur le bras fragile . . . Il sentait qu'il lui faisait mal. Il pensait aux enfants qui se sont saisis d'un chat sauvage et, pour l'apprivoiser de force, l'étranglent presque, pour le caresser de force.

[30] Sa maison était un navire. Elle passait les générations d'un bord à l'autre. Le voyage n'a de sens ni ici ni ailleurs, mais quelle sécurité on tire d'avoir son billet, sa cabine, et ses valises de cuir jaunes.

[31] Elle tapota le lit, rangea les fioles, toucha le fenêtre. Elle créait un ordre invisible et mystérieux.

[32] Les choses duraient plus que moi. J'étais reçue, accompagnée, assurée d'être un jour veillée, et maintenant je vais durer plus que les choses.

[33] Je dispose autour d'elle, comme autant de frontières, le réchaud, la bouilloire et le plateau de cuivre d'or, afin que peu à peu, au travers de cette assemblage, elle découvre un visage reconnaissable, familier, et un sourire qui n'est d'ici. Et ce sera pour elle l'apparition lente de Dieu.

[34] Puisque les buts n'ont point de signification . . . préparer l'avenir ce n'est que fonder le présent.

[35] Dieu est le parfait support symbolique de ce qui est à la fois inaccessible et absolu.

[36] J'en ferai une chose humaine.

[37] Et ceux qui espèrent un signe de Dieu c'est qu'ils en font un reflet de miroir et n'y découvriraient rien qu'eux-mêmes.

[38] Si j'ai perdu le bénéfice de l'explication religieuse, il faut au moins que je transpose les valeurs, car elles sont nécessaires et fertiles.

[39] Cette danse même, qui rassemblait les gestes pour en composer un langage, ne pouvait parler qu'à l'étranger.

WORKS CITED

Cate, Curtis. *Antoine de Saint-Exupéry*. New York: Putnam, 1970.

Chevrier, Pierre. *Saint-Exupéry*. Paris: Gallimard, 1958.

Delange, René. *La Vie de Saint-Exupéry*. Paris: Seuil, 1948.

Devaux, André-A. *Saint-Exupéry*. Paris: Desclée de Brouwer, 1965.

François, Carlo R. *L'Esthétique de Saint-Exupéry*. Neuchâtel: Delachaux and Niestlé, 1957.

Major, Jean-Louis. *Saint-Exupéry: L'Écriture et la Pensée*. Ottawa: U of Ottawa P, 1968.

Mounin, Georges. "L'Espérance de l'Homme." *Saint-Exupéry en Procès*. Ed. René Tavernier. Paris: Pierre Belfond, 1967: 125–35.

Ouellet, Réal. *Les Relations Humaines dans l'Oeuvre de Saint-Exupéry*. Paris: Minard, 1971.

Robinson, Joy D. Marie. *Antoine de Saint-Exupéry*. Boston: Twayne, 1984.

Saint-Exupéry, Antoine de. *Oeuvres*. Ed. Roger Caillois. Bibliothèque de la Pléiade. Paris: Gallimard, 1959; volume contains *Courrier Sud, Vol de Nuit, Terre des Hommes, Lettre à un Otage, Pilote de Guerre, Le Petit Prince,* and *Citadelle*.

—. *Carnets*. Paris: Gallimard, 1953.

Schiff, Stacy. *Saint-Exupéry: A Biography*. New York: Knopf, 1994.

Teilhard de Chardin, Pierre. *Hymn of the Universe*. Trans. Simon Bartholomew. New York: Harper and Row, 1965.

Weil, Simone. *La Pesanteur et la Grace*. Paris: Plon, 1948.

CHAPTER 3

VOL DE NUIT AND THE IMPASSE OF OMNISCIENCE

I.

*C**ourrier Sud* frustrates the reader with abrupt, unmotivated, and sometimes impossible changes of perspective. Yet the real frustration of these shifts is that all end up projecting the same *Sehnsucht*—the same longing after the next horizon—even though Saint-Exupéry lays no basis for such community of sentiment. Hence the novel's self-contradiction originates in something much deeper than a few missing cues. The book is not a true novel, in fact (as many have observed), in that it has no legitimate plot. It does not pose a problem and then find a solution: it states and restates a baffling enigma.

Vol de Nuit put right what the first book had got wrong, at least from the vantage of a conventional aesthetic. This novel clearly had a plot—a taut, suspenseful plot, at that. There is a Hollywood formula for action yarns where the hero becomes trapped in some wonder of modern technology gone awry: a stalled spaceship, a sinking *Titanic*, a burning skyscraper. Superficially, *Vol de Nuit* adheres to the formula. Fabien and his navigator are trapped aloft in a night storm, where their safety depends upon their receiving coherent directions or recognizing a landmark before their fuel runs out. Their strong-willed boss Rivière, unaccustomed to passive impotence, paces the office moodily all evening; and Fabien's young wife, aware that the flight has become long overdue, finally bursts into the control room demanding honest answers. Such moments make for high drama.

Of course, the formula requires that the marooned hero successfully extricate himself and his crew (though not without loss of life) from his high-tech mausoleum. Fabien does not come to so happy an end. Yet the novel remains distinctly cinematic in its rigidly linear sequence and its third-person, arm's-length perspective. As the scene shifts from Fabien to Rivière to the young wife to Rivière to Fabien, we are easily able to understand and appreciate the mounting tension. Robinson (62) thinks that Saint-Exupéry's technique may have been directly influenced by script-writing (though she also notes that the manuscript was heavily reworked at the editor's request). Gone are *Courrier Sud*'s sudden flashbacks and lyrical but disjointed reveries: every change of viewpoint presents the action as it unfolds and the characters' responses to the unfolding action.

Such responses are important to the camera: they are the visual representation of an internal state which would otherwise be quite inaccessible. Films cannot achieve a first-person perspective ("voice-overs" notwithstanding), and Saint-Exupéry has likewise abandoned it. At most, he reads in someone's mind an anxiety which a stare or manual gesture might convey, or—in the special case of Rivière—descants briefly on a philosophy which a monologue or voice-over might well deliver. This fluid shifting from one pair of eyes to another without sacrificing a kind of director's aloofness is typically (if clumsily) called limited omniscience. The reader is now spared any unease about how the narrator could have known the doomed Fabien's anxieties in a small craft a mile above the earth or the taciturn Rivière's meditations on the sidewalk or in a deserted room. There is no narrator's central, authoritative voice: there are only angular outlooks from the eyes of participants.

In what sense, then, is *Vol de Nuit* anything less than a stunning literary success? Those who have devoted book-length studies to Saint-Exupéry's literary career and philosophical evolution tend to view the second novel as a clear triumph. "One could scarcely attribute to the action of *Vol de Nuit* the character of an evasion or an artificial stimulus," writes Major. "Its fundamental and constant significance is limited to establishing a living rapport between man and the world" (123). Ouellet concurs: contrary to *Courrier Sud*'s essentially individual framework of action, *Vol de Nuit*'s "is narrowly bound to that of the community: Fabien's adventure infinitely surpasses the adventure of an individual" (39). Neither of these critics has chosen to see the later work's superior coherence as a function of its more defensible shifts. They believe that the story moves more fluidly, rather, because the author's moral vision is less fragmented.

Other observers who have devoted little time to Saint-Exupéry's corpus are repelled by Rivière's *Führer*-like dominance of the book. Robert Kanters generalized these concerns in a review published in 1948: "To labor in a grand cause is the conviction of the S.S. as of the soldier in the Red Army, as of the G.I.; of the missionary being roasted alive as of the cannibal who has just skewered him" (Vercier 72). Even Ouellet acknowledges the protagonist's distinctly Nietzschean approach to leadership (115). Ironically, the hostile interpreters are also registering an implicit praise of the novel's structural unity; for no one would take such exception to Rivière's authoritarian style if his voice, like Bernis's, were competing equally with a host of others. Hence we might say that an overwhelming consensus finds *Vol de Nuit* a work of resonant consistency.

And herein lies a new impasse: the novel is altogether too resonant—not from an aesthetic standpoint, but from an ethical one. Rivière is right, always right, and always wholly right: "he alone, unlike the others, is profoundly persuaded that he knows and holds in his hand the truth, and thus that an absolute power over all other men has been conferred upon him" (Borgal 51). Quesnel and Autrand stress that the four pilots of the novel, like the four points of the compass, rotate around Rivière's moral axis from start to finish (xxv). The beings of inferior vision who surround him—wives, bureaucrats, and pilots of the line—all fit unconsciously but perfectly into the niches which he has created for them. They are marionettes, and he is their puppeteer; or, if he lacks such a degree of control over their lives, he may at least be likened to a god on the order of Virgil's Jupiter. He knows his creatures' destined terminus and sometimes reminds them of their duty to strive after it, although both their motion and its bull's-eye seem capable of slippage.

In other words, an omniscience which should belong to the author is appropriated by his major character. Rivière's mind should be just one of many read by the story occasionally. Yet these occasions bestow upon it an authority over all other minds within reading distance—an authority, not simply a clairvoyance. The psychic narrator of *Courrier Sud* has now acquired a program of action and a power to transmit it. But whence comes such authority? Rivière is no more a practicing allegorist than *Courrier Sud* is an allegory: he has by no means plumbed the immutable depths of human nature. He is, instead, a brilliant motivator, the priest of *Courrier Sud* with a mission rather than a doctrine, a raised fist rather than open arms. Precisely because no immutable human nature worth mentioning exists, Rivière's infectious will becomes law. We are given no narrative or moral framework within whose broader contours we may judge his order. He creates cosmos *ex nihilo*: hence he is beyond good and evil. Mounin reflects provocatively, "To make of *Vol de Nuit* the meditation upon the human condition which it truly is, Rivière must be this unacceptable figure [because of his arbitrarily enforced will]; it must be the reader, and not the author, who *judges* Rivière: otherwise, the book would be a *roman à thèse*" (129). But *Vol de Nuit* is a quintessential *roman à thèse*: the reader is not provided the slightest textual leeway to recoil from Rivière's judgments. Indeed, far from being judged by either the author or the reader, Rivière dominates both along with the other characters.

Thus Rivière's triumph as an aesthetic creation, a guiding principle of coherence, bestows upon his private worldview an objective truth to which it has no philosophical claim. He gives the unaccountably echoing voices of *Courrier Sud* a source, making of their sporadic and diffuse cries a series of concentric circles, with Fabien's wife the farthest ripple and Fabien himself a much nearer one. More than anything about the chief's vision *per se*, it is this presence of so many waves encircling him—so many planets caught in his gravity—which magnifies his system to a quasi-objectivity. Neither Robineau's petty frustrations nor the young wife's domestic fears nor Fabien's last living thoughts are unanticipated by Rivière's philosophy, which easily transcends all such crises. Where now is the alternate culture of Geneviève? Where are the mutually defining polarities and opposing lines of force about which we read so much even in the posthumous *Citadelle*, and which reduce life in Saint-Exupéry's system to a profoundly individual—even lonely—exercise in creativity? Were Rivière the speaker of the novel, as the monarch is in *Citadelle*, we should at least confront this personal isolation honestly and directly. The transformation of chaos into cosmos would be taken on faith, as Saint-Exupéry required of it, rather than demonstrated by fact.

So the omniscience which was necessary to prioritize multiple voices—to supply a source for their mysterious agreement—inevitably laid claim to a knowledge of things beyond what the individual might ever find in his or her own heart. Because all ethical knowledge, to Saint-Exupéry, was subjectively based, he found himself before a new impasse. The full-fledged pilot-hero has accepted that the universe's ultimate truth is inscrutable—and, as such, irrelevant. One can only live *as if* one's metaphors describe reality. Commentators have often mentioned Saint-Exupéry's refusal to make radio broadcasts on the ground that one should not lecture over the air waves "if one hasn't a Bible to offer to people" (e.g., qtd. in Devaux, 63).[1] Here was a prophet who dreaded the thought of his message's profiting artificially from an aura of absolute truth—who perhaps had hunched over his own radio in the hope of salvation, like Fabien, too many times to steal for his voice the disembodied speed and pliancy of an angel. Yet something like an angel seems to flit between Rivière and the world, making it all just as he has ordained.

Hence *Vol de Nuit* would not only be the first but also the last experiment in third-person omniscience for Saint-Exupéry. He would move immediately to the first-person anecdotal style of *Terre des Hommes* and *Pilote de Guerre*, as if trying to distance himself as far as possible from the voice of authority which rendered the previous work's cosmos fully irresistible. Only the open subjectivity of the "I" can lay claim to a degree of objectivity, for only confinement within innumerable unique experiences and immeasurable stages of mental and spiritual development is common to all human beings (in the Exupérian system). In other words, paradoxically, the only culture which may be objectively affirmed is that which each individual may affirm in his or her own manner.

Rivière, it must be said, is no less aware of his isolation in the human order than of his free fall through the natural world's disorder. We should be mistaken to charge him with authoritarian arrogance, as so many have done, for he does not consider himself a god. The narrative framework makes him so: it forces upon him a majesty which he, like his author, would have wholly repudiated. Yet his innocence of tyranny involves him in another, perhaps more damnable crime: he incites others to worship a myth which he himself knows to be hollow. The humility of his agnosticism cannot belong to a mythic hero, who seeks to establish precisely that he is a god. Likewise, Rivière's concern for humanity has nothing to do with mythic heroism. His sense of vulnerability, both in others and in himself, is the basis of his philosophy, yet it contradicts and undermines the exemplary heroism toward which he would have his pilots labor. Were his ideal a truth which precedes and survives flawed human action, such striving would be noble; but since the ideal's value utterly depends upon everyone's believing it to be practicable—since the characters of *Vol de Nuit* have come to accept the historical reality of some nameless Herculean pilot—Rivière purveys a lie. The more mythic the feats of his pilots appear, the bigger liar he becomes.

II.

Chapter 1, told from the pilot Fabien's perspective, begins in a fashion remarkably similar to *Courrier Sud*'s second scene. Like Bernis, Fabien looks down from his cockpit and is struck by several appealing metaphors. "The shepherds of Patagonia go without hurry from one flock to another: he was going from one town to another, he was the shepherd of small towns" (81).[2] A little later, after a radio message warns him of impending bad weather (again in the style of *Courrier Sud*, although Fabien has a radio operator on board), he descends to a village along the route and shares Bernis's sense of conquest. "He was similar to a conqueror, in the day of conquest's dusk, who surveys from a height the empire's lands . . ." (82).[3]

In short, Fabien begins where Bernis went astray. He registers no memories which must be escaped, no trauma which requires exorcism—only the free, frolicking imagination of someone engaging the great interface of cosmos and chaos. He is the mythic pilot-hero in full bloom. As the opening chapter concludes, he is once more airborne, caressing his controls in the thickening darkness. "The five hundred horses of the motor produced a very gentle current through the plane's matter which changed its ice into a pelt of velour" (83).[4] A knight-errant who rides his charger through the clouds (and who even has a squire behind him), Fabien seems ready to do battle with fire-breathing dragons—and so he will.

Chapter 2 introduces us to Rivière, who, "responsible for an entire system, was pacing back and forth on the landing strip of Buenos Aires" (85).[5] Rivière is suffering the same crisis of faith as *Citadelle*'s aging monarch (e.g., in ch. 83, which begins, "There came upon me an extreme weariness" [700][6]). His duties never end. The day's mail, once safely deposited in Buenos Aires, must be dispatched forthwith across the Atlantic. "For the first time, this aging fighter was astonished to feel himself weary. The arrival of flights would never be the kind of victory which ends a war and inaugurates an era of blessed peace."[7] Like a Bernis or a Fabien, however (or like *Citadelle*'s monarch), he resumes mastery of his feelings by immersing himself in tasks which demand close attention. While examining a piece of faulty equipment, he chats somewhat playfully with the mechanic Leroux, another warhorse who has aged in the all-absorbing performance of his duty. Rivière asks if he has had much time in his life for love—a question which will seem less idle later on when Fabien's wife bursts in upon Rivière's world, begging that her own be granted equal status. The answer to her lament is implicit here, and it is a negative answer.

Rivière's sphere of comprehension is immense. With every step, and even as he scrutinizes loose bolts and rust, he evaluates his own life, the lives of those around him, and the meaning of human life generally. The reader can already have no doubt that his perspective represents the novel's ultimate authority.

The next several chapters continually reaffirm the ample circumference of Rivière's vision by constricting the perspective to a lesser character's, then subtly returning to the chief's. Chapter 3 revolves around the seasoned pilot Pellerin, who descends from his aircraft mute and stunned after weathering an incredibly powerful contest of winds in the Andes. His figure anticipates that of old Bury in the opening pages of *Terre des Hommes*: Saint-Exupéry always drew upon genuine experience. Yet Pellerin's ordeal is neatly assimilated into the novel's plot in a way that Bury's will not be. To begin with, of course, the unexpected winds foreshadow the Pacific storm's arrival east of the Andes—an event which spells doom for Fabien. The narrative's causal chain is already being carefully forged.

At a more profound and significant level, perhaps, Pellerin's perspective gives way almost imperceptibly to Rivière's in chapter 4. The chief instantly recognizes the full philosophical import of his pilot's stammering narrative. "He had just lived a few hours on the other side of the polite surface," muses Rivière (89),[8] understanding at a glance what his simple subordinate cannot put into words: the extreme fragility of human constructions and the extreme vulnerability of human life. Tiresome administrators will not grasp this truth, continues Rivière: they will see in the pilot's pilgrimage through chaos (and *pèlerin* means "pilgrim") only a brave man's brush with death. Again, the contempt of popular heroism running throughout *Terre des Hommes* is anticipated in Rivière's thoughts. Heroism lies not in facing death, but in facing life when its familiar pretensions to immutable, eternal order have suddenly been slashed and rent. The difference between the next book and *Vol de Nuit* is that Rivière constantly sends men like Pellerin to possible death. Under the circumstances, his confidence that Pellerin has glimpsed a "sacred" truth is shockingly high-handed. He presumes that any pilot would rather prophesy over the abyss than live in uninspired security. He is only Pellerin's boss, not his conscience.

Nevertheless, within the novel's intricate succession of perspectives, Rivière does appear to read straight into the pilot's heart. The same applies to his assessment of Robineau, the prototypical dusty bureaucrat whose job consists of making other employees feel guilty. "Ignorant of everything, he would cock his head, slowly, in front of all that he encountered," reflects Rivière in the next chapter. "That would trouble bad consciences and contribute to the proper maintenance of materials" (90-91).[9] Any satirical humor in this description must be considered beyond the artistic bounds of the novel, despite evidence that Saint-Exupéry had a particular bureaucrat of his acquaintance in mind (cf. Pélissier 129); for the smoothly shifting perspective takes us within Robineau's skin briefly. He turns out to be a pathetically lonely (if rather pompous) lackey, as earnest and thorough in fulfilling his function as ever a man might be. We are told that he receives with admiration Rivière's rigorous order to dock the pilots' pay for tardiness even when bad weather delays them. He senses "a sort of pride to have a boss so tough that he wasn't afraid of being unjust" (91).[10] Rivière repossesses the point of view just long enough to tell us that his rigor aspires not to be fair, but to "create a will" ("créer une volonté," 92)—a standard Saint-Exupéry formulation, once more, and one which recurs throughout *Citadelle*.

At issue here is the formulation's style rather than its intrinsic merit. Robineau is (as his name suggests—*robinet* means "faucet") a mere conduit, a tool without personality. He makes no case for fairness before his boss, he shows no embarrassment before his subordinates when executing unjust policies, and he scarcely even resists when Rivière directs him to sanction Pellerin for a trumped-up infraction lest their nascent friendship disrupt the chain of command. Léon Werth, particularly disturbed by this last incident, regretted that he had not related to his friend Tonio a similar occurrence from his own experience which would have supplied the petty functionary with just the right repartée (182–83). Too minutely sketched to be dismissed as a caricature (we even hear of eczema and amateur rock-collecting), Robineau remains nonetheless disturbingly two-dimensional. The omniscient viewpoint has given him a chance to tell his story, and he has nothing to say beyond parroting his boss. The perspicacious Rivière scores another triumph.

The plot thickens in chapter 7. We return to Fabien's aircraft, around which the Pacific storm reported by Pellerin begins to gather. The entire scene is represented through the eyes of the radio operator. Fabien himself is only "a head and a couple of motionless shoulders" (99).[11] His poised silhouette inspires the navigator with the same awe as the wind and clouds outside (whose force was said in the chapter's first sentence to bump the plane like a shoulder). Fabien has become a culture hero of mythic stature. As I proposed in chapter 1, this kind of hero must possess anti-cultural qualities in order to defeat the enemies of culture. He must be part barbarian himself if he is to beat the barbarians at their own game. Fabien has now attained the stolid impassivity of a mountain: he opposes nature's destructive abyss with nature's mute resistance. The navigator cannot even bring himself to touch the mighty figure before him. "Without doubt, those hands, closed upon the controls, were already riding upon the storm as upon the neck of a beast; but the shoulders, full of force, remained immobile, and one could sense in them a profound reserve." The operator concludes that "after all, the pilot was responsible."[12]

Responsible—the very word which was used to introduce Rivière!

In this Herculean wrestling match where shoulders are mentioned in every paragraph, the pilot-hero has freed himself of all artificial etiquette, all culturally acquired presumption about what can and cannot happen in the universe, to stand before blunt chaos and assert order. Whether he lives or dies, he has already won, for he has chosen order without any illusions about its being objectively founded in nature. He has kept the faith against the ultimate temptation: despair. The operator takes comfort in this titanic figure's shadow, not as strong himself but, in his weaker manner, just as faithful. He is fully content to orbit Fabien, to submit to Fabien's authority, just as Robineau, Pellerin, and Fabien himself all dance to the pull of Rivière's transcendently benign gravity.

And this is the crucial point: Fabien is clearly displaying his discipleship to Rivière in chapter 7 even though Rivière is physically absent. If the operator draws his strength from the pilot, Fabien, in turn, is nourished by the great "river" of life (Rivière's name is yet another of Saint-Exupéry's quasi-allegories). Lest this fact be lost upon us, we immediately recover Rivière's perspective in chapter 8. He is wandering anonymously through the crowds of nightclub-goers, clearing his mind, gazing up at the stars. Even in such casual circumstances, Rivière attains with ease the kind of ecstasy (in the true sense of the word) to which only a typhoon slipping across the Andes can elevate Fabien. Rivière recognizes at a glance the pitiful frailty of civilized order, an order in which the amusement-seeking groups and queues trust implicitly. A kind of conspiracy exists between him and the stars careening through their arm of the galaxy at ten thousand miles per second. He alone knows the true value of sidewalks and streetlights, for he alone among the crowd knows how suddenly they may all be swept away. "He lifted his eyes to the people around him. He sought to recognize those among them who were letting a creative genius or a deep love take the night air in leisurely steps, and his thoughts turned to the isolation of lighthouse watchmen" (101).[13]

The cost of mediating between man-made cosmos and the mindless forces of nature—those capricious gods of primitive times—is, of course, high. Like an ancient prophet who returns greatly aged from each possession, Rivière suffers in body from his spiritual vigor. A sharp pain in his right side stimulates further self-evaluation in chapter 9. The question of justice torments him again. In particular, he hesitates to sign the dismissal of old Roblet, a senior mechanic who has begun to make mistakes. The issue is not really complex in this case. Roblet arouses our sympathy, but his quite unintentional bungling might cause destruction and death. In fact, our image of Roblet reveals less about him than about the man through whose eyes we see him. Rivière fully recognizes the subjectivity of his judgments: "I don't know if what I've done is good. I don't know the exact value of human life, or of justice, or of grief . . . But to endure, but to create, to exchange one's perishable body . . ." (106).[14] Nowhere in *Vol de Nuit* do we see Rivière more intimately than here, and nowhere is his humanity more evident and attractive. Though a crazed dictator, sensing the approach of death, might similarly strive to "exchange his perishable body" for some stupendous work, Rivière is clearly thinking about the mortality of everyone concerned in the airline—and, by extension, about every member of his civilization. It is the third-person omniscient perspective which makes his outlook appear domineering, and not that outlook in itself.

An especially illustrative case in point is the very next shift of perspective, which carries us into the psyche of a pilot's young wife. As the radio operator admires Fabien's flexed shoulders from behind, so the young wife admires her sleeping husband after an official phone call from the airport awakens her. "He was still sleeping, but his sleep was the powerful sleep of reserves which will soon give forth. This slumbering town did not protect him: its lights would seem vain to him when he began to rise, like a young god, from their dust" (107).[15] The same depth of reserves, the same elevation above the herd's dull sense of security, and the same quasi-divinity as Fabien displayed show this young man to be one of Rivière's creations. And, of course, he is also responsible—"responsible for something major, like the fate of a whole town."[16] The wife dutifully wakes him and prepares him for his trans-Atlantic flight: the next link in the mail's passage once Fabien touches down in Buenos Aires.

For her part, this woman resembles one of the mechanics with whom Rivière constantly converses. She sees that her man gets rest and food, lays out his equipment, helps him into his gear, and generally attends to the small bit of the line entrusted to her care. Not that she understands her role in such a manner: rather, she confesses half-jokingly to a certain jealousy of the stars—her husband seems unflatteringly eager to leave his home for a week. Her objections end there, however. The pilot, as he departs, lifts her bodily back into bed "as one lifts up a little girl" and tells her to sleep.[17] She might as well be his daughter, or doll, or servant—or concubine. She seems to feel the same awe and mystery before him that *Courrier Sud*'s lady of the night felt before Bernis, and she seems fairly content with that feeling. Another wife would have asked her husband how long this routine was to continue, or what she was to do around the house for a week, or why he ever thought he needed a wife and home to begin with . . . but wives in *Vol de Nuit* do not raise such issues. Like other petty functionaries, they are moons of the manly planets orbiting Rivière's solar majesty.

As the point of view returns to Rivière in chapter 11, he receives the young pilot—the god about to shake earthly dust from his heels—with a stern rebuke. In an earlier incident, the young man had apparently declined to take off in an impenetrable fog, alleging mechanical failure. Rivière insists that he recognize his fear for what it is. Rivière, the creator of these young gods, must save them from their human foibles. "If I listen to him, if I pity him, if I take his adventure seriously, he will believe that he's returning to a land of mystery, and it's only of the mystery that we're afraid. There must be no more mystery" (110).[18] Pellerin had not passed the test of fear, either, if to be dumbfounded by the infinite confusion beyond the man-made universe is to fail the test. Yet Pellerin had held on as if there were hope, as if one might have a plan and follow it—and Pellerin had survived. He had triumphed, after all, simply because he had refused to allow mystery into his calculations: he had refused to betray order even when faced with its utter inadequacy.

This is vintage Saint-Exupéry again, coming straight from Rivière: hold on, and act *as if* you understood. As a philosophy, it is quite unassuming, certainly not fascistic. Conrad's Marlow had voiced similar sentiments in *Heart of Darkness* when confronted with the mystery that had seduced Kurtz.

> . . . How can you imagine what particular region of the first ages a man's untrammelled feet may take him into by the way of solitude—utter solitude without a policeman—by the way of silence—utter silence, where no warning voice of a

kind neighbour can be heard whispering of public opinion? These little things make all the great difference. When they are gone you must fall back upon your own innate strength, your own capacity for faithfulness. . . . The earth for us is a place to live in, where we must put up with sights, with sounds, with smells, too, by Jove! . . . And there, don't you see, your strength comes in, the faith in your ability for the digging of unostentatious holes to bury the stuff in—your power of devotion, not to yourself, but to an obscure, back-breaking business.

The fascist—the fanatic of Kurtz's stamp—is precisely the one who luxuriates in mystery. Marlow differs from Rivière only in his belief that the mystery harbors an essential but unendurable truth about human nature, a truth to which the safe hypocrisy of public opinion is necessarily preferable if one would survive. For Rivière (and Saint-Exupéry), raw nature is amorphous chaos, threatening man not with a positive disclosure of horror but merely with repudiation of his painfully adumbrated patterns. Perhaps, after all, this is what Kurtz found in nature, as well: a void in which he might create himself like a god.

Fabien has learned Rivière's lessons well. Even though the typhoon counters his every maneuver, he continues to resist with quiet confidence, *as if* he understood what was happening. The aircraft itself sets at his fingertips various representations of the order for which he fights, just as the classic culture hero at his most brutal moment still carries some token of civilization in his strategy or armaments (Theseus overcomes the Labyrinth with a spool of thread, and Herakles is a master archer). Fabien does not draw upon his technology to any particular end—indeed, he is growing increasingly aware that it cannot help him; but he is nonetheless reassured by its purposive, "cosmetic" geometry and calibration. "There, in the middle of gauges and numbers, the pilot felt a deceptive security: that of the ship's cabin over which a wave is washing" (113).[19]

Deceptive or not, he must cling to this one hope. His radio operator cannot communicate with ground stations through the storm, and neither terrestrial nor celestial lights can supply him a reference point in the dense envelope of cloud. The situation has now become a race to orient the craft before its fuel runs out. Rivière has arrived at the same realization back in his office. The action has so intensified that it leaves the shifting third-person perspective little leisure in these chapters to review, generalize, or justify.

With fine dramatic effect, Madame Fabien calls the office of operations at just this moment. Rivière immediately murmurs, "There's what I was afraid of" (119).[20] Before the perspective settles upon him, however, we are privy to Madame Fabien's anguish at the other end of the telephone line. She follows her husband's transit imaginatively whenever he is flying up from the south. This night is no different from any other: she peers through the curtains at the sky, like the young wife in chapter 10, and anticipates the moment when she can help her man unlace his gear. Indeed, the previous domestic scene has prepared us for the present one. Yet again, we must be impressed by the narrowness and predictability of the human world which Rivière contemplates from afar (just as his pilots study the physical world from aloft). Lives repeat themselves: husbands, wives, mechanics, and bureaucrats seem to move in fixed rhythms learned from the clocks they punch, the deadlines they race, and the meals they prepare or consume. Domestic contentment, of course, can turn routine into a ritual, a peace which soothes rather than bores. Nevertheless, it clearly holds no surprises, for Rivière or for anyone else. After all, we have now seen it twice, this warmth of the lamp burning in the window, and all the trappings are identical. The "objective facts" of the story, and not the chief's prejudices, have verified its monotony.

Hence Rivière is right to fear the female intrusion. Madame Fabien does not force a sobering reality upon the boyish games played at the aerodrome, as someone from outside the Exupérian universe might expect. Instead, she threatens to entangle the fliers' heroic struggle with reality—with the senselessness of uncultivated nature—in her charming but utterly naive routine. "Before Rivière there arose, not Fabien's wife, but another sense of life. Rivière could only listen and pity this frail voice, this song so sad but so adversarial. For neither action nor individual happiness can be shared out: they are in conflict" (120).[21] The wives of the world want their men to remain in a static, contented torpor: Rivière demands that they face the void, fight it, and grow.

Not that the chief's thoughts are phrased so confidently at this moment. On the contrary, Borgal believes that the night's sad events have forced Rivière to acknowledge as never before the struggle between the creative life and the contented one: "indeed, far from scorning the latter in the name of the former's presumed superiority, this Nietzschean figure finds himself humbled" (57). In particular, Rivière is haunted by the memory of a construction accident which left one worker mutilated for life. An engineer had asked him if the building of one bridge as a mere convenience to the locals was worth the sacrifice of the man's body. Rivière had answered, "Even if no price can be set on human life, we always act as if something surpassed human life in value . . . But what?" (120).[22] He poses himself that question again tonight, knowing that Fabien may well not survive: "au nom de quoi?"—"in the name of what?" Now as before, he finds no ultimate solution. Rather, he thinks of the Incas who scaled dangerous Andean slopes to leave immense monuments, all so that the desert sand would not efface everything—their bones, their entire race, yes, but not everything. They had worshiped a sun-god, to be sure, perhaps for lack of something better. But whether fully deceived or not by their religion, what mattered was that they had lived "as if" a purpose existed beyond the comprehensible.

A belief which leaves the agnostic wistfulness of its foundations so transparent can hardly be called fascism. Rivière is no mono-maniacal dictator. Instead, it is Madame Fabien who should make her case more thoroughly than she does. When she appears in Rivière's office shortly after the phone call, she seems no more insistent than a Roblet come to ask why someone else has been given his box of wrenches.

In the meantime, the perspective returns us to the cockpit of Fabien's plane. The pilot is beginning to realize that he cannot win this game of irresistible winds, impenetrable darkness, and diminishing fuel. He descends to a dangerous altitude hoping to find a flat plot of land where he might bring the craft down safely, and uses his only flare to illumine the scene. Inexplicably, despite his severe corrections against the gale, he is flying over the open sea. "He could have struggled still, could have tried his luck: there is no exterior fatality. But there is an interior fatality: there comes a moment when you discover that you are vulnerable. Then mistakes draw you down like a swoon" (124).[23]

This rueful reflection of Fabien's unconsciously echoes Rivière's philosophy, once again. The natural world's defiance of all measurement and calculation—all rhyme or reason—leaves Fabien numbed for a moment, deprived of his faith in order and his ability to create out of the void. He is saved, so to speak, by the sudden emergence of a few stars from the mist overhead—not physically saved, for he recognizes that climbing into the starlight will consume his fuel faster than ever; but he is saved as a coherent being amid the universe's turmoil, because from the stars he creates a metaphor to hold his life and death together.

The ascent into the heavens unveils a surrealistic prospect as Fabien at last tops the clouds and blunders upon the full moon. "His surprise was extreme: the clarity was such that it dazzled him. He had to close his eyes for several seconds" (124).[24] An atmospheric calm prevails along with the beatific radiance. Fabien's wonder becomes the rapture of a vision. "He had been taken into an unknown and hidden part of the heavens, the bay of the blessed isles, as it were" (125).[25] Even now, he understands that he and the radio operator are doomed. Below is the ocean, or perhaps soon (since he has veered due west) the Andean foothills, both surfaces waiting to destroy them in the dense gloom. The two of them are "like thieves in some tale of a mythic city who become sealed inside the treasury and know that they can never get out. They wander among the sparkling stones, infinitely rich yet condemned."[26] As a matter of fact, we never recover Fabien's perspective. We receive definite news of him again only at the end, when he, like Jacques Bernis, is found dead in the rubble of his plane. Nonetheless, he has triumphed. He has wrested from the blind, brute force of chaos an image, a meaning, which even the knowledge of his impending death cannot unravel. His humanity has asserted itself in the most inhuman of circumstances.

As elsewhere in *Vol de Nuit*, this prophetic rapture of the two aviators is so fully documented, so objectified, that it utterly vindicates Rivière's system and leaves messengers of lesser truths, like Madame Fabien, quite bankrupt of any spiritual authority. Indeed, the wives admire their men in the first place only because Rivière has forged them into silent, burly wind-warriors. His truth does not so much contradict as circumscribe theirs. He makes the men who serve something higher than women—the men whom women cannot resist. Such sexual pursuit of the unattainable perfectly fits into the grand chain of postponed meaning. The men, of course, must aim higher for the chain to maintain its upward thrust. As far as we know, Fabien's last thoughts were *not* of his wife—and we have just been privileged to read his next-to-last thoughts. No doubt, he more resembled the Saint-Exupéry of *Terre des Hommes* who faced death in the Sahara without regret than the Guillaumet of the same work who trudged for days over glaciers lest his wife be left alone and penniless.

Madame Fabien's agenda for life, then, may seem severely limited when viewed beside moonrise on a cloudbank, cities reduced to toys, and courage measured against cyclones—but it is ultimately a humble member of the same indefinite regression. Only in the immediate crisis does her perspective appear to be an obstacle. Upon entering the airline's offices, she realizes that "she was revealing to the people around her the sacred world of happiness" (128).[27] She knows every clerk's eyes avoid hers, then follow her pretty figure down the corridor, because, for the airline, she is the enemy. "She was coming to plead timidly for her flowers, her freshly served coffee, her young flesh" (129).[28] With her own kind of courage, she continues toward the chief's personal office. Here she senses herself so out of place that she finds her cause incapable of pleading ("sa propre vérité . . . inexprimable"). She all but apologizes for having come.

At this point, Rivière's perspective subtly takes over. Since he can read the wife's mind, apparently, the shift is almost imperceptible. After sympathetically imagining the slow process, now scarcely in its first stage, of awakening to her loss, he reflects soberly, "But she's helping me to discover what I was looking for . . ."[29] Like Fabien, he seeks an image to steady him in his disoriented free fall; and like Fabien, he thinks of the fabled isles on whose account early explorers built ships and dared the unknown. "Perhaps the end justifies nothing, but action delivers us from death. Those men would endure through their ship" (130).[30]

Rivière's humanity is once again evident in this scene. Far from avoiding or brushing aside Madame Fabien, as he could easily have done, he alone of all the gawking officials and bureaucrats sits with her and absorbs with her the shock of death. Nor does he profess some facile credo or fanatical assurance before her: as elsewhere, he keeps his philosophical insights to himself and pursues them even in his thoughts with cautious skepticism. If he appears to dominate the scene for any reason, it can only be because—as elsewhere—the supporting cast offers him no challenge. Robineau flits about clumsily from start to finish; but most conspicuously of all, Madame Fabien plays the role of a pretty doll whose owner has gone away and left it. Not only in Rivière's mind, but in her own, she represents Fabien's creature comforts. She satisfies his appetites, adorns his leisure, and chases away his boredom. She helps him endure standing still.

Major assesses this character perfectly when he remarks of Saint-Exupéry, "If he refuses a female presence in the destiny of his characters, it is to the extent that women 'substantialize' themselves and exact a rapport no longer founded on becoming" (230). Never does the young wife suggest that she can help her man mature rather better than a bumpy flight or a crash landing—that she can help him face and grow out of his bad temper, his stinginess, his lack of consideration, or whatever Fabien-the-human-being's pecadillos may happen to be. By no means does she hint that her universe possesses elements at least as permanent as an Inca sun god's temple. She makes no mention of family heritage or child-rearing (the two traditionally female exchanges of self which Geneviève had sought); and, as a character, she utterly lacks the depth which might have permitted her to offer her example—her charity or tolerance or honesty—as an active contribution which lasts forever, or whose resonances will die only when the world loses all regard for virtue. As the typical young wife of a typical flier, she remains credible enough. Unfortunately, she is one of the few characters in the novel's universe, so thoroughly explored by the third-person perspective, who might just as credibly have overthrown Rivière's absolute rule.

As if to register the textual universe's confusion during Rivière's few moments of disarray, the point of view wanders through most of chapter 20 without settling upon any figure. A few scraps of radio transmission are received from the doomed aviators: then nothing. An unidentified clerk remarks that the craft has now formally surpassed the maximum flight-time possible with its fuel reserves. "But order must reign, even in a house touched by death," ruminates Rivière (132), now alone in his office.[31] He consigns to Robineau a memorandum forbidding pilots to race their engines. After a few more moments of melancholy (during which Robineau, alarmed at the chief's despondency, lingers about for new orders), Rivière announces that the trans-Atlantic night flight will depart in fifteen minutes.

The chain has been repaired where one of its links had snapped, and the cycle begins again. Chasing the horizon will resume—there will be no idle scrutiny of values on company time. Out on the runway, the trans-Atlantic pilot (he of the dutiful wife in chapter 10, presumably), digests the news that the schedule has not been altered by Fabien's catastrophe. "His mouth opened slightly, and his teeth glinted in the moonlight like those of a young predator" (135).[32] Another of Rivière's ambassadors of culture who can beat the wilderness at its own game, he is part wild himself—just wild enough to relish the thought of making an ocean conform to his flight plan.

And so the cycle does indeed continue. The wind and the night have dealt Rivière a check, yet they have also provided the occasion for a great victory. By refusing to relinquish his vision of order even at a time of devastating failure, Rivière has proved that he will not relinquish that vision under any circumstances. Hence, in an anticipated fashion, he has prevailed over every incidental defeat. "The defeat which Rivière has endured is perhaps an engagement leading to genuine victory. The full act's evolution is all that counts" (136).[33] As he shuffles wearily among his cowed employees, "Rivière-le-Grand, Rivière-le-Victorieux" presides over the night's tragedy like a Shakespearian king delivering the final lines of a drama.

Everything falls into proper perspective, and the proper perspective is Rivière's. This is so not because he is an autocrat, but because the author has made it so. Life in *Vol de Nuit* really is an inscrutable enigma that must be lived *as if* it had a purpose, and people really will languish in dull complacency unless made to keep stringently the rule of the assumed purpose. Who is capable of bringing the issue into question? The mechanics? The pilots? The bureaucrats? The wives? Whose life is not positively enhanced by accepting the rule as gospel? The pilots, though mere mortals, dare to brave the stars, and even their wives are willing to risk bereavement for the privilege of loving, if only for a short while, heroes who fight dragons.

III.

The tirelessly shifting third-person perspective has given everyone a chance to speak, and the testimony of all has vindicated Rivière. Overbearing as his authority may seem, it is bestowed upon him unanimously by the novel's participants. As a result, the work was greeted with praise for its literary polish and awarded the Prix Fémina. Boisdeffre concludes, "The author of *Vol de Nuit* is straining toward classicism with all his being; we can sense in him a great effort to arrive there" (168). Yet it also drew dissenting—though still admiring—murmurs of alarm, like Clifton Fadiman's in *The Nation*: "a dangerous book . . . because it enlists a fine imaginative talent in the defense of a spiritual toryism" (qtd. in Cate 239). If today we incline to the latter judgment, mistrusting the resonant ideological triumph awarded to Rivière's views by the novel's aesthetic coherence, we may be sure that Saint-Exupéry shared our misgivings, even though he did not cry *mea culpa* to Fadiman's charge. He did something more impressive: he acted rather than spoke. He permanently discarded omniscience, knowing that one cannot ultimately know, unwilling to smooth over ethical complexity for the sake of superficial harmony.

The next novel, *Terre des Hommes*, would revert to first-person reportage, and no future novel would suspend it, even though later ones would select an "I" clearly not identical with Antoine de Saint-Exupéry. But how, then, would the impasse of *Courrier Sud* be avoided: i.e., how could a broadly (if not universally) valid moral insight be attained from a single person's perspective without implying that the basis of human values precedes experience? *Vol de Nuit* had already made a dangerous concession to the idea of universal, *a priori* truth. It had openly played at allegorizing several characters by tinkering with their names. The River, the Pilgrim, the Faucet—these are very blunt double entendres; and in the Europe of Saint-Exupéry's day, even "Fabien" would have been widely recognized as the heroic Roman cognomen "Fabius." Why does the author issue such a pleading invitation to read his novel as a parable of the human condition? How can the human condition be rendered parabolic unless its most influential causes are not historical or environmental, subject to change with time and place, but rational or psychological? And if this is true . . . well, why shouldn't it be true?

For Saint-Exupéry, such immutable truth would have implied the futility of action. If human experience is so thoroughly governed by pre-experience that we may forecast the outcome of ambitious endeavors, then one who expects to create something new under the sun is either foolishly ignorant of the cycle or arrogantly confident in his puny abilities. There is no room left for dynamic intervention—or not, at least, for the kind which Saint-Exupéry felt morally impelled to champion: not for the heroic kind. Mythic heroes, of course, display a variety of arrogance called hybris; but their abilities are not puny by any measure—even the gods must work up a sweat to crush them—and therein lies the difference. The heroic act effectively holds the gods' destructive caprice one more arm's length from fragile human cosmos. Society trembles a little less abjectly before what Rivière styles "mystery." Precisely because our future is *not* written in the stars, the possible range of allegory in Saint-Exupéry's world is frighteningly narrow; for radical freedom, as the existentialists knew, can be frightening.

But where, then, is the mythic act in *Vol de Nuit*, and who is its hero? At best, the heroic function is split between Rivière, who conceives of dueling with chaos, and Fabien, who steps forth to fight the duel. To give Rivière all the credit would be to elevate conception above execution—a dichotomy impermissible in Saint-Exupéry's system, since no great deed is fully thought unless bravely thought, nor bravely thought unless fully enacted. Perhaps the nagging pain in the chief's right side hints that he has already performed to his physical limit, and beyond it. Few of us would be so uncharitable as to begrudge him this limit, of course; but he remains less than heroic because of it, an old Aristotle with a dream of a world state awaiting an Alexander to be his pupil. Is Fabien, then, that Alexander? But the undertaking was entirely Rivière's leap of spirit. Indeed, Fabien has been berated by his boss (like practically everyone in the company) for showing too little boldness, too much respect for the enemy. Moreover, his death can hardly be said to complete a cycle under whose semi-divine shelter posterity will scramble in frail imitation. He, too, had only scrambled, and another young pilot is about to scramble across the South Atlantic without positively knowing Fabien's fate.

The real myth in *Vol de Nuit* is the one that does not get told. As in *Courrier Sud* (though less ostentatiously), the story and its players all seem to emulate some presence which none of them can see. Rivière's father, perhaps—the Odysseus who first crossed all seven seas and then instated an awed Telemachus to arrange a shuttle service across one of them. . . . The real myth is not told because it *cannot* be told. It would have to inspire all who heard it to repeat its motions, however feebly. It would have to lure passers-by like a Siren-song. Of course, Homer's Sirens promise only knowledge, without specifying content. They evade the issue of exactly what can so inspire men, perhaps aware that the *longing* for ultimate knowledge entices all men irresistibly. They can afford to be cynical: they are no moralists. Saint-Exupéry has not the luxury of evasion on this question. He cannot produce a specific answer because myth commits him to the notion that men have nothing basic in common—only what circumstance imposes, or only what grand manipulators like Rivière impose upon the imposing circumstances.

If action creates ethics rather than ethics requiring action, then one great act may truly anchor an entire cosmos; but if even those who have not yet been initiated into the cosmos recognize something compelling in the action, then the action itself cannot be the true source of cosmos. How can people believe in a myth that they have never been told unless what they really believe in is prior to myth?

In such a case, preaching the myth rather than its allegorical underpinning is merely selling people what they do not know themselves already to possess. It is a lie, a confidence game; and, but for the fact that he has sold himself the same familiar goods, Rivière would be no more than a fast-talking "motivational" wheeler-dealer. His idiom is most certainly seductive; and, unlike the priest's in *Courrier Sud*, it inspires immediate action. Where the priest's vision forgives, Rivière's holds responsible. Where the priest's vision consoles the broken, the failed, and the disillusioned, Rivière's incites all such wretches to deplore their past and present that they may claim a new identity in the future. Naturally, the priest's message, properly understood, is also about changing identity—but it would effect change by freeing people from the shackles of their actions. To Rivière (and to Saint-Exupéry), this kind of change is in bad faith. It is the self-indulgent fantasy of a soft-willed, uncommitted hypocrite.

Yet Rivière knows (as none of his pilots does, or even any of their wives) that action *is* ultimately futile as action. Though the day will come when night flights are routine and incur no risk, they will have accomplished nothing more at that point than to make society impatient for its mail. Then a new species of technology will be required to serve an increasingly pampered and ungrateful clientele. The process might as well be viewed as degeneration (the visage in which we postmoderns recognize it). Rivière does not so view it only because he aims to exalt not the society being served, but the servants. In terms which Saint-Exupéry employed elsewhere, "I don't admire men for serving the postal line, but I favor the myth of the line because it creates such men" (*Carnets* 51).[34]

Not to be served, but to serve . . . an old formula, but never an outdated one. When Jesus originally uttered it, however, the idea was not to serve society, for society wants service only on its own terms: service of its prejudices, of strictures which contract rather than expand the envelope of human cosmos. Jesus envisioned a service of *humanity*, of the divine spark in every person smothered (as often as not) by social convention. Rivière would have agreed with him in this—but Rivière believes in no divine spark which would allow him to make the necessary distinction. His pseudo-divinity is sparked by the *act* of service, an act which must always be deluded since it has found nothing worth serving.

At certain specific points in *Vol de Nuit*, however, the presence of the fully, truly desirable seems almost palpable. These moments involve stars. One of them belongs to Fabien, and it precedes his death only by minutes. The scene's breathtaking beauty is treacherous, as Fabien himself remarks. The more fuel he wastes in chasing constellations, the more he accelerates his ruin. Even Rivière finds a faintly similar exhilaration in contemplating the night sky while weaving through the crowded streets of Buenos Aires, and he, too, realizes (perhaps better than Fabien) that he is admiring his mortal adversary. The wife of chapter 10 feels a vague jealousy at seeing her husband groom himself "for the stars," a jest which he does not attempt to parry. Throughout the book, characters eye bright pricks of light as heavenly rewards, blessed isles, or answers to insoluble riddles—as the supplement to whatever void keeps consuming their efforts.

In such a capacity, the stars seem to symbolize sometimes a noble ideal, sometimes a cruel illusion. Jean Ricardou, whose frustration with these crossed signals was mentioned in my introductory chapter, upbraids Saint-Exupéry for allowing his symbols multiple and opposite meanings. "From metaphor, which respects the object's polyvalence while projecting its sense, we have passed on to symbol, which reduces the object to a monovalent signification," he explains of proper usage. "Then, through the progressive symbolism which it institutes, the symbol submits neighboring objects and, ultimately, all space to its totalitarian sense" (205). Stars have lured Saint-Exupéry to break these rules before. We have already seen how, in *Courrier Sud*, the star represents both the menace of chaos (e.g., the starlight filtering through the roof-tiles of the childhood home) and the object of informulable desires (e.g., the starlight in the priest's sermon). "Thus Rivière is the victim of a reassuring illusion," concludes Ricardou. "In him is played out, without his knowing it, the odd doubling back of Exupérian symbolism. The gentle message which he receives from the star is nothing other than the illusory perception of a meaning which he, along with his men, has projected there" (207).

Ricardou is mistaken, of course, to assume that symbolic meaning is properly "monovalent" and that recalcitrant symbols with many meanings must never have opposite ones. Archetypal symbols are usually of just this sort: water as drink and suffocation, white as purity and bloodlessness, fire as warmth and destruction. That a star should be unreachable yet ever so desirable to reach, or that constellations should festively announce in code the hour of Ragnarok, is a profoundly human paradox. Where *Vol de Nuit*'s stars are most surprising, however, is in their very harmony. Ricardou has missed the point, and Saint-Exupéry did not entirely succeed in sidestepping it: the stars do *not* trick. They say that bodily death cannot defeat the spirit. If this is "reassuring illusion," Rivière indeed succumbs to it—but what in the novel licenses us to call it illusion?

Jean Sonet, too, is blind to the stars when he proclaims, "everything happens [in *Vol de Nuit*] as if Saint-Exupéry believed neither in a personal and transcendent God nor in a personal life-after-death for man" (qtd. in Borgal 58). Saint-Exupéry no doubt entertained such disbelief—but how firmly did he do so? The honest, wholly credible reaction of his fliers to the stars implicates *him* in illusion (as he would have viewed it), suggesting that he did not feel intuitively what he believed rationally. How well did he comprehend his character Fabien when the young pilot tops the clouds and intrudes upon the moon? Is this doomed hero assessing his life in the sudden lunar glow and concluding that aviation has made it all worthwhile; or is he grasping epiphanically that his flying hasn't mattered, after all—that no act on this earth, nor any lifetime of acts, can escape being dwarfed to invisibility beside the infinite scope and power of Creation? Isn't the real meaning of the stars here that they are *not* adversarial whirlpools of chaos, but rather—thanks to the longing of every human heart that sees them—a gallery of truths set unassailably beyond this world's corruptive touch?

In fact, the omniscient narration declines to probe Fabien's last thoughts before the fatal descent, as if aware that this unstable source might emit bursts of static into Rivière's resonant Nietzschean broadcast. The same kind of epiphany will again perplex Saint-Exupéry's chaos-tossed heroes in the climactic moments of *Terre des Hommes* and *Pilote de Guerre*, and will prove less avoidable there. Indeed, confining such moments to the mythic truth of great deeds will become, in somewhat different ways, the major impasse in both works.

In the intervening years, *Vol de Nuit*'s omniscience would have much leisure to grate upon its author's moral sensibility. For, as we can see now, that narrative strategy's clumsiness at modeling ethical dilemmas does not arise just from its arrogant pose of reading God's mind. Rivière's humility, however narratively rendered, is itself a source of arrogance. A lawgiver who codifies his own prejudices because life seems to offer no unconditional truth is rather like the pardoner in Chaucer who lines his pockets by sermonizing on the evils of greed. It is high-handed enough that the other characters' puzzlement shelters feebly under the umbrella of Rivière's vast understanding. That he himself should consider the umbrella's contours wholly arbitrary—that he should not believe at least half-heartedly in some Inca sun god—so involves his egotism in the process that his moral authority evaporates. He seems to have graduated from the agnostic view that one cannot know anything to the nihilistic view that nothing exists to be known—that no conjecture based on the slender scraps of available evidence can ever be warranted. And what may we call this view, if not self-arbitrated omniscience?

NOTES

[1] . . . si l'on n'a pas une bible à offrir aux hommes.

[2] Les bergers de Patagonie vont, sans se presser, d'un troupeau à l'autre: il allait d'une ville à l'autre, il était le berger des petites villes.

[3] Il était semblable à un conquérant, au soir de ses conquêtes, qui se penche sur les terres de l'empire. . . .

[4] Les cinq cents chevaux du moteur faisaient naître dans la matière un courant très doux, qui changeait sa glace en chair de velours.

[5] . . . responsable du réseau entier, se promenait de long en large sur le terrain d'atterrissage de Buenos-Aires.

[6] Me vint une lassitude extrême.

[7] Pour la première fois ce vieux lutteur s'étonnait de se sentir las. L'arrivée des avions ne serait jamais cette victoire qui termine une guerre, et ouvre une ère de paix bienheureuse.

[8] Il venait de vivre quelques heures sur l'autre face du décor.

[9] Ignorant tout, il hochait la tête, lentement, devant tout ce qu'il rencontrait. Cela troublait les consciences noires et contribuait au bon entretien du matériel.

[10] . . . une sorte de fierté d'avoir un chef si fort qu'il ne craignait pas d'être injuste.

[11] . . . une tête et des épaules immobiles.

[12] Sans doute ces mains, fermées sur les commandes, passaient déjà sur la tempête, comme sur la nuque d'une bête, mais les épaules pleines de force demeuraient immobiles, et l'on sentait là une profonde réserve . . . après tout le pilote était responsable.

[13] Il leva les yeux sur les hommes. Il cherchait à reconnaître ceux d'entre eux qui promenaient à petits pas leur invention ou leur amour, et il songeait à l'isolement des gardiens de phares.

[14] Je ne sais pas si ce que j'ai fait est bon. Je ne sais pas l'exacte valeur de la vie humaine, ni de la justice, ni du chagrin. . . . Mais durer, mais créer, échanger son corps périssable . . .

[15] Il reposait encore, mais son repos était le repos redoutable des réserves qui vont donner. Cette ville endormie ne le protégeait pas: ses lumières lui sembleraient vaines, lorsqu'il se lèverait, jeune dieu, de leur poussière.

[16] . . . responsable de quelque chose de grand, comme du sort d'une ville.

[17] . . . comme on soulève une petite fille.

[18] Si je l'écoute, si je le plains, si je prends au sérieux son aventure, il croira revenir d'un pays de mystère, et c'est du mystère seul que l'on a peur. Il faut qu'il n'y ait plus de mystère.

[19] Là, au milieu d'aiguilles et de chiffres, le pilote éprouvait une sécurité trompeuse: celle de la cabine du navire sur laquelle passe le flot.

[20] Voilà ce que je craignais.

[21] En face de Rivière se dressait, non la femme de Fabien, mais un autre sens de la vie. Rivière ne pouvait qu'écouter, que plaindre cette petite voix, ce chant tellement triste,

mais ennemi. Car ni l'action, ni le bonheur individuel n'admettent le partage: ils sont en conflit.

[22] Si la vie humaine n'a pas de prix, nous agissons toujours comme si quelque chose dépassait, en valeur, la vie humaine . . . Mais quoi?

[23] Il aurait pu lutter encore, tenter sa chance: il n'y a pas de fatalité extérieure. Mais il y a une fatalité intérieure: vient une minute où l'on se découvre vulnérable; alors les fautes vous attirent comme un vertige.

[24] Sa surprise fut extrême: la clarté était telle qu'elle l'éblouissait. Il dut, quelques secondes, fermer les yeux.

[25] Il était pris dans une part de ciel inconnue et cachée comme la baie des îles bienheureuses.

[26] . . . pareils à ces voleurs des villes fabuleuses, murés dans la chambre aux trésors dont ils ne sauront plus sortir. Parmi des pierreries glacées, ils errent, infiniment riches, mais condamnés.

[27] Elle révélait aux hommes le monde sacré du bonheur.

[28] Elle venait plaider timidement pour ses fleurs, son café servi, sa jeune chair.

[29] Mais elle m'aide à découvrir ce que je cherchait. . .

[30] Le but peut-être ne justifie rien, mais l'action délivre de la mort. Ces hommes duraient par leur navire.

[31] Mais l'ordre doit régner même dans la maison des morts.

[32] Sa bouche s'entrouvrit, et ses dents brillèrent sous la lune comme celles d'un jeune fauve.

[33] La défaite qu'a subie Rivière est peut-être un engagement qui rapproche la vraie victoire. L'événement en marche compte seule.

[34] Je n'admire point des hommes de servir le courrier, mais je tiens au mythe du courrier parce qu'il forme de tels hommes.

WORKS CITED

Boisdeffre, Pierre de. "Notre Jean-Jacques." See Tavernier: 161–82.

Borgal, Clément. *Saint-Exupéry: Mystique sans la Foi*. Centurion: Paris, 1964.

Cate, Curtis. *Antoine de Saint-Exupéry*. New York: Putnam, 1970.

Devaux, André-A. *Saint-Exupéry*. Paris: Desclée de Brouwer, 1965.

François, Carlo R. *L'Esthétique de Saint-Exupéry*. Neuchâtel: Delachaux and Niestlé, 1957.

Major, Jean-Louis. *Saint-Exupéry: L'Écriture et la Pensée*. Ottawa: U of Ottawa P, 1968.

Mounin, Georges. "L'Espérance de l'Homme." See Tavernier: 125–35.

Ouellet, Réal. *Les Relations Humaines dans l'Oeuvre de Saint-Exupéry*. Paris: Minard, 1971.

Quesnel, Michel, and Michel Autrand. "Préface Générale." *Saint-Exupéry: Oeuvres Complètes*. Vol 1. Ed. Michel Quesnel and Michel Autrand. Paris: Gallimard, 1994: ix–lii.

Ricardou, Jean. "Une Prose et Ses Implications." See Tavernier: 187–95.

Robinson, Joy D. Marie. *Antoine de Saint-Exupéry*. Boston: Twayne, 1984.

Saint-Exupéry, Antoine de. *Oeuvres*. Roger Caillois, ed. Bibliothèque de la Pléiade. Paris: Gallimard, 1959; volume contains *Courrier Sud*, *Vol de Nuit*, *Terre des Hommes*, *Lettre à un Otage*, *Pilote de Guerre*, *Le Petit Prince*, and *Citadelle*.

—. *Carnets*. Paris: Gallimard, 1953.

Tavernier, René, ed. *Saint-Exupéry en Procès*. Paris: Pierre Belfond, 1967.

Vercier, Bruno, ed. *Les Critiques de Notre Temps et Saint-Exupéry*. Paris: Garnier, 1971.

Werth, Léon. *Tel Que Je L'ai Connu* . . . in René Delange, *La Vie de Saint- Exupéry*. Paris: Seuil, 1948: 131–86.

CHAPTER 4

TERRE DES HOMMES AND THE IMPASSE OF ANTITHESIS

I.

Just as *Vol de Nuit* had been awarded the Prix Fémina, so *Terre des Hommes* garnered several honors, including the Grand Prix du Roman of the Académie Française. By an odd twist of events, Lewis Galantière's English translation, *Wind, Sand, and Stars*, appeared even before the French "original" (which was also more rigorously edited: see Robinson 87-90 and Schiff 301-305). The English version was selected for distribution by the Book of the Month Club and enjoyed immense popularity in the United States. Indeed, it still does: it remains the single work of Saint-Exupéry's most likely to turn up in an American bookstore (always excepting, of course, *The Little Prince*). Highly accessible to all kinds of readers, the book is less novel, notwithstanding the French Grand Prix, than collection of anecdotes. The frequent divisions of its subject matter and the brevity of its vignettes make it pleasant reading, for instance, in an airport (as long as one is not about to board a plane).

The work's readability is perhaps deceptive in that it represents years of anguish, uncertainty, and physical trial. Robinson (76-87) and Crane (65-73) offer relevant biographical details. Schiff dramatically summarizes, "Nothing about this humane book so bursting with heroism and innocence suggests that it was written out of dire financial necessity by a man with an exhausting sentimental life, who had not flown a mail route in eight years and was never again to pilot an airplane in peace" (306). Let it suffice to say here that the impression of restless search in Saint-Exupéry's difficult literary transitions is fully supported by his personal struggles. Both author and man traversed these years of apparent infertility and frustration with the same eagerness to find a way out—a way to the truth.

The narrator of *Terre des Hommes* has discovered a promising corridor in the labyrinth. Not only has he resumed the first-person perspective of *Courrier Sud*, but now he identifies himself unequivocally as the author, Antoine de Saint-Exupéry. Hence his remarks have the genuine intimacy of confidences. Not that *Terre des Hommes* bears any resemblance to prattle—on the contrary, its frequent editorials aim at ethical insight and spiritual inspiration rather than idle witticism. The author's personal intrusion into his text is simply his way of validating all that he says. Neither the spectrally ubiquitous commentator of the first novel nor the omniscient mind-reader of the second, he has finally found a voice with whose authority he is comfortable: his own voice, speaking on his own behalf. That this voice is utterly free of self-aggrandizement should be stressed. Saint-Exupéry never hints at his election to the Legion of Honor for his exploits at Cape Juby (cf. Delange 45–46). The authority he seeks is moral, never social or political.

The book is divided into a total of eight chapters of greatly varying length. The shortest, "L'Avion" (ch. 3), consumes only a few hundred words, while the longest, "Au Centre du Désert" (ch. 7), considerably exceeds the limits of the typical short story. These chapters are not unrelated in subject, but neither do they follow a single sequence of events from start to finish. It might appear that they expand in a series of concentric circles, starting from the pilot's *métier* and moving outward to encounters with other pilots, encounters with foreign lands and customs, and so on; but this impression calls for several very subjective judgments. For instance, can the discussion of "Les Camarades" (ch. 2), whose focus is Henri Guillaumet's miraculous return from a crash in the Andes, really be viewed as more absorbed in particulars and farther from the universal than chapter 7, which minutely traces the author's struggle to survive his own crash in the Sahara?

Alternatively, Quesnel and Autrand contend that "*Terre des*

Hommes is constructed out of conflicts [from times past] recon-
sidered," as if the author had retrospectively discovered the proper
measure of things (xxxiii). This is more or less the standard critical
interpretation; yet it tends to accept the book's contrarian tone at face
value rather than to examine the polarizing technique responsible for
that tone. For *Terre des Hommes* is constantly fidgeting: it takes all its
cues from popular misconceptions, starting with the most infamous
and progressing to the most hidden, ignored, or subconscious. Hence
the first chapter, "La Ligne," introduces the author dancing to a
different drummer amid a tram-load of Toulouse clerks and scribblers.
Almost all of us can sympathize with his rejection of such existential
tedium. Then several careless platitudes about "daring adventurers"
like our author—and especially about "heroes"—are set straight. By the
time we reach the lengthy chapter 7, Saint-Exupéry is showing us that
we have misunderstood death itself, and, by extension, the ultimate
value of life. The final chapter emphasizes this point not in the sands
of the Sahara but in a crowded European railway carriage.

Thus these portraits, if viewed in the proper light, all contrast
with and challenge well-known caricatures that have come to be
accepted for the real thing. Just as Saint-Exupéry opens with the tram
ride through a dreary suburban dawn in the company of sundry
dozing bureaucrats, so he continues to conjure up images of Western
civilization in its oblivious, business-as-usual slumber and of the
mawkish melodrama cynically, formularly mass-produced to titillate
it between naps. Like an ecstatic prophet in the throes of a vision,
Saint-Exupéry grabs this civilization by its gray flannel lapels, shakes
it, and shouts warnings and delights. Nothing is as it appears—
nothing. The very earth upon which we stand, far from being as safe
as a mother's womb or as solid as bedrock, is but a geological
aberration, a wonderful, life-giving accident; for most of the planet is
salt water, most of its land is uninhabited, and much of that is simply
uninhabitable. The very existence of human culture is a miracle.

This point will be most vividly illustrated in the chapter called
"Au Centre du Désert," when the stranded aviators discover how unfit
for human occupation the earth really is once the tenuous "umbilical
cord" to a water source has been severed. Yet the popular notion
persists, not only that culture is natural, immutable, and indestruc-
tible, but that a particular culture is the true one, the standard against

which others must measure up. We are less than morally proper beings, Saint-Exupéry implies, when we fall so far short of grasping one essential truth, the *sine qua non* of moral conduct: that we are free to choose, even within the illusorily ample layers of culture—and (for this is the same truth) that we are responsible for our choices, even if we merely defer to our culture's conventions. The earth may crack or the sky may fall. Where will we take our stand as moral beings then? Only the person who can face chaos steadily—who can die of thirst slowly on the Sahara—and say, "I would live the same life all over again," has understood both freedom and responsibility.

In a manner of speaking, *Terre des Hommes* is Saint-Exupéry's Sermon on the Mount. With the best of intentions, he seeks to shake his readers up and turn their world inside-out. (Perhaps he would even be pleased at the plight of those who naively scan his first chapter before boarding a flight: the plane *might* crash, after all, and people should live their lives acutely aware of the vehicle's fragility.) Not the least of the resemblances between his book and the Sermon is antithesis, the rhetorical strategy of posing two starkly opposite alternatives. "You have heard it said . . ." cries Jesus over and over, "but I say unto you this. . . ." The generous text of Matthew does not show a contempt of convention; indeed, each of Jesus's charges requires a more spirited and thorough obedience to the traditional wisdom. Nevertheless, the technique of antithesis communicates a certain tension between the two, a tension arising from motive. One must do the right thing not because tradition endorses it, but because it is right. An excessive reverence for traditional wisdom may cause one's moral fabric to deteriorate, since one is apt to forget that tradition draws its only true authority from rightness rather than the other way around.

With the exception of this final insight (Saint-Exupéry never developed any coherent concept of abstract rightness), *Terre des Hommes* follows Jesus's approach. Despite a tendency for many readers to see in it an attack on earth- and desk-bound functionaries, it attacks only their motives. After all, Rivière was a bureaucrat of sorts. Saint-Exupéry does not want citizens everywhere to rise up and forsake their offices for the life of the nomad. He only wants them to understand that their rules and procedures serve a higher end, and could be reversed or contradicted by another system of rules and procedures which would work just as smoothly. The goal is to create the miracle of order, not to grovel torpidly before any one manifestation of order.

Terre des Hommes, of course, proceeds in what may be called an antithetical motion rather than by using the particular rhetorical schema of antithesis. It is not a sermon, but a series of narratives on related subjects. This more leisurely literary medium by no means suppresses the message's urgency. Pélissier assures us that "all those who have truly become Saint-Exupéry's intimates know that he would *speak* his books before writing them" (68). The integration of message with events chosen from daily life, rather, is crucial to establishing the message's veracity for Saint-Exupéry, who always declined to locate a realm of absolute truth above and beyond the specific pressures of living. Hence each anecdote identifies a common but flawed presumption, then sets about illustrating the alternate perspective with a story. "You have heard stories like this," the book seems to say, "but let me tell you another."

Such an approach is a reasonable adjustment of the impasses in the first two novels. *Courrier Sud* forced the first-person viewpoint into repeated contradictions by mysteriously announcing the same revelation through its many voices without allowing revealed truth more than a circumstantial basis. *Vol de Nuit* addressed the contradictions by discarding the first-person vantage for an omniscient one. Now the novelist could explore the sense of things at any given moment without having to tender an explanation . . . but this ploy only enhanced the credibility of the story's mind-reading: it did not explain how every mind could be orbiting the same center if truth is created by circumstance. Such a validation of message by aesthetic unity rather than ethical teleology is, alas, ethically invalid. Saint-Exupéry permanently rejected it. Indeed, he seems to have so mistrusted the "easy beauty" of omniscience that he reclaimed the role of first-person participant for the rest of his literary career. *Terre des Hommes* revels in first-hand experience and in intimate testimonials to comrades; and, in answer to the old problem of how a participant may be everywhere at once to plumb the sense of events, it simply renounces the conventional complex narrative. The author carries us as far as he can on his own direct knowledge, and no farther. Intricate stories about several characters doing various things at various locations become impossible to tell from such a perspective, but at least what the author tells is what the author has lived.

There is no obvious reason why this aesthetic failure to traffic in intricate unity should constitute a moral failure, any more than the aesthetic success of a unified narrative necessarily validates its moral lessons for the real world. I proposed in my introductory chapter that narrative coherence reflects a moral quest for integrity; but one might as well argue, as Bakhtin does, that disruptions of such coherence reflect a morally salutary "dispersion [of paradigms] into rivulets and droplets of social heteroglossia" (263). Though Saint-Exupéry was no great exponent of empowering the masses, he would have agreed that life's complexity is best made comprehensible not through a rigidly archetypal pattern, but through a creatively flexible idiom. Hence *Terre des Hommes*'s favoring of numerous vignettes over a single inexorable sequence of events would not have left him embarrassed. He had decided early on that an inspired metaphor is as close to objective truth as man may approach. The test of truth is "ce qui simplifie le monde"—"that which simplifies the world" (*SV* 156). Never again after *Vol de Nuit* did he trouble to weave an intricate plot as a means of evoking practical reality. What he writes of aircraft design in chapter 3 of *Terre des Hommes* could readily be extrapolated to other circumstances, such as creating a work of art or an ethical system:

> It seems that every industrial effort of man, all his calculations, all his wakeful nights spent over the drawing board, find their consummation, as visible signs, only in simplicity—as if the experience of several generations was necessary to set free, little by little, the curve of a column, a prow, or an airplane's fuselage until the elementary purity of a breast's or shoulder's curve was bestowed upon them.[1] (169)

Thus the impasse posed by *Terre des Hommes* was not its relative incoherence as a story, but the unprofitably antithetical links between its sub-stories. Are they various enactments—better and better, closer and closer—of the primeval story, the myth? But where, then, is that myth? More even than the two previous novels, this book leaves us feeling that the arch-narrative, the Hero Slaying the Dragon, is just beyond the horizon—or, more exactly, in the very center of things and casting its huge shadow in all directions, yet unaccountably unnamed. Each new tale seems to correct or qualify the previous one concerning some subtle but not inconsequential error. On the basis of what blueprint are these modifications added? If that blueprint is a mythic act, what hero is its author; and if it is an eternal verity under whose preemptive rule all human acts tend to allegory, then what god has authored this verity?

The Sermon on the Mount has good reason to contrast the letter and the spirit of the law: While the spirit is invisible, the letter both incarnates it and renders it conspicuous by its absence. Jesus invites people to dwell upon the deficiencies of what they can see in order to convince them that something must exist which they cannot see. *Terre des Hommes* plays this game to no purpose, however, since it replaces an unsatisfying picture only with another picture, and another, always finding its offered images incomplete but never willing to concede that it seeks the unimaginable. It is a self-deluded hall of mirrors which hardly awaits deconstruction, which virtually deconstructs itself in its restless rounds of substitution. Its gospel depends wholly upon unbelievers and persecutors to usher in revelation. It forces falsehood to precede truth. The creative spirit which dares to confront chaos and affirm order is deeply beholden to dusty, pharisaical bureaucrats for its lofty disdain.

Cate has observed that such uneasy surrender to absurdly arbitrary meanings and values less approximates existentialism, despite the frequent claims of that school's zealots, than the "resistentialism" of Ortega y Gasset (368). His classification seems well justified from the standpoint of comparative ethics; but could Saint-Exupéry really have found comfort in this uncomfortable truce? He would virtually have been asserting that right depends upon wrong, since no *esprit fin* would be able to awaken us to moral distinctions if some cruder but more dominant character or group had not first imposed a body of prejudices autocratically.

One must conclude that, though Saint-Exupéry was poignantly aware of the problem here, he was never fully aware of it. In *Citadelle*, he would continue to wrestle with the arbitrary egotism of certain creative acts and the self-annihilating nobility of others. At no point in the posthumous work did he overtly determine that right and wrong rest upon abstract, *a priori* principles rather than upon the dynamic struggle of interests. Jesus had used antithesis to destabilize his hearers, to make them see an imperative which transcends tradition. In contrast, Saint-Exupéry's antithetical technique risks establishing its own kind of pernicious stability. It polarizes, chiding incurious brethren not so much for what they do as for doing it too lethargically; and the passage from lethargy to creativity to lethargy is, of course, as easy as the swing of a pendulum. Even a Bernis or a Fabien can grow jaded—even cyclones and constellations get old.

Life therefore becomes an unending process of reanimation, weariness, and reanimation. The creator—a human creator, motivating through new images and idioms—constantly pushes off, in antithetical fashion, from yesterday's novelty, just as Russian theoretician Viktor Shklovsky had proposed. Weariness is the great sin, the only sin; and we are protected from it only by new, electrifying revisions. *Citadelle*'s monarch even eulogizes his enemy at numerous points for giving his kingdom something against which to strive. "I will even say," summarizes the king, "that I have more effect on my enemy than on my friend, for that man who walks in the same direction as I offers me fewer occasions of meeting and exchange than the one who goes against me and does not ignore either my gestures (for he depends upon them) or my words" (859).[2] One might be forgiven for wondering if Saint-Exupéry himself, anticipating with near-clairvoyance the disarray into which post-war Europe would tumble, did not sense a certain gratitude to the Nazis. "What frightens me more than the war is the world of tomorrow," he once wrote to his mother (*LM* 219).[3] The post-war world would require substantial answers founded in immovable moral truths. Sure enough, such answers were not forthcoming once the great adversary was defeated.

Yet *Citadelle* speaks in just as many places about the vital importance of spiritual evolution. The fervent individual needs more than an enemy to fight: he or she needs a destination toward which to emigrate. The swing of the pendulum must become the coil of an ascending spiral. If this all-important but ever-elusive fulfillment is often pessimistically identified not with heaven, but with the peace of death, its persistence in *Citadelle*'s unfinished manuscript nonetheless proves that Saint-Exupéry was no inveterate relativist. The jolt of an outlandish novelty is not enough. Otherwise, why would *Terre des*

Hommes invoke devotion and sacrifice from start to finish? For all the book's vignettes have this in common, after all: one must exchange oneself for something higher. The difference between mere change and growth is that, while the former evades identity, the latter redefines it against an immovable objective.

So the various examples and counter-examples are really exemplifying an already well-established truth . . . but what, then, is that truth? What makes the object of one's sacrifice higher than oneself—how can the exhilaration of service arise merely from serving, so that the object's worth is bestowed retroactively? Children and lunatics may lock away and bury a cheap trinket, but what does a sane adult hold dear? If the antithetical strategy of *Terre des Hommes* cannot draw its insights to a higher plane, it must end where it began, a futile tug-of-war between equally vexed alternatives. Yet the strain which would give these opposed energies an upward thrust can only originate in such abstraction, not in the heat of a terrestrial competition. There is no way to illustrate immaterial realities with purely material exempla.

Terre des Hommes brought this genuinely philosophical impasse to the surface in a way that its predecessors, hampered by problems of narrative mechanics, had been quite unable to do. As a writer, Saint-Exupéry was now fully in his element. The perspective was his, its authority was his, the time was composed of moments from his own life, and the message was one validated by his own suffering. Now, at last, he must have begun to see that he had not declared what life is, but only what it is not. He had been offering counter-stories rather than The Story.

II.

The book's first chapter, "La Ligne," examines the commercial pilot's profession, a reversal in many ways of what society believes a profession ought to be: safe, steady, and offering opportunities for material advancement. Yet even before any explicit contrast with the typical bureaucrat is drawn, Saint-Exupéry begins to imply that the world is not what we think. He generously offers his own ignorance as an example. The seasoned pilot Bury had once upon a time scoffed at the aristocratic young trainee's questions after having navigated a ferocious storm (140–41), leaving him with grave self-doubts. Months later, Saint-Exupéry's friend and mentor Guillaumet confirms this encroaching sense that surfaces deceive. On the unforgettable night just before Antoine is to make his first official flight, Guillaumet takes him aside and initiates him into certain mysteries of the trade. On a map of Spain spread before a lamp, Guillaumet tells him of the three orange trees near Guadix and of the river west of Motril—treacherous enemies waiting to destroy the pilot forced to make an emergency landing. "And, little by little, the Spain of my map became, under the lamp's light, a fairytale land. I marked with a cross the points of refuge and the traps" (145).[4] No more is his map that "white paste [which] used to be for me the frontier between the real and the unreal, between the known and the unknowable" (143).[5] Now the world of his transit is a land of men, a world referred to human culture—to the practical needs of a pilot in distress—and not just a series of altitudes oriented to the points of the compass. Now he knows faces in addition to possessing the "facts." In a placid field lay a snake that devoured planes: a narrow riverbed. Who would have guessed it, just from looking at the map? Only experience makes the facts real.

These encounters with Bury and Guillaumet had already appeared in a fictional context, the former in *Vol de Nuit* and the latter in *Courrier Sud*. The young Saint-Exupéry's walk home after conferring with Guillaumet even suggests Rivière's stroll through the evening crowds, punctuated with conspiratorial glances at the stars, those companions of night flight. There are many other resonances of the two novels, indicating how heavily Saint-Exupéry had drawn upon personal experience when ostensibly not writing about himself. He is clearly comfortable with the direct and unpretentious narration of *Terre des Hommes*, a comfort reflected in the fluidity with which he makes subjectively motivated transitions.

At the same time, we must notice that these magical moments share some of the self-contradiction found in the earlier novels. Why the conspiracy with the stars? Ricardou had insisted that Rivière was deluded when he felt himself more drawn to the heavens than to the human throng around him: after all, nature is the hero's adversary in the Exupérian scenario. Likewise, the map brought to life by Guillaumet is not really a "cultivated" human construct so much as Morgan Le Fay's libretto of spells, charms, and trade secrets. Its cosmos is that of the chaos-resisting warrior who depends upon his enemy for employment, not of normal families raising children and transmitting customs. Saint-Exupéry's fervor for his new *métier* is already being fueled by a certain anti-social independence.

The next scene, in fact, shows as much disdain for social ritual as any passage Saint-Exupéry would ever write. He has clambered on board the tramway (as Schiff warns us to translate *omnibus* [139 at footnote]) that will take him to the aerodrome. It is three o'clock: he is still half-asleep, like all of his fellow passengers. Their fellowship is more appearance than reality, he muses. The others go to their offices, while "the pilot of the line, mixed with the functionaries," is destined finally to disembark as from "a gray chrysalis from which the man would emerge transfigured" (146).[6] In his contemplation, Saint-Exupéry's contempt turns to pity: "Old bureaucrat at my elbow . . . you don't look at all like the inhabitant of a wandering planet, you pose yourself no questions without answers. . . . By this time, the clay of which you were formed has dried and hardened, and no being within you would know how to awaken the sleeping musician, or the poet, or the astronomer, who perhaps originally used to live inside you" (148).[7]

The content of this scene is particularly important insofar as it lays bare the essential difference between pilot and bureaucrat. The former is a creator, while the latter simply consumes the cosmos which others have designed. In Major's words, "Even in the presence of the bureaucrats who accompany him in the bus at dawn, Saint-Exupéry formulates, not a condemnation, but an uneasiness, a need to rediscover man" (116). In a subtle way, the tram ride foreshadows the final image of *Terre des Hommes*: that of the infant Mozart asleep in the railway carriage, lost forever, in all probability, to squalid poverty and an existence of brutish routine.

This slightly disdainful compassion is rather humane, even noble—and certainly a stark contrast to its object, the vegetative victim of the urban treadmill. What waits at the other end of the contrast, however? What will save us all from a similar degeneration? As Major implies, the formula must potentially transform us all, not just those of us who are pilots, deep-sea divers, and cowboys. We can anticipate how splendidly the maiden flight will differ from this dismal procession; but what we still need to be shown is how the sad bureaucrats might take their own flight one day. If everyone flew, would "flight" be possible—or is a prerequisite of flight precisely that it is impossible for most?

A bit surprisingly, the first flight ends up producing no incident worth recounting. Saint-Exupéry's antithetical frame of mind even toys with our expectation of a good yarn. Instead, he makes the most unlikely of moves: he shifts his glorious profession through metaphor so that he is no longer a flier so much as a slightly mad scientist in a laboratory. Flight, he tells us, is most often a kind of alchemy wherein the pilot, hunched over his dials, descends with perfect timing to pull his creation from the oven. "Gold is born from the Void: it beams in the refueling strip's beacons" (149).[8]

Having thus deprived his *métier* of its anticipated drama, our pilot-author then lurches in the opposite direction and speaks of those exceptional outings—those fairy-tale occurrences through which we might have wished to see him navigate a few pages earlier with his fairy-tale map, courtesy of Guillaumet. Such was the experience of Mermoz when he was first to cross the South Atlantic in a hydro-plane. At the climax of his crossing, "He broke in upon a realm of fantasy."[9] A series of waterspouts had worked its way around him, forming a kind of gigantic colonnade down which he could only steer his craft in awed wonder. "And this spectacle was so overwhelming that Mermoz, once the Black Pot was behind, perceived that he had not been afraid" (150).[10] Another reversal of expectation: the hero was so busy slipping under giants' coattails that he had forgotten to be afraid! The absurdity of heroism as conceived by uninvolved on-lookers will remain the major subject of the next chapter.

Saint-Exupéry concludes this opening section with the personal flight adventure which he had begrudged us earlier—an incident where the wrong gold came out of the pilot's oven, one might say. Traveling at night over Africa and sealed off from the continent by fog, he and his navigator had lost their bearings. Finally they located a distant beacon; yet it stood impervious to their flashed signals, until they realized that they were hailing a star. "From that point, we felt ourselves lost in interplanetary space . . ." (151),[11] a predicament reminiscent of Fabien's in *Vol de Nuit*. Obviously, this crisis had a happier resolution. What fable of disorientation could possibly employ more evocative symbolism, however? A pioneer, a pilgrim, lost in the stars and looking for the one in a million which calls truly, which is his home's window ... what could be more antithetical both to the laboratory precision which Saint-Exupéry has deceptively put in our minds and to the melodramatic heroism of which we were probably thinking from the start?

Yet the author's shifting cannot stop here: too much is still missing. Why, after all, did Mermoz forget to be afraid, and why is the "lost in the stars" fable so evocative? To answer that both incidents surprise their participants would be inaccurate and manipulative. They do and they do not. Anyone who has ever witnessed a spectacular thunderstorm or become completely disoriented while alone in a foreign city knows the feeling. It consists somewhat of our being severed from conditioned prejudices about the normal universe, yes—but is it simply a vacuous confusion created by the absence of prejudice, or does something precede and survive prejudice which even the most stunning shock cannot dispel? The ecstasy of these pilots implies that their inner life has not merely gone numb, ready to be annihilated by the environment's chaotic power; yet what we observe them clinging to is no robotically imbibed protocol or fanatically trusted formula (Rivière's mystery-retardant swagger and drill). Whatever in their minds endures the rude impact of chaos is no image of a mythic hero toughing out a greater impact. It is essentially human, and it *interacts* with rather than tunes out the external threat in order to elevate the soul. In a small way, Saint-Exupéry is anticipating *Pilote de Guerre*'s central impasse.

The mention of Mermoz seems to arouse in Saint-Exupéry certain observations about camaraderie with which he begins chapter 2, "Les Camarades." Having tirelessly accepted one risk after another, Mermoz finally disappeared on a relatively routine flight over the South Atlantic. Saint-Exupéry remarks with wonder that, although pilots of the line rarely encounter each other more than once in several months—and then only briefly—the loss of Mermoz nonetheless left a gap in the lives of other fliers. Their common dedication to a single end had created a context within which even rare and brief encounters became rich in meaning. "There is only one true luxury," he concludes, "and it's that of having human ties" (158).[12] People bound together in a shared enterprise enjoy a wealth which the materially wealthy must envy and may never understand.

In illustration, he relates another anecdote about a Christmas-like evening which he and two companions passed in Morocco, surrounded by the Sahara, hemmed in by hostile tribes, needing daylight to make necessary repairs on a damaged craft. For all their material poverty, they were rich in spirit: another paradox, another reversal of expectation. One would have to live the life of devoted service to comprehend how three men on the brink of starvation or massacre could sing and joke such a night away.

Thus two slender shafts of elucidation have been admitted into the gray question of what makes life worth living: the ties between comrades and the nobility of sacrifice. But is this elucidation really an optical illusion? Do fraternal ties create an atmosphere of willing sacrifice for others, or does the ethic of sacrifice create closely bonded comrades—which comes first? Does the sacrifice have to be valuable in some abstract sense to cement people together—or will any cause, however absurd, suffice as long as its servants believe in it? If people already have the capacity to feel warm dedication to each other, why do they need a cause—and if they are not innately so inclined, what kind of cause works this magical transformation? Could it be that these examples have really explained nothing at all?

The bulk of chapter 2 is saved for its greatest paradox, the unheroic heroism of Henri Guillaumet. Saint-Exupéry painstakingly frames this narrative in antithetical terms. He has read another account of his friend's ordeal, he says, which portrayed Guillaumet as dismissing his situation's dangers with frivolous wisecracks—"as if courage consisted of lowering oneself to a school kid's rails and jeers" (160).[13] The real Guillaumet had been forced down on a crest of the Andes during a terrific storm. Unable to take off again from his precarious perch, he had begun the long trek back on foot. After an indeterminable number of days on the move, the castaway had only wanted to lie down and sleep: any instinct of self-preservation had long since vanished. Yet he would repeat to himself, "My wife, if she believes that I'm still alive, believes that I'm walking. My friends believe that I'm walking. They're all placing their trust in me. And I'm a scoundrel if I do not walk" (164).[14]

So he continued to walk, not belittling his peril or fighting with animal tenacity—not displaying the heroism of a popular romance—but clinging to a thin thread of meaning which extended beyond the unspeakable void. "What I did, I swear to you, no animal would ever have done," later he declared to Saint-Exupéry (165).[15] Only a human being has the imagination to sustain a patently absurd struggle which even an animal would relinquish: only a human being can make order where there is none.

Such is Guillaumet's heroism. Like Fabien, he succeeds in discovering and affirming order in the very face of his own annihilation. Saint-Exupéry echoes Rivière's comments about mystery when he adds in epilogue, "Only the unknown frightens people. Yet for whoever confronts it, it is already no longer the unknown" (166).[16] This is so, apparently (Saint-Exupéry becomes rather vague here), not because the void conceals a hidden prize of knowledge, but because its human combatant imposes the dictates of his own heart upon nullity. In Guillaumet's case, he saw in the white oblivion around him the faces of those who were waiting and hoping. "His greatness was to take responsibility upon himself."[17] Released from a narrow culture into an immeasurable infinity, Guillaumet had the courage, or the modesty, or the gravity, or the heroism, to re-create and reassert his cosmos.

The remark about tolerating a drudgery which no animal would have accepted reveals that in Gillaumet's mind, at least, the inner power driving us at such moments is indeed in our own hearts. But if we are instead asserting the circumstantial order programmed into us, as Saint-Exupéry implies, then the response is infinitely less noble. We have simply been wound up to go, like mechanisms running on cogs and springs, and the first catastrophe activates our auxiliary power. Does this describe Henri Guillaumet? Are the Andes so much vaster than his feeble imagination that he can only focus on a light burning in a window? Is his concern for his wife a quaint and curious relic of a special little love nest, as journalists and romance-writers would have it—or does it manifest that consideration for others understood by every decent human being (if acted upon by rather fewer)? In any event, how would a circumstantial order—a loving wife, a circle of close friends—ever fill up the void of chaos? Earlier examples have portrayed chaos sweeping away like a house of cards the flimsy prejudices of those wretches who stumble into it. So which case is true? Do these moments where one's cherished sense of the norm is obliterated before one's eyes not erase everything, after all? Perhaps the idea is that some elements of cosmos, certain collaborative ties, are less flimsy than others . . . but which ones, and why?

The third chapter, "L'Avion," is so short that its very brevity offers something of an antithesis to what the reader might have anticipated in this book about the wondrous new field of aviation. Surely the aircraft itself, as great a technological miracle to Saint-Exupéry's generation as space travel would be to the next one, rates more than a couple of pages . . . and even these few pages are occupied with discounting rather than emphasizing the machine's triumph over human limitation. The airplane, like any other invention, is merely a new appendage, an extension of the human being's capacity to act upon his or her environment. Just as he cleansed Guillaumet's arduous journey of all heroic mystique and presented it as a profoundly human accomplishment, so Saint-Exupéry translates the machine from the rationalized tool of Satan which romantics would make of it to an expression of human creativity—a poem. Indeed, the perfect machine, like the perfect work of art, blends with nature almost imperceptibly. "And just as everything clearly mechanical in the flying instrument has been effaced, little by little, and an object as natural as a pebble polished by the sea has come into our hands, even so is it marvelous how the machine, in the very process of running, has caused itself to be forgotten little by little" (170).[18]

Thus plane and pilot become one just as, in an earlier age, plow and farmer became one. In our silly presumption, we expect a contraption from H. G. Wells to transform us without requiring our active participation. The truth is that we can only be transformed by ourselves, and then only by fully engrossed and devoted participation. The poet Pierre Reverdy had written at about this time, "The essence of an act is in the soul; action and activity concern the machine, the human mechanism in motion" (207). Saint-Exupéry had the same thing in mind. . . .

Or did he? Reverdy's reflection implies the dichotomy between thought and act which Saint-Exupéry always rejected. To some extent, gadgetry seems an indispensable part of the pilot myth—perhaps less because it is a myth about pilots than because it is a myth. What would Perseus be without his winged sandals or Bellerophon without his Pegasus? Whereas Reverdy's focus on the human soul insinuates that Saint George and George Bernard Shaw are, after all, made of the same basic stuff, however differently combined, Saint-Exupéry seems very reluctant to grant that any soul contains more than what its environment has put there. The pilot hero needs his airplane to test the honesty and durability of his thought: his brave aspiration can only be validated by take-off. His action defines him, in high mythic fashion. Creative energy moves back and forth reciprocally between him and his plane. If it were otherwise—if the airplane were the utterly dependent brainchild of a daring intelligence—then why might not the bureaucrats on the tramway have been draftsmen and designers? Why would their dare be less than the pilot's?

Chapter 4, "L'Avion et la Planète," also begins in an aggressively antithetical vein. The airplane has unmasked the deception practiced upon us by our highways and byways, says Saint-Exupéry. We could not be more deluded about our planet's habitability if we were royalty at whose passage the oppressed peasants had been told to cheer. We believe that our world teems with green pastures and flowing rivers because our culture, naturally, concentrates itself around such points of fertility. From several miles up in the sky, however, the pilot discerns traces of human civilization only with study and patience, like a biologist searching a sterile drop of water for a patch of green and its colony of protozoans. How precariously rooted in the earth is that urban order which we deem as natural and irresistible as the sunrise!

Two graphic illustrations of this fragility occur to Saint-Exupéry, both of which his aircraft has allowed him to discover. The inactive craters which one observes in flying over Patagonia are not immediately impressive, for people seldom reflect upon the vast history of terrestrial violence lying literally under their feet. Upon these craters are tenuously grafted (as the northbound flier observes) the green fields of Punta Arenas, the southernmost town in the world. Who would ever suspect that charming, placid Punta Arenas sits upon an unstable and temporary surface? Saint-Exupéry recalls a local girl who smiled to herself while drawing water from a fountain. "From thoughts about her lover, from his voice, and from his silences, she was able to build a Kingdom, and from then on, beyond that pale, there were only barbarians for her" (175).[19] On the very fringe of the habitable universe, people are already building their castles in the sky.

This passage, far from clarifying anything, reverses the chapter's opening reversal. In Punta Arenas, if anywhere on earth, we might have expected to find a land of men trembling in constant humility before the forces of chaos. Yet wherever humanity can find a foothold, apparently, it proceeds to fashion grand illusions. Are the girl's naive daydreams about her lover, then, to be viewed as assertions of cosmos in the same way as Guillaumet's feat of endurance? Is frivolous naiveté of the same order as mortal self-sacrifice? Again, is the encounter with chaos supposed to jar silly ideas loose from human minds, or only to provide an occasion for showing just how silly those ideas are?

A similar incident involves Saint-Exupéry's discovery of minute meteorites on Saharan plateaus. Utterly inaccessible except by plane, these raised surfaces have never been walked upon by human foot since they broke off from the surrounding terrain—an event which must have occurred long before *homo sapiens* was walking anywhere. "A tablecloth laid under the stars can catch nothing but stardust" (176),[20] so this evidence of the planet's antiquity strewn amply around him on every plateau must be authentic. The universe has not anxiously awaited humanity's appearance, nor, perhaps, will humanity's presence have measured more than a split second on this chronometer of shooting stars.

As with the section about the craters, Saint-Exupéry seems unwilling to hand us a sublime image of our fragility and move on. He appends another Saharan incident, a case where a malfunctioning craft has again left him stranded far from help in the territory of marauding nomad tribes. Gazing into the night, with no point of earthly contact except the dune at his back, he feels a momentary vertigo, as if he were in free fall through the galaxy. Yet the sensation quickly passes, succeeded by an absurd but wondrously reassuring memory of his childhood governess. He envisions her precisely folding, counting, and distributing the linens; like Guillaumet in the Andes, his fall through the void has been arrested by a thin but invincible tie to an order far away. Frail as human culture is—a microevent between two drops in a meteor shower—it is nonetheless man's answer to the senselessness of the world around him. Its fragility renders it not pompous, presumptuous, or contemptible, but invaluably precious.

Here we find less enlightenment than ever. An old woman folding linens . . . one could have hoped for a nobler, or at least more devastating, assessment of human cosmos from the brink of the abyss. Conrad's Marlow admires Kurtz precisely and only because of his final pronouncement: "The horror!" Emily Dickinson's persona hears a fly buzz when she dies—a witless tease which undermines all possible summary assessments. Yet Saint-Exupéry offers his linen closet in good faith. Chaos yawns over you, everything goes dark, and then from your crackling neurons comes the image of . . . a pillow case! Emily's fly makes more sense in its senselessness. Of course, hiding behind this image may be an entire childhood, a redeemingly universal range of innocent loves and hopes. Has not Saint-Exupéry eulogized his governess so incongruously just *because* he sensed the imminence of something universal? But universality imbalances all his equations. Myth requires that the hero bring back to his village a lustrous and unique prize—a golden apple or a Pandora's box. He must not simply declare to his expectant clan Socratically, "What you need to know is what you already know."

Still, is any of these revelations more than a mirror held before the prophet's eyes? In his mistrust of immaterial, *a priori* truths—in his need to discover something substantial "out there"—Saint-Exupéry paradoxically condemned his thought to non-ascent, to impasse. The linen closet turns out to be an apt metaphor for his entire system, images doubling back upon themselves, the door shut tightly upon the lot of them.

The maiden at the fountain and the housekeeping governess pose yet another antithesis to the preceding matter: through them the female appears, an unlikely intruder into this evolving "land of men." *Courrier Sud* had already manifested Saint-Exupéry's tendency to equate the female with home, childhood, and the extra-vital security of the womb. *Vol de Nuit* had denigrated such associations—but then, it had straightjacketed the vagaries of Saint-Exupéry's other favorite images, as well. Now *Terre des Hommes* re-elevates females to their original pedestal. While these tutelary spirits are themselves incapable of heroics, they inspire the chaos-tossed pilot to retain his cultural conditioning in a crisis. They remain mysteriously immune to the corruptive social grind which that hapless variety of male without woman or *métier* cannot resist. They never rise as high as the pilot, but neither do they sink as low as the bureaucrat. They could negotiate the mummifying Toulouse tramway without batting an eyelash.

Chapter 5, "Oasis," continues the study of uncorrupted, nymph-like femininity. The chapter is extremely brief and need not even have been inserted. Its irrelevance is so visible, in fact, that Saint-Exupéry begins by advancing a rather playful and thoroughly unconvincing defense: he wishes to visit an oasis, he says, before plunging back into the desert for some while. An image coined earlier is also flipped to reverse its truism. Those green traces of life which the pilot-biologist must scrutinize so intently from his flying laboratory are not, after all, negligible in the surrounding expanses of rock and sand. Parts of the earth are quite lush. A sudden descent into them would reveal other kingdoms presided over by other virgin goddesses, like the water fountain at Punta Arenas.

This time the kingdom is an ancient mansion in Paraguay, and the deities are two in number: the young daughters of the eccentric proprietor who eye their guest from the heavens suspiciously at the dinner table. Schiff calls them "another incarnation of the kind of fairy princesses he [Saint-Exupéry] had always known existed" (180). The girls have turned the whole rainforest into their personal zoo, it seems—or, better yet, "a new terrestrial paradise. They were reigning over all the animals of creation" (183).[21] At first, they are not entirely sure that the dinner guest deserves to be admitted into their inner circle. Fortunately, he passes the ultimate test. Upon being informed that the slight rasping sound beneath the table is a viper family returning from a day of hunting, he nods calmly and suppresses a twitch of horror.

Evidently, Saint-Exupéry regards it as a great privilege to have been accepted by two little princesses who, like his own Little Prince later on, remain unsullied by adult prejudices and can evaluate animals and people on the basis of performance, not talk. Yet he is also dis-turbed at the thought of what the two girls may have become over the intervening years. Each one, beguiled in her turn by a fool who pretends to understand nature, will probably have given away that heart "which is a wild garden to one who loves only well-trimmed parks. And the imbecile leads the princess away into slavery" (185).[22] Such sympathy for the plight of the female in many domestic arrangements will no doubt startle those who know Saint-Exupéry best from his later works. The monarch of *Citadelle*, for instance, seems to like his women held well in check—and even Mme. Fabien prefers arranging flowers to stroking scaly pets.

Does this sympathy rest with oppressed women, though, or with the fragile order of flowers, linens, and nurseries which they anchor? Perhaps the slavery of a "well-trimmed park" resides in its lack of Eden's elusive intricacy: perhaps it substitutes the all-too-transparently feigned world of the social butterfly for the ritual-intensive domestic one of the barefoot farmgirl. Perhaps the strictures of the public man's cocktail-party protocol bite and mangle not because they are too many, but because they bind in all the wrong places. The cruel Herlin wanted Geneviève to re-create her idyll in his terms, and Bernis could not rescue her (nor she him) precisely because he had stolen her from the garden.

Could it be that a woman liberated from her domestic domain can no longer replicate or imitate that ultimate destination toward which the pilot guides his craft—that peace which always awaits him just over the next horizon? Does a fairy princess need to be nestled in the jungle because, anywhere else, she might possibly be found? Is that what Saint-Exupéry holds against young imbeciles?

The authorial smirk about visiting an oasis before wandering off into the desert may be more serious than we (or Saint-Exupéry) thought. It may reveal a genuine sense of gap, of embarrassment—of postponed meaning—haunting the desert episode and supplied here in anticipation. Saint-Exupéry will in fact find himself hard pressed to explain why he staggered through the Sahara as Guillaumet did through the Andes. He will scarcely mention his own wife, perhaps because he was too keenly aware that, for Consuelo, he was the point of indefinite regression, the burly god with wings. Let us be honest: Genevièves and Mme. Fabiens occur intermittently throughout all of Saint-Exupéry's work. Take all their occurrences together, and you will find no clear development whatever in the author's understanding of the female. Instead, they are two contradictory sides of Woman: the Princess Unattainable to all lovers and the lover of the Unattainable Prince. Obviously, this female Janus has an exact male analogue: the pilot in quest of mythic fulfillment and the pilot sealed forever in his fulfilled myth—Bernis in Nôtre Dame and Bernis in the Parisienne's bed—Fabien in the clouds and Fabien before the moon.

The only difference in the cycles is their sequence. Woman is created complete. She is already edenic in her ignorance and innocence. Her inaccessibility in turn creates heroes who hurl themselves into the abyss to reach her—whereupon she may then hurl herself after the hero of her choice.

What real advance of understanding is to be found in this coy game of displacing ends? What does it all mean . . . what is it all for?

Just as an oasis has no poignancy without a surrounding desert—just as a desert has none without at least the illusion of an oasis—so *Terre des Hommes*, despite its self-reversals, is steadily leading up to chapter 7, the longest and most intimate section of the book. Chapter 6, "Dans le Désert," sets the scene for Saint-Exupéry's dramatic reenactment of Guillaumet's ordeal. A desert, of course, is a place of great emptiness and silence: but its barrenness is also fertile, Saint-Exupéry reminds us. Here we find enhanced the essential meaning of life, the minimally adorned struggle of cosmos to declare itself in the void. The mere existence of a well to the north when you are parched with thirst orients the universe rigidly around a single source of magnetism: each step acquires significance according to how directly and how quickly it approaches water. "A raid also transforms the sands" (187);[23] the mere knowledge that a hostile tribe is on the move in the south makes the unveiling of each new vista from the crest of each new dune a minor climax of suspense. In the Sahara's harsh simplicity, life is always full of purpose.

Hence the Arab chieftains whom Saint-Exupéry's airline once flew to Europe in a gesture of goodwill (or, more honestly, in an attempt at intimidation [cf. Robinson 42]) were most dismayed not by aircraft or railways, but by an incessant Swiss waterfall. The complex toys of the Europeans only demonstrated their well-known frivolity, but water—water was life, and the wooing of it was the sense of life. Yet God had squandered inconceivable amounts of water upon the infidels. . . . The chieftains decided not to report what they had seen. "It is better to say nothing about certain miracles. It is better, even, not to think about them too much: otherwise one no longer understands anything—otherwise one begins to doubt God" (195).[24] They had witnessed the very keystone of their cosmos being plucked out—had glimpsed the ensuing senseless chaos—and they had chosen to reassert that cosmos by covering their eyes and forgetting. Even thoughtlessness, if willful, can be an act of creative denial, it would appear. Just so had Rivière dissuaded his pilots from thinking too much about the night's dangers.

Chapter 6 offers other vignettes in illustration of the desert's taut, grandly primeval "lines of force," such as the windblown insects which betray the approach of a terrific sandstorm from green plantations far to the east. At these moments, the text obviously opposes our preconception of a desert as an empty expanse without reference points. By implication, it challenges the presumption that a cosmos full of material wealth is necessarily more humane and rewarding.

Yet perhaps this chapter's most vigorous antithesis is again with itself. Having presented the desert as a return to simplicity, a kind of romantic wilderness where people may strip the corruptive dross of civilization from their souls, Saint-Exupéry also would have it be a Darwinian chaos of mindless power. Just as the Arab chieftains who visit Europe suppress their nullifying experience in order to cling to their worldview, so the Europeans—the more heroic of them, at any rate—cling to their distant ties in the face of a yawning abyss where "the gifts of the earth trickle through one's fingers like the fine sand of the dunes" (186).[25] The old sergeant languishing in a desert outpost who fêtes passing Frenchmen and speaks constantly of his cousin in Tunis is the source of Jacques Bernis's last human encounter, as Saint-Exupéry himself reminds us ("I have told this story in a book . . ." [188]).[26] His full significance to the author is much clearer here, however. *Terre des Hommes* supplies a context (as *Courrier Sud* never could) in which this mildly comic castaway's devotion to a dormant, invisible culture assumes heroic proportions.

Likewise, the story of Bark, the slave who lives only to repossess his freedom and return to Marrakech, exemplifies the victory of tenacious, creative faith despite overwhelmingly unfavorable circumstances. Bark—or Mohammed, as he insists on being called (his name before enslavement)—does make his return, after all, thanks to Saint-Exupéry's personal intercession. He celebrates his liberation by lavishing the village children with gifts: that is to say, he celebrates reabsorption into his culture with a spree of forging ties. His cosmos has recrystallized from the desert's vacuum, none the worse for a few years' suspension.

So what is the desert's true identity—chaos or cosmos? Though introduced into *Terre des Hommes* as a stark contrast to tired, bored, spoiled societies, the desert seems to have no inspirational power of its own: only blunt force. The strong-willed individual who blunders into it while struggling against advanced social decay is precisely the one best able to resist its influence. His native ethos, for all its present corruption, awaits revival in him, and a push into the chasm does the trick. As a site for spiritual regeneration, then, the desert turns out to be indifferent, neither more nor less suited to inspire a human being than any other alien location. Switzerland has the same effect on the Arabs. Though Chevrier asserts, "The experience of the desert ... will prove to be of the utmost importance" (20), and though others tend to concur that Saint-Exupéry found God in the desert, Devaux is surely more correct in observing that Saint-Exupéry does not belong on the long list of those who "have experienced in the desert the intimate certainty of God Incarnate's familiar presence, the God with whom it is sweet to converse" (66).

While Saint-Exupéry's rhetorical strategy calls for a setting which vigorously opposes Paris or Toulouse, then, his message cannot sustain such antithesis. A Parisian pilot stranded in the Sahara preserves his Parisian values if he is a substantial, loyal person, just as the old sergeant pines for Tunis and Bark dreams of Marrakech. The relativity of all value systems so often declared explicitly in *Citadelle* is already implicit in the subtle doubling back of *Terre des Hommes*. Just as he sometimes consigns women to subservience and at others elevates them worshipfully to guardian angels, Saint-Exupéry condemns a decadent Europe only to raise it up again when least expected. In the final analysis, he finds no objective basis for considering the desert more spiritual than the city or a man more energetically devoted to cosmos than a woman. Another tale, and another, keeps coming to clarify his point—or to obscure it for those who seek too facile a clarification. Yet while the antithetical approach appears to insist upon a system different from or opposite to Western status quo, it actually manages to reinsert the existing system in disguise. The shocks which it creates are illusory.

The desert . . . a nothingness which might be anything, an anything which might be everything. Does it need an oasis, after all? Rather than green palms and sweet water, isn't the most powerful image of essence that "white out" of sensory overload—that stripping away of the flesh which leaves one naked before another voice within—as if the pilot were to steer his craft straight into the sun? But Saint-Exupéry, as he nears the blinding corona, closes his eyes and dreams of childhood. Devaux was right: he misses the missing god whose presence becomes almost palpable in utter absence.

Into this milieu of garbled reversals is inserted chapter 7, "Au Centre du Désert." Originally an article for *L'Intransigeant* (Cate 301), the chapter's sense of tension is understandably quite polished. The very title promises an unveiling of some mystery, a penetrating of some luminous core or some heart of darkness. Again, the antithetical wording has created an illusion. The marooned aviators, Saint-Exupéry and Prévost, discover nothing in the heart of the Sahara but animal tracks and mirages: no guardian angel or Angel of Death, no passage to the Underworld, no Jacob's ladder. At best, the befuddlement of their faculties as they battle heat and dehydration may unmask a certain existential truth; for what are human beings in any circumstances, if not castaways who project their subjective order onto the neutral (or at least impassive) screen of reality? Hardly inspirational . . . but Saint-Exupéry has suggested throughout his thrashing book that a bath in the void can put new sparkle into one's cultural conditioning. This is as visionary as it gets.

Like Guillaumet in the Andes, then, Saint-Exupéry preserves his ties with a world immeasurably distant from the present setting. "We discover that we are not the castaways. The castaways are those who wait! Those whom our silence threatens; those who are already torn apart by a terrible mistake. One cannot *not* run toward them" (232).[27] The images which the stranded pilots pursue from horizon to horizon are those of comrades and family: it is for them that Prévost weeps, and for them that Saint-Exupéry keeps walking even after his eyes cannot be trusted. The bonds, the lines of force, which encumber men and women before they set foot in chaos, are that arbitrary but indisputable substance which they re-create out of chaos. "For his part, Prévost will not feel, either, that anguish before death which they never tire of telling us about," concludes Saint-Exupéry. "But there is indeed something which he can't stand, no more than I. . . . Each second of silence murders a little more those whom I love" (223–24).[28]

The anguish before death: this staple of melodrama has been handled by earlier vignettes, always disparagingly. Mermoz "forgot to be afraid" while clinging to a vision of stability in the midst of sublime upheaval. No monsters reared up to swallow Guillaumet, either. As it returns to an oft-visited polarity, however, chapter 7 does add something new: the authority of personal experience. How can one contend that resisting oblivion does not require an extraordinary heroism accessible to very few unless one has personally faced such moments—how can one know death from the testimony of others? The fear of death stands behind and looms over all the lesser fears which keep the bureaucrat commuting on his bus and the academic caviling in his ivory tower. If such people were to break out into the open air, where would they end up? Would any spiritual satisfaction suffice to compensate them in the event of homelessness or starvation? Saint-Exupéry's own experience in the Sahara teaches him that the answer is affirmative. "Taking everything into account, I've had the best life can offer. If I were to return, I would begin where I left off. For me, life is to be lived" (237).[29]

Saint-Exupéry does not offer his example that we may go forth and dare fate in Hemingway-like fashion: "This formula is pretentious. I have no great admiration for toreadors" (238)[30] He is simply confirming, through personal experience, that death has no hidden horrors. Its nullifying power has been grossly exaggerated by popular fictions. The best antidote to the fear of death, naturally, would be firm belief in an afterlife; but such faith, like physical courage, seems to be given to some more than others, and Saint-Exupéry wishes to offer a hope available to all. The life of enthusiastic action extends this hope. Anyone can dare to live by his or her own conscience rather than the group's inertia: it only requires the energy to wake up. Once awakened, the active, dedicated human being will enjoy the double reward of having a purpose for living and of having lived for a purpose when the time comes to die. As Saint-Exupéry sums it up in the following chapter, "When we become aware of our role, even the most inglorious . . . then only can we live in peace, for that which gives a sense to life gives a sense to death" (256).[31]

To be sure, the offered hope takes several things for granted. Saint-Exupéry does not distinguish, either during his brush with death in the Sahara or at any other time in *Terre des Hommes*, between a life led according to real principles of conscience—a life of selflessness and self-discipline—and one led in counterconformity and whimsy. A dying bank manager might draw as much satisfaction from knowing that he had honored his community's trust as a dying pilot would draw from knowing that he had resisted his family's pressure to become a bank manager. Still, in a very roundabout way, chapter 7 asserts a fundamental truth necessary to any viable moral system: that the prospect of death cannot obviate the imperative to do right. Even the concept of an afterlife is pusillanimous if not combined with the concept of eternal goodness, whereas goodness alone has an enduring character in which the good person always lives on, though he or she should believe in no individuated afterlife. The Saint-Exupéry who urgently reports to us that death is nothing beside life seems to have reached a very similar conclusion.

Why, then, such shyness about saying so? Though faith is a gift, rationality is a given; and no insight is more accessible to a thinking (if occasionally hallucinating) mind in moments of vital crisis than that money, prestige, power, fame, and all the other acquired dross of our social context must pass from us like chaff in the wind. If the grains which fall back into our examining hearts carry the faces of loved ones, are we therefore grasping at the social order which formally defines our love? Are we not, rather, seizing upon a basic goodness— an honesty and innocence—which remains after the forms are swept away? Would a good friend be less of a good friend if we were farmers or teachers instead of pilots? Why does Saint-Exupéry represent as his ultimate insight that he would be a flier all over again—does *this* sentiment capture the essence of the moment? In a similar moment, beholding the unearthly glory of the golden moon over his empty petrol gauge, was Fabien thinking about his wife—about a love which would continue to bind him and his wife beyond this life—or was he murmuring to himself, "I'm glad I was a pilot"?

How can that rude chaos which strips the scales of social conditioning from our bleary eyes set before us in the next instant, mended and ready to blind us anew, the same social conditioning?

Saint-Exupéry and Prévost's ordeal ends when they stagger toward a group of Bedouins, one of whom happens to look around. "By a mere movement of his torso, by the mere wandering of his gaze, he creates life, and he seems like a god to me" (242).[32] This sanctifying language continues. Their savior is not just a man: Saint-Exupéry cannot even remember his face now. Instead, "You are Man, and you appear to me now with the face of all men at once" (243).[33] Yet the castaways have supposedly been dredging from the sandy abyss the highly memorable faces of unique people and finding therein their firmest ties to meaning. Just when Saint-Exupéry seems to have learned that spiritual salvation lies in something like a clear conscience—a network of honest, self-sacrificing relationships—he transfers his salvation to . . . what? To mankind? As opposed to his special circle of friends and loved ones? As opposed to the transcendent power of love? Of course, the Bedouin offers a salvation of the body which well-wishers in France cannot extend. But he seems to offer the other kind, as well; otherwise, why does his gift assume divine proportions, particularly after chapter 7 has applied itself so well to dissolving the mystery of death?

At the very least, this ending abruptly transforms the anecdote into a conscious allegory, factual precision notwithstanding. One man's offer of life-giving water is mankind's offer of communion at life's altar. So much for myth! The pilot-hero's duel with the elements has concluded not in awe-inspiring tragedy, but in comic dissolution as an ordinary passer-by turns his head. Pierre-Henri Simon has finely criticized Saint-Exupéry's pseudo-mystical humanism, here and elsewhere: "in the midst of the human, it neglects or ignores the supernatural which . . . fertilizes and imprints it to the core of its being" (qtd. in Borgal 87). As an allegory, however, the passage actually succeeds in adumbrating the presence of the spirit much better than recollections of family and the "no regrets" retrospective on an uneven career. Precisely because the Bedouin has no name—or even a face—he passes much more credibly for the persona of Charity, of Disinterested Love. This time, Terre des Hommes has reversed its apparent motion so accurately that no trace of a myth is left. It has undone everything Saint-Exupéry thought he was setting out to do.

In another sense, naturally, this man—this Man—is the ultimate tactical evasion. The myth was not working, anyway. He has arrived just in time not to offer a new or different salvation, but to whisk away into the dunes that original salvation which Saint-Exupéry could handle no better than Jacob could the angel. Meaning conveniently escapes in the Bedouin caravan, and the author can claim a kind of literary salvation from the harsh judgment of readers who fail to notice that the kidnapping was arranged.

The tone of the "salvation scene" prepares the way for chapter 8, "Les Hommes," wherein the focus of the book's final pages recoils to include all of humanity. Its motion is consciously (perhaps self-consciously) synthetic rather than antithetic. Saint-Exupéry seems to realize that his earlier strategy has involved him in several contradictions. "It's a well-known fact that everything about the human being is paradoxical," he observes in a kind of tacit apology. "You assure this person of his bread so as to permit him to create, and he goes to sleep; the victorious conqueror turns soft; and the generous man, if you bestow wealth upon him, becomes a thief" (243).[34] Thus the reader would be mistaken if he or she saw in *Terre des Hommes* a mere praise of life in the air or in the desert, since life can become complacent anywhere. The pilot who rejects the city's tedious servility may later surrender his own enthusiasm just as abjectly. "I have betrayed my purpose," concedes the author finally, "if I have appeared to draw you into admiring men primarily. What is primarily admirable is the kind of ground which has served as their foundation" (245).[35]

This renunciation of the misconception/antithesis strategy is itself a shocking reversal, of course. By now, we have grown used to the salutary shock of Saint-Exupéry's brilliant contrasts. Yet we are to forget the contrasts henceforth, or rather to overlook their apparently contrastive nature. Indeed, the taste for stark contrast—the insistence on sharp dividing lines between truth and falsehood—"is perhaps why the world of today is beginning to crack all around us. Everyone is dedicating himself to some religion which permits him a sense of fulfillment" (252).[36] Truth lies not in antithesis, but in synthesis; it fuses contradictions rather than deciding between them. "Truth, as you all know, is what simplifies the world and not what creates chaos. Truth is the language which expedites the universal" (254).[37] As Newton found an idiom which could explain both the fall of an apple and the rising of the sun, so the truth unites human beings in all of their diversity rather than liberating these and executing those.

Saint-Exupéry has already alluded to Spanish Fascism in a section which (as we should have come to expect) finds the perfect example of warm, selfless humanity in the midst of civil war (246–48). Now he refers specifically to Nazism, unwittingly anticipating the occasion of his next work, *Pilote de Guerre*. One can readily become inebriated on one's glorious Arian heritage "down to the bottom of the bottle. It's a lot easier, certainly, than pulling out of the bottle a Beethoven" (255).[38] Instead of reveling in our differences, we must seek our purpose in a common end which will enlist all of our efforts equally. Even so does the physician serve mankind in treating sick men and women; even so is the shepherd a sentinel for an entire culture as he stands guard over his sheep.

The combined images of shepherd and sentinel will recur in separate and elaborated form throughout the pages of *Citadelle*—as, for that matter, will the image of the physician, of the ground fertile for the right seed, and of many other passages in chapter 8. Saint-Exupéry's antitheses, to the extent that they have wrestled their way through any progress at all, seem to be taking a distinctly parabolic turn. A hint of things to come, the book's closing vignette completely abandons the mythic pilot and his elemental struggle. It is a contemplative portrait of a sleeping baby glimpsed amid a train-load of Polish laborers. The tram of bureaucrats in Toulouse had already hardened into soulless beings. Here the clay is yet soft—but what chance has it to be molded into a Mozart? How can a society take such care to select and cultivate prize roses while consigning its human potential to the "machine à emboutir," the assembly line's stamp-and-eject fatality (260)? Mozart is doomed.

We are not told why this particular baby shows signs of genius, nor is any anecdote appended which traces a similar child in similar circumstances. Instead, the story is presented in a supremely simple collection of images, like a fable. The final reversals of *Terre des Hommes*, it seems, have managed to yoke their energy and direct it toward the same general objective: the elevating, all-embracing upper-cased domain—Man, Woman, Child—of allegory.

III.

But allegory is essentially anti-mythic. Neither the watchful Bedouin nor the baby Mozart introduces or reflects an order which did not exist before. Neither explores or defines new limits to human experience: on the contrary, their power as figures resides in what they succeed in conveying about the human condition's universality. For Saint-Exupéry to claim that he has not intended to stir admiration for men, but rather for the "ground which has served as their foundation," is as good as a renunciation of his mythic undertaking; for if the emphasis in "Land of Men" falls on the first word—on the *ground* which nurtures the hero—then we must acknowledge a realm of rich and consequential pre-experience. If actors of great deeds are not to be wondered at, prayed to, weakly emulated, and prudently shied away from, then we must not be living on vulnerable cultural islands held together by arbitrary feats of creation. We must instead be comically blundering our way through a *plus ça change* kind of dance where our actions—for better *and* for worse—will end up falling into the same old patterns. So where does this leave the Exupérian imperative to go forth and act?

At least *Terre des Hommes* has zeroed in on a purely philosophical impasse. It has cleared away the rubble of inhibitive literary conventions which obstructed Saint-Exupéry before—not always to the detriment of art, perhaps, but certainly to that of moral truth. The author/moralist is speaking at his own pace, with his own emphasis, and from his own experience for the first time. He seems, indeed, to work his way down a list of foolish misconceptions which have long vexed him, but which he can freely oppose and discredit only now. At the time of the book's composition, Saint-Exupéry was often being commissioned to write articles of a distinctly editorial twist. His clear and intelligent ruptures with unexamined prejudice made good copy. The episodes in chapter 8 of the Spanish sergeant awakening and the Polish infant sleeping draw almost verbatim from reports which he filed in Spain and Russia (cf. Crane 70). Everybody is probably capable of producing one electric, curmudgeonly editorial. Saint-Exupéry had a positive gift for the genre.

The problem with this strategy is the impression it inevitably leaves that alternative conceptions of a superior truth value exist—a problem which vanishes, of course, for those who happen to believe in higher truth. Saint-Exupéry was not prepared to assert so much, nor would he be at any time in his literary career. One may do practically anything in his view, apparently, as long as one does it creatively and devotedly. Yet it would be a mistake to regard Saint-Exupéry's ideas as interchangeable with those of any relativist.

He has been treated by some as a soulmate of Merleau-Ponty, for instance—a highly dubious equation which would have the former's praise of diehard dedication share a bed with the latter's disparagement of fidelity. Why do such unlikely associations keep obfuscating Saint-Exupéry's work, even half a century after his death? Partly because he invited them—because his work obfuscates itself. Could not the mature Saint-Exupéry have written the following: "Hate is a virtue from behind. To obey with one's eyes closed is the beginning of panic; and to choose against what one understands, the beginning of skepticism" (Merleau-Ponty 60)? If certain kinds of hate are simply and irredeemably vicious—if choosing against what one understands may sometimes slide from skepticism into shut-eyed panic—what will save us (to echo Baudelaire's prayer) from becoming what we most despise?

Is Saint-Exupéry's thought really this lubricious? Is there not, after all, an objective and absolute kind of value behind his relativism of service, sacrifice, and fidelity? If one cannot conceive in material terms of any god deserving such worship, may one not nevertheless assert—from a purely practical perspective—that the least self-interested acts are those which we most admire? The snag lies in defining that for which one gives oneself up—but is the triumph over selfishness any the less noble in the absence of such a clear definition?

Saint-Exupéry's relativism was, to say the least, relative. His pilot-myth in *Terre des Hommes* circles around a narrower set of coordinates than it had managed to identify before, as if finally picking up a strong signal, a beacon from home. Perhaps the book's antitheses are less linear reversals than vectors systematically adjusted around that faint but life-saving energy source. Without doubt, there is no leather-jacketed strongman or Chairman Rivière sitting in this control tower—no hero who has died in action or been carried home crippled but inspired. It is a different face, and we know whose it is: a face with two sides, neither of which is visible. One belongs to the Bedouin in the desert, bringing his water of common humanity. The other belongs to an infant, but not the one we see in the railway carriage. The child's real face awaits him in the future, where he may never claim it if the Bedouin does not find him, too. Yet he *is* the Bedouin, in a sense. Both are designated bearers of essential humanity, the one dispensing it to his brethren, the other soliciting it from them.

How to make people see this? How to tell them that they must serve and be served, act and reflect, resist society and confirm society, love each other yet not indulge each other? Live through, with, and for mankind by refusing to settle into the comfort of human institutions? How can this all be formulated to make sense? If the mythic act is stressed, then the end of action becomes virtually irrelevant. If the end of action is stressed in its fully worthy perfection, then the act becomes either sublime or trivial (depending on whether "perfection" is understood to demand thoroughness or to license mercy), and the would-be agent either falls into despair or grows shallow and insipid.

Whose face is that behind the Bedouin's veil? Whose face does the infant hope to claim one day?

Pilote de Guerre would try again. On the one hand, it merely reprises the digressions into childhood memories, comradely anecdotes, and so on, which characterize every previous novel except for *Vol de Nuit*. Yet even these pleasant excursions are warped back into the central sequence of events with a determination reflecting Saint-Exupéry's desire to uncover the Ultimate Myth, if there is one. In another sense, then, the wartime novel picks up where the final two chapters of *Terre des Hommes* had left off: self-sacrifice for an unknown god, almost certain death, and then . . . and then, epiphany. Saint-Exupéry had returned to find his Bedouin, this time hoping to lift his veil.

NOTES

[1] Il semble que tout l'effort industriel de l'homme, tous ses calculs, toutes ses nuits de veille sur les épures, n'aboutissent, comme signes visibles, qu'à la seule simplicité, comme s'il fallait l'expérience de plusieurs générations pour dégager peu à peu la courbe d'une colonne, d'une carène, ou d'un fuselage d'avion, jusqu'à leur rendre la pureté élémentaire de la courbe d'un sein ou d'une épaule.

[2] Je dirai même que j'agis mieux sur mon ennemi que sur mon ami, car celui-là qui marche dans la même direction que moi m'offre moins d'occasions de rencontre et d'échange que celui-là qui va contre moi, et ne laisse échapper ni un geste de moi, car il en dépend, ni une parole.

[3] Ce qui m'effraie plus que la guerre, c'est le monde de demain.

[4] Et, peu à peu, l'Espagne de ma carte devenait, sous la lampe, un pays de contes de fées. Je balisais d'une croix les refuges et les pièges.

[5] . . . glu blanche [qui] devenait pour moi la frontière entre le réel et l'irréel, entre le connu et l'inconnaissable.

[6] Le pilote de ligne, mêlé aux fonctionnaires . . . une chrysalide grise dont l'homme sortirait transfiguré.

[7] Vieux bureaucrate ici présent . . . tu n'es point l'habitant d'une planète errante, tu ne te pose point de questions sans réponse. . . . Maintenant, la glaise dont tu es formé a séché, et s'est durcie, et nul en toi ne saurait désormais réveiller le musicien endormi, ou le poète, ou l'astronome qui peut-être t'habitaient d'abord.

[8] L'or est né du Néant: il rayonne dans les feux de l'escale.

[9] Il déboucha dans un royaume fantastique.

[10] Et ce spectacle était si écrasant que Mermoz, une fois le Pot-au-Noir franchi, s'aperçut qu'il n'avait pas eu peur.

[11] Dès lors, nous nous sentîmes perdus dans l'espace interplanétaire. . . .

[12] Il n'est qu'un luxe véritable, et c'est celui des relations humaines.

[13] . . . comme si le courage consistait à s'abaisser à des railleries de collégien.

[14] Ma femme, si elle crois que je vis, croit que je marche. Les camarades croient que je marche. Ils ont tous confiance en moi. Et je suis un salaud si je ne marche pas.

[15] Ce que j'ai fait, je le jure, jamais aucune bête ne l'aurait fait.

[16] Seul l'inconnu épouvante les hommes. Mais, pour quiconque l'affronte, il n'est déjà plus l'inconnu.

[17] Sa grandeur, c'est de se sentir responsable.

[18] Et, de même que, dans l'instrument, toute mécanique apparente s'est peu à peu effacée, et qu'il nous est livré un objet aussi naturel qu'un galet poli par la mer, il est également admirable que, dans son usage même, la machine peu à peu se fasse oublier.

[19] Elle a pu, des pensées, de la voix, et des silences d'un amant, se former un Royaume, et dès lors il n'est plus pour elle, en dehors de lui, que des barbares.

[20] Une nappe tendue sous les étoiles ne peut recevoir que des poussières d'astres.

[21] . . . un nouveau paradis terrestre. Elles régnaient sur tous les animaux de la création.

[22] . . . qui est un jardin sauvage, à lui qui n'aime que les parcs soignés. Et l'imbécile emmène la princesse en esclavage.

[23] Le rezzou aussi transfigure les sables.

[24] Il vaut mieux taire certains miracles. Il vaut même mieux n'y pas trop songer, sinon l'on ne comprend plus rien. Sinon l'on doute de Dieu.

[25] Les biens de la terre glissent entre les doigts comme le sable fin des dunes.

[26] J'ai raconté ça dans un livre . . .

[27] Nous découvrons que nous ne sommes pas les naufragés. Les naufragés, ce sont ce qui attendent! Ceux que menace notre silence. Ceux qui sont déjà déchirés par une abominable erreur. On ne peut pas ne pas courrir vers eux.

[28] Prévost ne connaîtra point non plus cette angoisse devant la mort dont on nous rebat les oreilles. Mais il est quelque chose qu'il ne supporte pas, ni moi non plus. . . . Chaque seconde de silence assassine un peu ceux que j'aime.

[29] Tout compte fait, j'ai eu la meilleure part. Si je rentrais, je recommencerais. J'ai besoin de vivre.

[30] Cette formule est prétentieuse. Les toréadors ne me plaisent guère.

[31] Quand nous prendrons conscience de notre rôle, même le plus effacé . . . alors seulement nous pourrons vivre en paix et mourir en paix, car ce qui donne un sens à la vie donne un sens à la mort.

[32] Par un mouvement de son seul buste, par la promenade de son seul regard, il crée la vie, et il me paraît semblable à un dieu.

³³ Tu es l'Homme et tu m'apparais avec le visage de tous les hommes à la fois.

³⁴ Tout est paradoxal chez l'homme, on le sait bien. On assure le pain de celui-là pour lui permettre de créer et il s'endort, le conquérant victorieux s'amollit, le généreux, si on l'enrichit, devient ladre.

³⁵ J'ai trahi mon but si j'ai paru vous engager à admirer d'abord les hommes. Ce qui est admirable d'abord, c'est le terrain qui les a fondés.

³⁶ . . . c'est peut-être pourquoi le monde d'aujourd'hui commence à craquer autour de nous. Chacun s'exalte pour des religions qui lui permettent cette plénitude.

³⁷ La vérité, vous le savez, c'est ce qui simplifie le monde et non ce qui crée le chaos. La vérité, c'est le langage qui dégage l'universel.

³⁸ . . . jusqu'au soutier. C'est, certes, plus facile que de tirer du soutier un Beethoven.

WORKS CITED

Bakhtin, Mikhail. *The Dialogic Imagination*. Trans. Michael Holquist. Austin: U of Texas P, 1981.

Borgal, Clément. *Saint-Exupéry: Mystique sans la Foi*. Centurion: Paris, 1964.

Cate, Curtis. *Antoine de Saint-Exupéry*. New York: Putnam, 1970.

Chevrier, Pierre. *Antoine de Saint-Exupéry*. Paris: Gallimard, 1949.

Crane, Helen Elizabeth. *L'Humanisme dans l'Oeuvre de Saint-Exupéry*. Evanston, Ill.: Principia, 1957.

Delange, René. *La Vie de Saint-Exupéry*. Paris: Seuil, 1948.

Devaux, André-A. *Saint-Exupéry*. Paris: Desclée de Brouwer, 1965.

Major, Jean-Louis. *Saint-Exupéry: L'Écriture et la Pensée*. Ottawa: U of Ottawa P, 1968.

Merleau-Ponty, Maurice. *In Praise of Philosophy*. Trans. John Wild and James M. Edie. Chicago: Northwestern UP, 1963.

Ouellet, Réal. *Les Relations Humaines dans l'Oeuvre de Saint-Exupéry*. Paris: Minard, 1971.

Pélissier, Georges. *Les Cinq Visages de Saint-Exupéry*. Paris: Flammarion, 1951.

Quesnel, Michel, and Michel Autrand. "Préface Générale." *Saint-Exupéry: Oeuvres Complètes*. Vol. 1. Ed. Michel Quesnel and Michel Autrand. Paris: Gallimard, 1994: ix-lii.

Reverdy, Pierre. *Le Livre de Mon Bord: 1930–36*. Paris: Mercure de France, 1948.

Robinson, Joy D. Marie. *Antoine de Saint-Exupéry*. Boston: Twayne, 1984.

Saint-Exupéry, Antoine de. *Oeuvres*. Roger Caillois, ed. Bibliothèque de la Pléiade. Paris: Gallimard, 1959; volume contains *Courrier Sud, Vol de Nuit, Terre des Hommes, Lettre à un Otage, Pilote de Guerre, Le Petit Prince*, and *Citadelle*.

—. *Lettres à sa Mère*. Paris: Gallimard, 1955.

—. *Un Sens à la Vie*. Paris: Gallimard, 1956.

Schiff, Stacy. *Saint-Exupéry: A Biography*. New York: Knopf, 1994.

CHAPTER 5

PILOTE DE GUERRE AND THE
IMPASSE OF REVELATION

I.

The absurdly futile effort of the French standing army to resist the Nazi onslaught of 1940 (a small part of which effort would be chronicled in *Pilote de Guerre*) plunged Saint-Exupéry into a new crisis. If the dissolution of the Aeroposta Argentina had ushered in years of painful soul-searching, the dissolution of his nation and his culture left him infinitely more in need of an active, coherent program for living. His fellow Frenchmen were bitterly divided over the appropriate posture to assume. The United States, whose energetic support would be utterly indispensable to any successful opposition of the invaders, inclined more than ever to neutrality before the spectacle of partisan bickering offered by vociferous French refugees. Though Saint-Exupéry himself "refused to be drawn into these fratricidal squabbles" (Cate 437), he became increasingly aware that the United States would not offer support unless awakened to certain realities—to those facts of historical and cultural kinship which he continued to call "spiritual."

Such was the environment in which *Pilote de Guerre* was conceived. Intended to present the French cause as all of Western civilization's to the American audience and to marginalize the rivalry among expatriate factions (cf. Robinson 104), it was Saint-Exupéry's way of striking a blow for freedom. Never was there a better example

135

of authorship as vigorous participation in life's drama. The blow proved a telling one, to judge from the sales of the English translation by Lewis Galantière, *Flight to Arras* (Crane 118). For obvious political reasons, the translation was made available immediately: in fact, it appeared somewhat before the French "original." Robinson documents the book's triumphant reception among American critics (111–12). Schiff, developing the same point, observes that the victory was Pyrrhic in that it made the author a more attractive target for partisan sniping than ever (363–66).

The plot of the work is supremely simple. During the general rout of the French forces, Saint-Exupéry and his crew are ordered to fly a reconnaissance mission over Arras in western Flanders. Only one in three aircraft returns from any sort of mission in the present circumstances, but this outing seems especially suicidal. In order to obtain photographs of the requisite precision, the pilot must pass over a German-occupied, heavily fortified area at seven hundred meters; and even if, by some miracle, the photographs could be made and delivered, they would never come under the scrutiny of the French high command in time to do any good.

Nonetheless, Saint-Exupéry grudgingly accepts his doom. His attitude in the book's early chapters is curiously sympathetic with rather than antithetical to the popular American sentiment that France's resistance is inept. He seems more disposed to win over his readers than to challenge their judgment openly. The flight progresses from one malfunction to another before the dangerous target is approached. No aircraft can be properly serviced in the ongoing retreat, and most of them are ill equipped from the outset for the missions which they must fly.

Hence the descent to Arras is almost an escape from a greater peril, since it causes the plane's controls to unfreeze. Then the German artillery opens fire, and survival for even another moment seems impossible. The fact that Saint-Exupéry does survive thus assumes the character of a rebirth, the whole experience leaving him inspired with a new vision of his and France's purpose. They must be the eventual victors, precisely because they have consented to fall first in an absurd struggle. Their death will have a meaning because their life has a meaning—a meaning bestowed upon it by centuries of humanitarian endeavor. In the book's concluding chapters, Saint-

Exupéry attempts to specify the values which define his culture, which Nazism threatens, and which must prevail simply because their language translates the common humanity binding together all people everywhere. The miserable rout is transformed into a resonant victory.

Were such a work from such an era to adopt a strategy dictated by expedience—that is, were it to transmit propaganda—nobody would be surprised, and few would be censorious. Saint-Exupéry manages largely to avoid the surges of opposition to popular wisdom so fundamental to *Terre des Hommes*, and others have remarked that his overt celebration of Christianity strikes a note of religious conformism heard nowhere else throughout his corpus. Could this be the same author who contemptuously disdained manipulative writing—who insisted that his own books were the full and faithful expression of his moral being?

Yet the impression of dissonance is misleading: Saint-Exupéry has indeed remained true to his convictions. *Pilote de Guerre* is nothing if not a direct transcription of an intimate moral struggle. The protagonist clings to a view of right conduct even when certain death and irresistible senselessness seem to oppress him, then exults in the vision of order which his brave tenacity forges from chaos. That much of this order is traditional does not obviate its need to be re-created in individual striving; on the contrary, the purely traditional character of the Christian faith in *Pilote de Guerre* seems to be responsible for its preciousness. It simply exists, an arbitrary set of references upon which one may take bearings in the void. Hence Saint-Exupéry's passionate defense of it is quite sincere, as is his defense of all his cultural heritage. He is equally sincere in never suggesting that Christian values enjoy any sort of *a priori* foundation in the human consciousness which would render their defense ultimately unnecessary. Such students of Catholic orthodoxy as Devaux (51–53) and Crane (148–51) observe that the profession of faith concluding *Pilote de Guerre* reflects no knowledge or experience of God the Son, the loving intercessor. In so doing, they are merely stating in their preferred idiom that Saint-Exupéry's Christianity is entirely contingent upon the extrinsic factors which collaborate in building culture.

In the same fashion, Saint-Exupéry's repression of the antithetical strategy is surely a closer approach to his profoundest convictions rather than a cynical wooing of the audience. We have seen in the previous chapter that vigorously contradicting a series of truisms involved him in certain self-contradictions during the composition of *Terre des Hommes*. There could be no body of absolute truths for Saint-Exupéry, since truth was only a culturally created and sustained framework within which life might have direction: a sense of things, not *the* sense of things. Hence there could be no absolute falsehood, either. One system of truth surpassed another only to the extent that its framework was more securely impressed into individual lives (i.e., grounded in tradition) and that its framework embraced a greater volume of lives (i.e., grounded in liberalism). The book that would truly express his philosophy, therefore, must offer not contrastive propositions, but synthetic ones. As it tells the story of his life on a given day, it must also be telling the story of his life on every day, and of every life on any day.

In short, Saint-Exupéry had decided to write an allegory of life in a universe where no deep allegory is possible. *Pilote de Guerre* is a magnificent last attempt to incarnate the motive ecstasy at the pilot-myth's heart. Without doubt, a climactic burst of patriotism helps the book to accomplish its desired political ends—but the novel's objectives go far beyond the political. After all, the struggle to survive was nothing new to Saint-Exupéry: in a manner of speaking, every work he ever wrote was a tale of war. *Pilote de Guerre* merely substitutes an openly declared war between national powers for the eternal war between spiritual life and death wherein social apathy and natural chaos assail the conscientious individual from either side. The declared war with fascism was really no more important than the largely unrecognized war with cultural atrophy or the more dramatized—but much misunderstood—war with uncultivated nature.

We would thus be gravely mistaken to suppose that Saint-Exupéry would suspend his quest for enduring practical truth just because the European crisis obliged him to write polemics. If anything, he viewed the Second World War as less of a menace than the vast demoralization which, as he foresaw so keenly, must inevitably succeed it. His notorious "Lettre à Général X" (*SV* 223–31), though often used to exaggerate his depressed state of mind, proves at the very least that he considered the war within a broader perspective than most of his contemporaries could imagine. "I am sad for my generation, which is void of any human substance . . . ," he laments in this never-posted correspondence. "There is only one problem, a single one around the world: to give to people a spiritual meaning, spiritual concerns" (224).[1] The defeat of Nazism would scarcely constitute the end of the beginning in so great a struggle.

Pilote de Guerre is "a book of transition, consequently," writes Borgal, "for which the war was certainly not the cause, but at most the occasion" (117). It can and should be read as a continuation of the author's striving to formulate a deeply philosophical message—a spiritual significance for life. That someone who believed in no absolute truth could feel this need for significance so strongly is one of the essential paradoxes of Saint-Exupéry, the writer and the man. (Cf. Devaux: "Is the drama of Saint-Exupéry not to have united paradoxically in himself an idealist and relativist philosophy with a basically mystical temperament longing for an absolute?" [84–85].) For the very reason that truth is relative to the individual's creativity and to his or her cultural heritage, a life free of arbitrary order is a terrifying, vertiginous spin in a black vacuum. Nothing—nothing whatever—will slow the spin or resolve it into a purposeful orbit if one does not impose gravitational lines of force by an act of will, an act either of inventing purpose *ex nihilo* or of adhering tenaciously to an indoctrinated purpose. The necessity of a framework, of gravitational lines, is itself the great truth: not the particular structure of the framework or the particular direction of the lines, but the sheer generative energy of the anchored reference.

What ethical system could be more aesthetic? The creation of order becomes self-justifying, just as a stone surface sculpted by mindless wind and rain does not depend upon authorial intent for its beauty, but only upon a lucky collaboration of accidents. The sculpture would be considered artistic merely if several beholders discerned within it a face, a form. A culture-based ethical system, too, might be deemed superior to the extent that more people remarked pattern in its performance. Beyond that, there could be no objective criterion for beauty, no rule which challenged the collective judgment of taste—and none for goodness, according to this formula. A tireless laborer in modern man's "forging a language to think about the world of his time" (*SV* 153),[2] Saint-Exupéry puts before us seductive arabesques of feverish activity rather than marble tablets of commandments. His work is perpetually ordered by the ethic of the well-turned curve. The curves need not even form letters—or if they do, we need not even understand the script.

Of course, there *are* letters, and we *do* understand them. In fact, the crude contours of a would-be myth had emerged from every earlier novel: the emissary of culture cast into the abyss halts his plunge by willing a cultural lifeline—a stable asteroid, a land of men—into existence. As often as Saint-Exupéry had told this tale, however, he had never succeeded in telling its original version, the primeval struggle which grounds all subsequent struggles. At least *Pilote de Guerre* tells only the one story (though not without digression), and tells it only from one perspective. As a result, the reader may look within the narrative's structure for ultimate meaning rather than having to scan several narratives simultaneously for an evasive common denominator. Whatever the author has to say must reside in this single chain of events. The supremely simple *praxis* of a myth is at hand.

The mythic enterprise is favored, too, by the unusual subject matter. International warfare is hardly a normal situation, and opportunities for heroism abound. Since the book's ostensible purpose was to animate this war before the eyes of American readers, Saint-Exupéry also had an ever-present incentive to resist allegory, that great subverter of myth; for had he explicitly allegorized the nature of human existence in the flight to Arras, he would have vitiated the desired political effect. War would have become not a monstrous malaise, but the state of daily life.

Yet it bears repeating once more that *Pilote de Guerre* is in no way a concession to popular taste or political expedience. Instead, Saint-Exupéry was confronting in its pages, more forthrightly than ever, the impasse of formulating a mythic act with the heartfelt magnetism of a universal allegory. How could he represent the pilot-hero's epochal sacrifice—the gift of peace left behind when he and the war dragon carry each other into the chasm—as a common man's feat, or at least as an inspiration to the common man? How can myth claim the vast moral applicability of allegory while defying all cosmic powers whose normal operation suppresses the mythic hero's lonely creativity? What can a man do which has not been done before; and, if it *has* been done before, how can it create meaning only now?

The author's mild, persistent bemusement helps. The book's opening words at once invite fantasizing: "Sans doute je rêve" ("I must be dreaming"). Never has Saint-Exupéry's first-person narration been more accessible, more lovably bungling, more Charlie Chaplinesque. We are instantly drawn to this dreamy narrator. Here is no sober chronicle of Hitler's aggression (the original text did mention Hitler, but the reference was expurgated [see Schiff 365 at footnote]). Rather, we have something more like Proust gone to war or Baudelaire contemplating fireworks. Each step into the grim reality of rout and flaming death sends nostalgic echoes down the corridors of things past or stirs far-ranging metaphors splendidly alive. Schiff must have had *Pilote de Guerre* prominently in mind when she wryly observed, "A common literary construction for Saint-Exupéry is 'over A I was thinking of B'" (x). None of his works so well justifies François's supposition of a surrealist influence, for never were his imaginative leaps more numerous, more brilliant, or better integrated into the narrative's flow.

Yet surrealism can be quite arcane and hermetic. Saint-Exupéry's day-dreaming serves rather to wear away the forbidding edges of his heroic undertaking and to place it within the reach of ordinary human beings. The contemplative passages draw the combat mission out of its death-defying no-man's-land. They mingle the quaint with the awe-inspiring, the sentimental with the tragic. They insist that precious moments of childhood really are contained in a brush with death, and that murderous artillery fire really does have some of the joyful beauty of fireworks. As always, the exigencies of dials, gauges, and switches also deflate any aura of semi-divine mystery. Says Anet of *Pilote de Guerre*, "at the moment that musing borders on the dryness of an excessively abstract expression . . . ," an urgent call to physical maneuvers wrenches it back into "the warmth of life" (152). In fact, what appeared in Jacques Bernis's craft as a deadly contest for his attention between control panel and terrestrial regret is here a strange collaboration aimed at bringing us on board. One way and another, this epochal defeat of chaos is not so intimidating, after all. It combines child's play with elementary mechanics.

So well does the self-effacing pilot hero of *Pilote de Guerre* convince us that we might be flying his mission that the weight of contradiction shifts to the other polarity. How can such lackluster subjects as we ordinary mortals ever dream of heroically establishing our culture's frontiers? At the book's most crucial juncture, the answer literally explodes upon us: our heroism lies not in the deed itself, but in the vision to which we gain access through the deed. Action is required, for this rare epiphany will entrust itself to no mere contemplative. Yet the quality of the action need not measure up to Herculean standards, for the whole-hearted *attempt* suffices to unveil the inspiring goddess of cosmos. All of us who venture so far execute the original myth together: all of us are the first hero in the purity of our face-to-face encounter with the divine.

But *does* revelation literally explode upon Saint-Exupéry—*is* it the barrage of detonating flak over Arras? Or is the flak, instead, just another metaphor behind whose mystery meaning slips away, like the faceless Bedouin of *Terre des Hommes*? Perhaps not. Stranger things have happened than meeting one's irreducible, eternal part in the naked instant of a psychic mushroom cloud, an Awful Horror. Just as Mermoz forgot to be afraid while piloting through the colonnade of waterspouts, so Saint-Exupéry is completely engrossed in the majesty of the onslaught released upon him. What remains when one is scared out of being scared?

The philosophers of the Enlightenment thought they knew: they believed that remnant to be God, or what of us is in God. In his *Critique of Judgment*, Immanuel Kant described the encounter with the "dynamic sublime" as a triumph of mentality over corporality, an escape from the body's severe limitation into such limitless concepts as perfect goodness and eternity (cf. ch. 26). Saint-Exupéry feels something of the kind. Aware of his extreme physical peril scarcely at all, he is consumingly, rapturously caught in an inspiring spectacle wherein the pains of the flesh shrink to infinitesimal points. His experience while stranded in the Sahara had similarly raised him above bodily concerns, but not so rapidly or so loftily. Such is the true nature of his revelation. It is the death-defying spiritual bliss of one who has trespassed upon chaos and found in its midst an unspeakable, not-of-this-world cosmos—a Fabien stealing into the moon's exclusive domain.

This is indeed so, I believe, up until Saint-Exupéry's concluding summary of why he fights: his so-called profession of faith. As magnificent a philosophical manifesto as the conclusion surely is, and as politically effective upon the American audience as it surely was, it remains unrelated to the thrilling experience over Arras. It is an entirely manufactured vision. Saint-Exupéry was not thinking about his Christian heritage or Western culture as he ran the gauntlet of artillery fire, nor did the ecstasy of surviving from moment to moment draw any of its power from a sudden appreciation of those traditions. Of course, such liberation from contingency is *not* what he had hoped to find, for it untangles chaos without the aid of mythic action. It intimates that moral chaos is only ever an illusion, and that the true antidote to such apparent chaos precedes and survives culture. It subsumes material circumstance under a metaphysical mantle which he is not prepared to embrace—or which he *has* embraced in the dark, by default or grace or accident, but cannot draw out into the harsh light of empirical study.

In the "profession" section, therefore, Saint-Exupéry energetically retreats from the unconditional shimmer of his revelation. He endorses Western democratic Christendom with a fervor wholly incongruent to the religious misgivings of his private correspondence. No more here than elsewhere is he simply surrendering to the political expedience of selling the war to the Americans as a crusade. *Pilote de Guerre* has been too faithful to his deepest convictions throughout to begin propagandizing at its conclusion. Manufactured though this retrospective interpretation of his epiphany is, it reflects no intent to deceive. It actually managed to vex much of its Yankee readership; for, as translator Lewis Galantière wrote later in *Atlantic Monthly*, "Americans wanted to be told what to do, not what to be, wanted a book on Democracy, not on Man" (qtd. in Migeo 265). As a sabre-rattling battlecry, the book's end is a complete flop.

The truth is that *Pilote de Guerre* successfully unveils the life-saving Bedouin and successfully divines the face in Fabien's moon. Since this success establishes the inadequacy of all possible myth, all purely circumstantial systems, it spells failure for Saint-Exupéry's cherished faith in creative action. The Bedouin's face is not that of Man, but of the God who made men and women in His image. Saint-Exupéry requires heroes who make God in their image if his culturally dependent ethic is to trace its mythic pedigree. In this sense, revelation has indeed failed him. It has revealed what the eye cannot see—or, more precisely, *that* the eye cannot see; and his enterprise, like

Rivière's, may proceed only if its warriors are able to chase mysteries back into their caves.

II.

The "dream" which opens the story is in fact the author's conscious flashback to his schooldays. Loitering with his comrades of the 2/33 Group in a farmhouse which constitutes their temporary barrack, he cannot believe in the war. Like loosely supervised students marking time before the hour of dismissal, the unit's members converse languidly, toy with their equipment, and practice card tricks. Even when Saint-Exupéry and Dutertre are called into Commandant Alias's office to receive instructions—their turn has come up for a reconnaissance mission—the war seems infinitely distant. It has no connection to anything real.

> But one impression dominates all others in the course of this war's ending: that of the absurd. Everything is cracking around us. Everything grows bloated. The impression is so total that death itself appears absurd. It lacks seriousness amid the rubble . . .[3] (267)

The chaos so prominent under one guise or another in all of Saint-Exupéry's works is especially explicit here. Rather than a cyclone or a desert, it offers itself as the literal breakdown of man's carefully nourished culture. A new daydream invades the author's consciousness: a nation full of unwound clocks. Clocks in church towers, clocks in railway stations, clocks on mantelpieces . . . all of them stilled on a different hour. As the image develops, he envisions gardens gone to seed, vehicles broken down, fountains empty or overflowing. First and foremost, war is hours, days, and seasons deprived of meaning, a nightmare of topsy-turvy, gravity-less floating. And so one flies reconnaissance missions to take comfort in a posture of organized resistance. (Webster defends this particular mission, by the way [212]). Though the craft are few, battered, and exponentially outnumbered—and though their hard-won intelligence would never reach headquarters through the German blitz in the unlikely event of a "successful" mission—one must pretend that one's clock keeps a soldier's time. "Everybody strives his utmost to make the war look like a war. It's a pious undertaking. Each man forces himself to play exactly by the rules" (269).[4]

The absurdity in this instance is too great for the imagination to resist, however. Guillaumet could overcome the Andes, in all their immensity, by putting one foot in front of the other; but here action produces no advance of the most minuscule proportions, as if it were engaging the wrong dimension. "And it isn't that I'm not thinking about the war, about death, about sacrifice, about France—quite the contrary—but I'm missing a directive concept, a clear language" (271).[5] The reality is unthinkable for want of an image, and the only images which crowd in upon Saint-Exupéry are "rêves" because of their irrelevance to any possible action. Thus the first chapter has posed the problem in terms of how to translate war into the imagery of a daydream; or, in other words, how to constrain a chaotic reality into a reality with meaning. Saint-Exupéry is not struggling against the "facts," but against a senseless disorder which renders the facts incomprehensible.

Both the first and second chapters end with Saint-Exupéry's comparing himself to a believer whose faith has abandoned him (much to the fascination of those who have sought to decipher his religious inclinations). In another faintly religious construction, the author claims in chapter 2 that he is "shocked by a plain fact that no one admits: the life of the Spirit is intermittent" (275).[6] Surely this idea must have occurred to him before—it is strongly implicit already in *Courrier Sud*. Nevertheless, Saint-Exupéry devotes much space here to remarking the ebb and flow of meaning, as if only now has he really become aware of how much the sense of things depends upon one's subjective state. In the general exhaustion which is overtaking Group 2/33, he has observed that comrades become caricatures of themselves: "We are ourselves divided into pieces. This voice. That nose. This nervous tic. And the pieces do not stir any emotion" (276).[7] Thus, for the moment, his exclusive mental image of his friend Israël, who recently failed to return from a mission, is the flushed nose which betrayed his irritation as he marched silently to a flying suicide similar to Saint-Exupéry's assignment. In the same fashion, Commandant Alias mutters something about Saint-Exupéry's always being out of matches. Their weary intellects are all prickling with minutiae, but the spirit which makes sense of detail has deserted them. Under such circumstances, death itself has no meaning, for one can scarcely notice an empty chair when one is being moved from barrack to barrack in ongoing retreat. Thanks, perhaps, to these experiences, the periodic lapse of spirit will become a major rubric of *Citadelle*.

The next two chapters dissolve into the meticulous preparation necessary before take-off. Their staccato style mimics Saint-Exupéry's own turbulent state of mind, forced to occupy himself with the hoses and valves of his cumbersome flight suit when he would rather be composing his thoughts to meet an almost certain death. "At that instant, one traverses the very center of the interior desert about which I was speaking" (278).[8] So he is again in the desert's heart, as in *Terre des Hommes*, surrounded by the same loss of bearings, the same senselessness of direction: at no other point in the book does chaos so ravage his identity. The first sentence of chapter 5 tacitly acknowledges as much: "Anguish is due to the loss of a genuine identity" (281).[9]

Very soon, however, he is airborne. "Now, at last, time has stopped flowing emptily. I am finally installed in my proper function. No more do I project before me a future without a face" (281).[10] Thus, in the novel's first few dozen pages, the interior desert has already been not exactly traversed, but magnetized and oriented toward an oasis. Whether Saint-Exupéry survives his transit or not, he now has a direction to go. The aircraft, with its rigid and quite finite set of options in any given crisis, imposes its law incontestably. Switches, dials, and gauges demand the pilot's constant attention and must channel every response to danger. The reality of which Saint-Exupéry could shape no image has been transformed into readings on his instrument panel. "The combat between the West and Nazism becomes, in this instant and at the level of my acts, an operation upon handles, levers, and spigots" (284).[11] Indeed, returning to a religious metaphor, he treats the operations of flying like stages in a reverend, beloved ritual. "The love of his God, for a sacristan, expresses itself as a love of lighting candles."[12]

In this chapter, as in no previous passage of Saint-Exupéry's works, one glimpses the true importance of aviation as a *métier*. It poses that arbitrary but insistent rule of conduct whose authority he could never recognize in religious dogma or philosophical argument. At the same time, I should emphasize that the pilot has already traversed the "desert phase" of his myth, just as the Saint-Exupéry of *Terre des Hommes* had spiritually defeated the desert once he had discovered inner coordinates for guiding his trek home. The preceding book, having thrashed about for most of its length, had discovered still another phase, a new phase: revelation. *Pilote de Guerre* already circles this destination. The pilot has heroically (if humbly) reaffirmed his cosmos. Now he is ready and waiting to see whatever *else*—what of the external to or greater than himself—may appear when sense meets senselessness.

And circle he does. In the ensuing chapters, Saint-Exupéry continues to recover his sense of things with loving leisure. The more aware he becomes of the plane as an extension of his own nervous system and appendages (in the fashion described in *Terre des Hommes*), the more deeply he meditates. His works offer no better example of the merging of thought and action. When Dutertre warns that he is veering off course, he marvels that his body (or what we would call his subconscious mind) can subtly defy his waking will power by steering away from the zone patrolled by German fighters.

This observation carries him back again to his schooldays. He reflects that shirking the mission would ultimately prove as sterile as feigning sickness to skip classes. In either case, one ends up losing the delights of active participation just to coddle one's body in a dull security worse than death. In fact (he pursues), such has been his motive for continually rebuffing those who would plant him safely behind a desk or dispatch him on diplomatic assignments far from the front. Though he cannot counter their logic, the spirit has reasons which the intelligence does not understand. Along with this vague, perhaps unintended echo of Pascal, he uses another ecclesiastical image: "I know of what temptation consists as well as any priest of the Church . . . it is . . . to yield to the reasons of the Intelligence when the Spirit sleeps" (287).[13] Like a blind man "whose palms have led him to the fire" (288—an image destined for frequent repetition in *Citadelle*),[14] he has stubbornly followed the warmth of his imagined role through a night of demoralization and obstacles.

François, intrigued by a surrealist connection, stresses that "by the thread of physical sensations and wholly spontaneous associations of ideas, Saint-Exupéry climbs back up the slope of memory and reconstructs his childhood" (145) throughout *Pilote de Guerre*. Yet one need not have read Breton's *Surrealist Manifesto* to suspect another objective, equally artistic and much more practical, behind these excursions into childhood, old acquaintance, and epic simile. The more they accumulate, the closer an all-embracing revelation looms, and the better we see that the real war being waged is with human existence.

Many commentators have difficulty in perceiving the transformation, for several thick trees obscure this forest. They marvel, rather, that Saint-Exupéry should be so incurably—and unhealthily, in the present circumstances—inclined to day-dreaming. By his own admission, Saint-Exupéry tends to become flustered at Commandant Alias's demands for detail during his debriefings (cf. 351 and 358). We know from other testimony, too, that he could display alarming absent-mindedness in the cockpit even as a young pilot (cf. Robinson 52 and Schiff 156–57 and 224). He had nearly killed himself while training at Orconte, preoccupied, as Cate suggests, with a scientific problem (390). Leleu, a sympathetic witness, nonetheless concludes, "Saint-Ex's distraction was not always all that harmless, and it played more than one trick on him in the course of his flying career" (91).

Something of the sort appears to happen at the end of chapter 7 and into chapter 8, as Saint-Exupéry's reverie is rudely interrupted by a German fighter patrol. In flying an evasive pattern, he exerts too much energy on the frozen controls. The high altitude will not allow such vigorous activity. He faints briefly, and upon reviving says of himself, "J'ai été stupide"—"What a fool I was" (290). One might be forgiven for reading in this incident the author's confession that a combat mission is no place for poetry.

Speaking from historical fact, however, we can hardly suppose that Saint-Exupéry would have jeopardized his comrades' lives if he had truly thought himself incapable of the necessary concentration (though Schiff wonders if he was not quite careless even about his own unsteady health [330]). Furthermore, his argument that scouring the skies for marauders is wasted effort (a position motivated less by his absent-mindedness, perhaps, than by his inability to twist sideways due to previous injuries) has a certain logic. Once the fighters see you, he suggests, your time is up: "At the very instant when you recognize that there is a combat, the fighter, having released his venom in one blow like a cobra, looms over you, already neutral and inaccessible"

(297).[15] The pilot might as well remain as motionless as possible and hope that he will be lost in the sun. Since this very stratagem saves plane and crew, miraculously, in the present instance (and cf. a similar incident related in Delange 116), Saint-Exupéry's daydreaming might even be said to approach the proportions of a heroic sang-froid. It is worth noting that he had been officially commended a few weeks earlier for having stuck to his flight plan in a severely crippled craft (Delange 91).

In any case, Saint-Exupéry's first authorial concern is with beauty and goodness, not historical fact; and his integration of poetic image-making and aeronautical combat, whatever it may intimate about his professional competence, remains ingenious as a means of raising—at one and the same time—both average readers and daily moral stakes to mythic stature. We might be this hero: our puny concerns would not be lost in his universe's convergence upon Arras, and would, indeed, assume a certain grandeur as we clung to them. The naively personal, almost confessional viewpoint of *Pilote de Guerre* joins every shift of space and time comprehensibly to the main narrative without insisting that the concatenation has other than a subjective value. Rather, the appealing subjectivity with which each experience is recorded serves as the foundation of its objective value. Each brush with death becomes an occasion where any individual is bound to expose his or her true nature. As Quesnel and Autrand summarize, "It isn't objective reality which Saint-Exupéry seeks, but the path to a keener apprehension of the self" (xx). Were we in Saint-Exupéry's cockpit, we might prefer different metaphors to his, and we would most certainly hearken back to different memories, but we would all surrender to metaphors and memories. He has won us to the notion, not that combat nourishes his imagery, but that it would nourish ours, or anyone's—that, like the desert or his other emblems of nullity, it is a polished mirror wherein we see those images most precious to us. It is an opportunity to recollect one's past, one's ties, one's beliefs, etc., and defend them from oblivion with a clinging embrace.

Dutertre's announcement of the hostile fighters' approach elicits still another reminiscence from Saint-Exupéry, which consumes all of chapter 9: only in the following chapter does he realize that his steady progress into the sunlight has succeeded in veiling their escape.

Meanwhile, as he awaits a lethal hail of missiles impotently, he recalls Sagon, a fellow pilot who had bailed out of his craft when it was similarly overtaken by a patrol and riddled with bullets. The resemblance which strikes him, however, is not their specific predicament, but the sensation of waiting which he now endures, and which Sagon described to him haltingly from a hospital bed. Saint-Exupéry summarizes: "Thus Sagon preserves the memory of having waited, from the beginning to the end of his adventure. Waited for more flames. Then waited for who knows what, on the wing. And waited again, in free fall, plunging straight toward the earth" (293).[16] Despite the life-or-death struggle, despite the physical exertion of extricating himself from the plane, Sagon found in combat "un abîme" ("an abyss") above which his spirit paced tediously. No revelation, no transformation—only Sagon in slow motion, in the motion peculiar to Sagon the man. Saint-Exupéry briefly refers to his own near-drowning while test-flying a hydroplane (the only reference in any of his works to the incident), and also to a man trapped for several days under a collapsed house during the Spanish Civil War. Both cases, he proposes, illustrate the same truth as Sagon's: "No circumstance awakens in us a stranger whose qualities we would never have suspected. To live is to be born slowly" (295).[17] War, like any other suspension of normal order, favors our displaying in spectacular fashion an allegiance to whatever order we have truly imbibed.

Such a state of mind scarcely sounds receptive to revelation; but why, after all, are we being told this story—the broader story of the flight to Arras—if it will only show us the pilot-hero in waiting? Certainly we have been made to view his heroism as within our grasp: we, too, can wait. If we can expect no sudden wonder or horror which will expose a new side of our pilot or ourselves, however, any more than Sagon tapped some hidden reservoir of strength, may we not at least expect enlightenment of some kind? Is not waiting a prelude to revelation—must there not always be something for which one waits? Even when Sagon was dangling in infinite leisure from his parachute, did not his continued waiting reveal to him precisely that his inner being, his sense of coherence as a moral agent, could not be so easily annihilated as he had feared?

Yet Saint-Exupéry persists in understating the sense of anticipation. As if to justify his meditative state, the ten kilometers

separating the aircraft from the earth impose an irresistible sense of
remove, and even age. The metaphor of the scientist peering through
a microscope so effective in *Terre des Hommes* recurs here, for roads
and canals only emerge as hair-thin networks at such an altitude. Also,
and more gloomily, ice begins to appear everywhere. Crystals of it
may be heard crinkling when our pilot-author squeezes his oxygen
hose, and he imagines the old man's white beard of frost which must
be under his mask. The machine-guns are frozen now, too, as are the
gas controls. Though he cannot see it, Saint-Exupéry knows further
that condensation trails must be forming in the wake of the hot
engines, leaving a path for fighter patrols to follow. Yet his most acute
impression is of time grinding to a halt rather than of imminent
gunfire or suffocation. He recalls from childhood a print of several
sailing ships trapped in Arctic pack-ice, the very billows of their sails
caught permanently in the hard freeze. Like those hapless polar
explorers, he has drifted beyond the reach of his world. His craft's
motions have a planetary torpor about them, for all their speed. "The
earth, despite its forty-two kilometers per second, makes its circuit
around the sun slowly. It requires a full year. We also, it seems, have
slowly entered into this gravitational exercise" (298).[18]

Saint-Exupéry concludes that war has no adventure to offer—or
not the aerial war, at any rate, where a split second of machine-gun
fire in "un vide presque sidéral" ("an almost astronomical void") poses
no problem and admits of no solution. One simply dies in the midst
of contemplating the puny frailty of human civilization. The greatest
adventure of the war so far, he decides (still sliding easily from image
to memory to metaphor), was his room in a farmhouse at Orconte.
More exactly, the adventure was jumping out of bed to start a fire,
returning to the warm covers as the wood kindled, and finally racing
back to the hearth to enjoy its mature and steady flames. "Thus I had
three times . . . crossed the empty, frozen steppes of my room" (301).[19]
In his portrayal, the entire experience turns out to allegorize the
body's progress through life, representing first "a child's body clinging
to a mother's breast, enfolded and protected; then a soldier's body,
trained for suffering; then a man's body, nourished with joy by the
fire's civilization, wherein the hearth is as a totem pole" (302).[20]

What Saint-Exupéry does not seem to recognize fully is how far
this allegory's breadth surpasses his would-be myth's. Every anecdote

he has yet related, every fantasy he has yet conceived, is but another polar desert traversed to reach another fire—a literal conflagration in the case of Arras, as we shall see. In similar fashion, *Terre des Hommes* had shown him leaving the comforts of Toulouse to fly over the Sahara in search of that same rebirth of culture and order, that same "civilization of fire." Thus the Orconte adventure is less a subtle inlay in the broader narrative than the simple equal of that narrative and of all others in Saint-Exupéry's book: the struggle to get airborne and recover his sense of purpose, the ordeal of playing sick at school which taught him the rewards of participation, the plunge through a watery void in his hydroplane which brought him face to face with death, and so on. Collectively, they trace but a single tale from a single arch-mold. A myth will not emerge from this flight's morality play unless the fire at its heart seethes from a unique, as yet undreamt-of dragon.

The crossing of the celestial desert at ten thousand meters is itself "inlaid" into a broader trek through chaos, as Saint-Exupéry is forced to realize in chapter 12. The various frozen controls pose several dilemmas. Essentially, they offer him a choice of disasters which cannot be avoided: he must risk one catastrophe or another. Unlike the marvelous reducing of cities and villages to microscopic proportions, an experience available from any cockpit, this mechanical dissolution of sense reflects a malaise in the culture which has sent the scientist and his microscope aloft. The scientist was never meant to go so high, and the lens cannot be focused. War has disrupted the experiment's established procedure. "All of this is absurd. Nothing is to the point. Our world is made of wheels which do not engage each other. It's not the materials which are at fault, but the Watchmaker" (303).[21] No Saharan sandstorm could be more disorienting than this vast failure of culture to repair its own watches, to light its own fires—to defend itself by functioning as it was meant to do. Accompanying Saint- Exupéry, all of Western Europe staggers through a region of senselessness. We are not just being invited to heroism through this narrator: we are being summoned.

The next several chapters communicate the crisis in France with relative objectivity, often adopting a style similar to Saint-Exupéry's journalistic writing. In many ways, this section is the heart of *Pilote de Guerre* as an exercise in political persuasion. We hear of the civilian population fleeing the German blitz as if a nineteenth-century column of marching soldiers were closing in; but Panzers and Messerschmidts do not present a solid front and do not require billeting in occupied villages. The refugees simply congest the roads and ravage their own countryside in a spectacle of staggering futility. "The significance of the village's incineration must equal the significance of the village. As things stand, the role of the burned village is no more than the caricature of a role" (308).[22] Like the French military, the French citizenry is trying to play out a preconceived game of war in the absence of any stable reference point.

As a literary maneuver, this adroit series of flashbacks to the war's historical and social context—to the initial causes of Saint-Exupéry's now finding himself embarked on a suicidal mission—continually renews its credibility and coherence by referring to the author's present ordeal. He has once again wrestled with the frozen controls too vigorously, and an enforced meditation helps him to recover his strength. "Were it not for this pain which has come to life in my heart," Saint-Exupéry says of a twinge in his side, "I would slip into vague daydreams like an aging tyrant" (310).[23] The chosen image is especially interesting in that it anticipates the invented narrator of *Citadelle*, the aging Berber monarch (in fact, the first pages of the unfinished manuscript were already written). Like his fictitious desert king, Saint-Exupéry is now descanting upon affairs of state—upon nothing less than political science viewed, in Aristotelian fashion, as the highest branch of ethics.

Curiously, he manages to insert another childhood reminiscence here. At five years old, he had crept out of bed, hid himself along a dark vestibule, and listened uncomprehendingly to two uncles discuss world affairs while pacing back and forth (the memory had always enchanted him [cf. *LM* 160]). The scenario should seem familiar. A warm sleep deserted, a marginal space explored, and the wisdom of two gods "qui savaient tout [et] collaboraient à la création du monde" (313)—" who knew all and were working together to create the world". . . the five-year-old boy is already the pilot-hero!

The moral which Saint-Exupéry draws from this vignette justifies its appearance and leads back to universal experience. From the august, enduring order of the recollected house, he understands and can define civilization.

A civilization is a heritage of beliefs, customs, and knowledge slowly acquired over the course of centuries, sometimes difficult to justify with logic, but which justifies itself—as do roads, if they lead somewhere—since it opens unto man his interior range and depth.[24](314)

Not only is the image of the road which goes one way and not another heavily worked in *Citadelle*, but such blunt statements of the arbitrary authority behind any inherited system of values occur only in *Pilote de Guerre* and the posthumous work. The passage also prepares us for similar sentiments a few chapters further on, in the glorious concluding "profession of faith."

As grand as they sound, the words nonetheless leave right and goodness adrift in the limbo between various cultural declarations. The final phrase suggests a way out—a way to absolute and immutable justification: the "interior expanse" which, perhaps, could open upon something resembling a soul. The Dominican friar kneeling at his prayers, Pasteur bent over his microscope, and Cézanne recoiling to study his fresh strokes are all said to manifest this internal life. Could it be that goodness, truth, and beauty have their foundation in something deeper than mere cultural conditioning, after all? Is this what the pilot-hero, having already imposed his order upon chaos since take-off, still waits for? But if it is, why would any hero be needed to substantiate its reality, which is inwardly fixed rather than outwardly fabricated?

Finally, the plane approaches Arras. Amid all the memories and reflections, Saint-Exupéry scarcely allows us to notice that he has begun his descent at a ruinous speed so as to unfreeze the controls without going into a tailspin. The enormity of this present crisis dissolves into further meditation (another example of the pilot's absent-mindedness, perhaps—or of his cool-headedness). He remembers the proprietress of a small café near one of their many temporary barracks who sought their help in launching an ancient car into the mass exodus. "Before she gets ten kilometers from here, she will already have rammed three cars, stripped her gears, and punctured her tires. Then the sister-in-law and the seven kids will start to cry" (319).[25] Yet the woman could not be convinced that her duty was to remain. Saint-Exupéry himself undertook to begin a counter-surge of opinion in the village (we have already remarked his gift for antithesis!); but his nascent party of common sense disintegrated when someone observed, "Le boulanger est parti. Qui fera le pain?" (320): "The baker has left. Who will make the bread?"

So the flight which began as a desperate attempt to find meaning in confusion—to make war comprehensible by following the old wartime rules—continues in recollections of insuperable senselessness. On the congested highways, a woman dies in childbirth here, a baby starves for lack of milk over there, yet the mass keeps growing. The refugees are not even aware of suffering as they sicken and starve. "Wrenched from their framework, their occupations, their duties, they have lost all sense of meaning. Their very identity has been used up. They are not very much of themselves—they do not exist very much" (324).[26] They perfectly exemplify human beings whose humanity has been annihilated by chaos. Robbed of all reference, they can hardly register the most visceral pain: they can hardly recognize death in the present absurdity of life. A vague rumor circulates that the government has forbidden further evacuation . . . but no message can be disseminated through empty towns and impassible roads. "The government is immersed in a polar void" ("Le gouvernement baigne dans le vide: un vide polaire" [325])—a void like that through which the aviators now fly, or that in which the ships of the print were locked forever. Even French soldiers in the field, the remaining visible sign of authority, are absorbed into the throng. How can they play by the rules when their armored cars crush pregnant women and their bullets strike babies? They must yield before the tide of futility, turning south because of "the general incoherence which divides them from each other, and not from any horror of death. They feel horror before nothing: they are empty" (330).[27]

Yet this France which is no more than "a deluge of pieces, none of which presents a face" (331),[28] had anticipated and accepted its fate before entering the war. The nation should be judged "sur son consentement au sacrifice"—"on its consenting to the sacrifice." Hence, in the chaos of utter rout, Saint-Exupéry sees the same nobility as the soldier in the vanguard shows in agreeing to become the first target and, in all probability, the first to die. France's very willingness to assume so unsavory a role, furthermore, proves that the vital spirit of Western civilization has not departed. Others will step over the fallen vanguard and press on to the common goal: "Defeat, despite its ugly flaws, can reveal itself to be the only path to resurrection" (332).[29] Also mistaken is the popular assumption (Saint-Exupéry takes care not to emphasize the source of these typically American attitudes) that the French view their "drôle de guerre" ("joke of a war") frivolously. Having once consented to sacrifice their nation in the first round of fighting, they have every right to laugh at their own immediate ineptitude. They are not toreadors upon whose bravado a ring-full of paying spectators sits in judgment (and we may remember from *Terre des Hommes* what Saint-Exupéry thinks of toreadors). Instead, it is they who judge the spectators: the heaviest responsibility is not that borne by France for crumbling, but that borne by other Western democracies for looking on as France crumbles.

Nestled within this brilliant defense of French national policy is the narrative detail that the controls have thawed. Saint-Exupéry seems only to recollect the fact because, in stating the absurdity of his present situation ("I am plunging toward the German army at eight hundred kilometers an hour and at three thousand five hundred revolutions per minute. Why? Why else?—to terrify it!" [333]),[30] he suddenly realizes that the situation has altered and that he exaggerates its gravity. Perhaps the almost comic abruptness of transition here is due to Saint-Exupéry's having compressed into one tale a high-altitude and a low-altitude mission, as Cate maintains (450); the flight report of Lieutenant Dutertre, reproduced by Estang (77), bears out this contention, as does the description of combat missions offered by Pélissier (59–61: the mission to Arras occurred on May 23 [60]). Saint-Exupéry the author attempts to smooth this rough seam by quickly diverting our attention to a wholly new problem. The ground-fire has now become much thicker and more accurate.

We should not be surprised to discover that the aircraft's approach to the greatest danger it has yet faced also puts Saint-Exupéry in touch with the very earliest of his memories, as if the last moments of life were merging into the first and closing the circle of consciousness. He recalls Paula, the young Swiss governess who had left his household before he was old enough to remember her features and to whom he was made to write occasional polite notes. "It was a little like saying prayers, since I didn't know her . . . ," he muses (336).[31] Indeed, as he zigzags to elude the flak, he invokes Paula very much as another person might murmur a prayer. This idealized figure, with her Alpine connotations of permanent snow and glinting sunshine, of ageless beauty and immeasurable distance, is the poetic equivalent of an Exupérian star. Perhaps she was the first such figure ever to ascend above'the young Antoine's horizon, or at least the first ever to radiate through his subconscious being. She is far more complex than the wood nymphs of *Terre des Hommes* who congregate around rustic fountains and ruined mansions, trusting naively in fragile truths. She is the goddess at the center of their dance. In her are gathered cultural riches from the past, an orienting magnetism over the present, and an aloofness from direct future contact: all of the attributes necessary to Saint-Exupéry's image of the divine. He sways over the earth at low altitude as a child would caper through a green field. "I have entered this countryside. So much for window-shopping! I'm a poacher who has jumped over the wall. I walk with big strides through the damp green grass and I steal plums. Paula, it's a joke of a war" (337).[32]

Is this the face of revelation, then—at once virginal and maternal? Has the hero transported his orderly vision thus far into the wilderness so that he might discern behind its strained lines of force the womb which bore him? But what, then, of the virgin, the Snow Princess? In her waits the future: she gives life its moral urgency. There is still something to come, a destiny, an appeal which makes pilots forsake their culture's secure sleep within untested presumptions.

But the womb dominates at this moment. Our pilot is pervaded by an ineffable peace: "I have at my fingertips all my memories, all the provisions which I have stored, and all my loves. At my fingertips is my childhood, which recedes into the darkness like a root" (338).[33] We are entering the climax of *Pilote de Guerre* as Saint-Exupéry enters the ecstasy of meeting death—or, more precisely, of closing life's design. As an author, he had always puzzled over this moment, the instant of unveiling. He had evaded it either with an enigmatic demise or with an apocalyptic illumination whose flash of radiance blinded. Now he has reached the critical point again.

He describes the vast conflagration below him, the remnant of Arras, in a shocking metaphor—shocking because it would become his favorite metaphor of life. "Behold . . . a tree. This tree has captured

Arras in the network of its roots. And all the juices of Arras, all the provisions of Arras, all the treasures of Arras, ascend to nourish the tree, transformed into sap" (339).[35] The incinerated city seems, indeed, to symbolize his own ecstasy. Like him, it has devoted all the "provisions" of its past to feeding a flame of consummatory experience, of revelation: it is the tree of life whose highest branches, the ultimate end of so much drained soil, touch the floor of heaven.

Quesnel and Autrand insist that this glimpse of life in death, of florition out of destruction, is absurd under the circumstances, despite the author's manifest enthusiasm (xxxvii). Undeterred by the image's ambiguous optimism, however, Saint-Exupéry recharacterizes Arras as "un château mystérieux et enchanté" ("a mysterious, enchanted castle") which poses the knight's destination in a fairy tale—which was their destination when, as children, he and his young friends would run for home ahead of a gathering storm's first raindrops. The child whom the rain touched last won the right to be dubbed "le chevalier Aklin" until the next such occasion. "I'm still playing the game of Chevalier Aklin. I run flaggingly, at the end of my breath, toward my castle of fire" (340).[35]

Just as the first raindrops soon multiply into a deluge, however, so the artillery begins to send aloft innumerable tracers that seem to seal the aviators' fate. Saint-Exupéry realizes that he was wrong to think of emerging as "le chevalier Aklin" from Arras: this game offers no hope of winning. Nevertheless, what follows is less a condemned man's surrender to his doom than a boy's attempt to redefine the game, or a poet's to find a more appropriate metaphor. In the earnest exuberance with which it shows Saint-Exupéry groping about for the perfect image, chapter 20 must be considered one of the most self-revealing passages that he ever wrote. Its bursts of colorful imagery in tight succession are at least the equal of the tracers' visual spectacle. A log in the fireplace which suddenly cracks to release a million sparks . . . an avalanche which suddenly tumbles down when a mountaineer thoughtlessly coughs . . . a team of jugglers in an intricate dance . . . a broken string of pearls . . . slow tears turned to lightning . . . lances in a joust . . . swords in a duel . . . such are the pictures which interpret the hail of bullets. Never did a poet mix metaphors more shamelessly. "It's not a matter of danger! The luxury in which I am steeped simply dazzles me!" (343).[36]

In a letter to Benjamin Crémieux, Saint-Exupéry would defend the realism of this poetic strategy. "The most unpoetic of persons," he explained, "once activity prevents him from choosing his words and he lets his flesh do the thinking, does not think in technical jargon, but outside of words, in symbols" (qtd. in Devaux 99).[37] Properly understood, he is simply reiterating that the spirit's reality is greater than the body's. Instead of seeking to restrain the imagination, the "realist" must give it full rein in order to achieve escape velocity from the corporeal world. Illusion is in the object as object.

In this instant of rapture over Arras, Saint-Exupéry abandons even his memories. He has not merely completed life—he might have done that in his submerged hydroplane or while lost in the Sahara. Instead, he has discovered the ultimate substance of life, the treasure trove supposed to lie hidden within the enchanted castle. The tracers are pure energy ascending into heaven. They are virtual crystallizations of spirit. The pilot-myth, after all, is exclusively about spiritual energy: the unthinkable energy required to create something from nothing, and to do so perpetually. Now the tokens of such vitality are raining almost into his lap. For once, the pilot does not have to create sense out of chaos: this time, the void has split at the seams and yields an astonishing display with which his imagination can scarcely keep pace. Saint-Exupéry could not be more inspired if he were flying into the Milky Way's vortex.

Recollecting his situation somewhat in chapter 21, he begins new evasive maneuvers. Yet even in this slight recovery from awed jubilation, he remains fascinated that his body's imminent peril is of so little account to him. Many of the shells explode with blunt impact right beside the craft—which was, in fact, badly damaged during the mission: the oil reservoir was completely shattered (Cate 402 and Pélissier 60). Vaguely reprising his antithetical style of challenging presumptions in *Terre des Hommes*, Saint-Exupéry remarks, "Life has always belied the fanciful images that I would invent. But this time it was a matter of walking bare beneath an unleashing of mindless fists, without even a folded elbow to protect my face from them" (345).[38] He concludes that on such occasions, a person's sense of identity shifts from his body to his act. His reality changes from how he appears in an instant of frozen time to what he does with a unit of running time—the most basic of moral insights. "You dwell within your very act. Your act is yourself" (346).[39]

To exist in this state of action, of being in becoming, is the highest human reality. (Again, it is tempting to interpret the tracers analogously: essential motion whose most instantaneous glimpse remains blurred, they require an imaginative calculus.) To stress the point, Saint-Exupéry recalls the death of his young brother, an incident which scarred him deeply at the time and to which he refers directly nowhere else in his published work. The boy had sensed that he was dying and had explained to Antoine serenely, "I can't keep myself from doing it. It's my body" (347).[40] He then took obvious pleasure in bequeathing to his brother a bicycle and a few mechanical playthings which he must have known Antoine would appreciate. Placid tolerance of a body that has failed . . . altruistic delight in changing oneself into a gift for others . . . such is the moment of death not in cases of fabulous heroism, but in the orderly souls of children and of certain adults uncorrupted by grown-up egotism.

One must wonder if, occupied by eluding the artillery, Saint-Exupéry could really have recalled his brother consciously and in coherent illustration of a moral insight. When, toward the end of the chapter, the shells strike particularly close, the emotion he describes is decidedly *not* that of sacrifice to a cause.

> And I begin to feel a stunningly unexpected pleasure. It's as if my life, at every second, were being given back to me; as if my life, at every second, were becoming more perceptible to me. . . . I am no more than a fountain of life. The intoxication of life is claiming me. They talk about "the intoxication of combat . . .": this is the intoxication of life![41] (349)

Without doubt, the meditation on the body's puniness and the spirit's limitlessness which Saint-Exupéry offered us shortly before belongs to this kind of encounter, if only at a subconscious level. As I suggested earlier, philosophers of the sublime had long ago described the same sense of physical intimidation succeeded—and utterly dwarfed—by a sense of moral identification when one contemplates a mountain chasm, a waterspout, a desert, etc. Charles Baudelaire, whose works were among Saint-Exupéry's favorite bedside reading, registers a classically sublime impression from a mountain precipice in the following terms, which often approximate those of the flight over Arras:

> The memory of terrestrial things reached my heart only in weakened and diminished form, like the sound of bells tied to an imperceptible flock passing far, far away, on the slope of another mountain. . . . And I remember that this solemn, rare sensation, caused by some huge yet perfectly silent motion, filled me with a blend of joy and fear. In short, thanks to the god-bestowing [*enthousiasmante*] beauty which surrounded me, I felt in perfect peace with myself and the universe . . . (*Petits Poèmes en Prose* 71)

With the reminiscence of his brother, however, Saint-Exupéry manages to slip into the equation a new constant: the exchange of self for others. The intensely intimate awakening to spiritual reserves which he portrays so well in his sublime encounter with the tracers has no immediate social dimension, properly speaking (one of the reasons, no doubt, why the Romantics found the transition from sublime awareness to political action so problematic: Baudelaire's meditation above ends in a grating encounter with sordid social realities). In celebrating the "intoxication of life," Saint-Exupéry exhibits a personal awakening to his identity as an agent, a metaphysical force dwelling beyond physical danger. The social repercussions of his discovery remain merely implicit, at best. Nonetheless, he inserts his code of service to cultural order wherever he can. Rather than acknowledge a new proximity to the creator of his soul, he claims to find in these instants a new solidarity with circumstances left far behind. We are being prepared for the safe return to base with its long "profession of faith" in Western culture and Christian tradition.

Of course, the suicidal mission is safely completed, after all, and the aviators veer from Arras in the gathering darkness. *Pilote de Guerre* contains another seven chapters, but the narrative is essentially over at this point. Saint-Exupéry savors his return to Group 2/33, well satisfied that he has today shouldered his part of the burden and indignantly defying (though diplomatically leaving unnamed) those who would have him retire from active service. "The professional observer has always filled me with horror. What am I, if I do not participate?" (354).[42] He decides that his day's work has changed him—that he is now filled with that sense of purpose which had so painfully deserted him at the novel's beginning. Ultimate victory will be theirs precisely because they—he, his comrades, and his country-men—have consented to a senseless resistance in a show of solidarity. "If I accept to be humiliated by my family, I can act upon my family. It is part of me, just as I am part of it" (368).[43] Such unity of vision is invincible.

Saint-Exupéry's first allusion to the West's Christian heritage occurs here. As always, his images are marvelously eloquent, but also—this time—disturbingly skewed to the very tradition which he claims to understand. "I understand for the first time one of the mysteries of the religion from which the civilization which I claim as my own has come: 'To carry the sins of the world . . .' Indeed, everyone carries the sins of the world" (369).[44] Not only does every person *not* bear the sins of all people from a Christian perspective, but no person can bear even his or her own sins. To tolerate the cowardice or short-sightedness of one's fellows is another matter: though difficult, it remains a moral obligation. But sin, the perverse desire to spoil the life of the spirit, to rake everything down to the meaningless level of rubble—not the fact of error, but the taste for error—this is a concept which, one must conclude, Saint-Exupéry never managed to understand. Devaux expresses similar reservations about later passages:

> The profession of faith with which *Pilote de Guerre* concludes is, taken altogether, a vibrant homage to Christianity . . . but it is also a farewell to Christianity and a hail to the new religion of Man, wherein the human being will henceforth be the "common measure" necessary to guarantee the universality of those values which alone make life endurable. (51)

The pilot-myth foresees only faint hearts and laggards, not positive friends of disorder. The world can be transformed if its people will simply awake—with heavy emphasis on "simply"!

Chapters 25 and 27 contain Saint-Exupéry's assessment of alter-native new political systems, their various failures, and the traditional system's reasons for success. The cult of Man must always dominate the cult of the Individual to nourish a free society (the author insists upon upper-case lettering for these different political entities): otherwise one has only a mass of stones lying about in disarray and declaring their existence egotistically, never a cathedral in which they have gloriously collaborated. On the other hand, the responsibility of each person for all people must not be interpreted as allowing the Community's interests to prevail over the Individual's survival. Such a society would produce not a cathedral, but an anthill. To achieve the difficult balance necessary, Western civilization has generated a concept of God. "The contemplation of God would anchor the equality of men, because they would be equal in God. And this equality had a clear meaning. For one cannot be equal except in reference to something" (374).[45] Thus one serves humanity rather than a communal hive by honoring the presence of God in all people, a presence which manifests itself universally yet individually; and thus the community is bound to risk its very existence for the sake of one prisoner, for God's presence cannot be carved up and meted out according to some inane arithmetic.

These profound and moving pages deserve to be studied in much more detail than I have offered. Fortunately, most commentaries on *Pilote de Guerre* do exactly that, devoting far more space to Saint-Exupéry's political theories than to the book's actual story. My purpose has been to trace how Saint-Exupéry adumbrates his philosophy through his art; and, since the "profession of faith" rests entirely outside the narrative's chain of cause and effect, it does not justify further delay. Yet we must note that Saint-Exupéry is quite unaware of having strayed beyond the tale's rightful lines of force. Estang thinks him merely caught up in "a lyricism which does not always escape grandiloquence" (76), a criticism which Robert Brasillach and others had originally leveled at the book's concluding section in much more vituperative terms (Chevrier 63–64); but to these closing chapters the author seems also to have transferred all the work's previous tension, exhilaration, and triumph. Indeed, when encapsulating his observations of chapters 25–27 into what he specifically calls his "credo," Saint-Exupéry explains, "I wish to remember what I have seen" (383).[46] He is fully convinced that his discovery of the human spirit's active endurance beyond bodily fear and pain has been a socializing experience—that it has revealed the value of circumstantial ties rather than the individual's exclusive worth in his or her will to choose goodness. By no accident, then, the Christianity which he expounds at the book's conclusion is a formula for civil harmony rather than a hope in the spirit's eternal life. "Had he belonged to a Buddhist or Islamic civilization," notes Borgal, "Saint-Exupéry would no doubt have embraced the great principles of either of these religions in the same manner" (128).

The pilot-hero returns bearing the magical seeds of culture, or so he believes . . . but how well has he examined his pocketful of tracers? And, in any case, had his faith in cosmos not already been confirmed as soon as he had reduced the world to readings on his control panel? What, if anything, has truly been revealed?

III.

One can only suppose that, yes, Saint-Exupéry's near-death experience had helped him to view life in a new light—but that he had misreported the event. Why did he handle it so ineptly? His pilot-heroes had long been awaiting some clap of thunder to give their lives coherence. *Courrier Sud* was alone among the previous novels to leave its characters clinging to patently relative principles. Fabien is already implicitly at odds with Rivière when he gate-crashes upon the moonlit heavens. An ally of natural chaos, the full moon nonetheless lifts his soul far above the level of his boss's mystery-resistant cult of duty. Likewise, the Saint-Exupéry of *Terre des Hommes* who had serenely resigned himself to death in the Sahara has already reached Rivière's stage, and is inexplicably elevated from it by an encounter with a charitable nomad. Now the Saint-Exupéry of *Pilote de Guerre* has arranged almost from the book's beginning to resume that wait identified before with the final crescendo. Before, the moon's face had escaped unread and the nomad's unremembered. Now, with so long and deliberate a wait, surely the countenance of essential truth would be captured. . . .

Yet the wait does not drag on in order to prepare author or reader for the revelation. On the contrary, most of the intervening chapters seem to reject the possibility of a greater truth, like a frantic Sybil fleeing her divine voice at the moment of possession. For one thing, Saint-Exupéry's spiritual liberation during the tracer-storm is the one stage of an oft-repeated pattern that finds utterly no parallel in any "waiting" recollection or digression. What he discovers over Arras is not, after all, what he discovers in his farmhouse-billet or his childhood home. The fireplace at Orconte spreads the warmth of blankets to the rest of the room, extending the boundaries of culture. The two uncles also warm young Antoine in their indecipherable but obviously capable wisdom. For his part, Commandant Alias clings to the rules of the game as the best means of kindling the human spirit. All of these instances, and all of the book's other vignettes, involve blind devotion to an arbitrary, life-giving power. Serving the fireplace hand-and-foot, cowering in darkness before the wise uncles, punctiliously obeying a code that demands one's death . . . these are sacrifices to an inscrutable, almighty god. They lead to no revelation except the self-fulfilling kind. The warmth that rewards them is the warmth that preceded them, though enhanced by an active involvement fostering a sense of collaboration.

The "revelation" in the heat of combat might easily have been tailored to suit the same pattern. The pilot, terrified, would mumble a prayer learned long ago by rote—not to Paula, goddess of transcending perfection, but to the hearth god, patron saint of home and safety. Perhaps, too, the pilot would remember his family and friends—not a dead brother, but a living wife whom he wants to hold once more (like Guillaumet during his Andean ordeal). Forcing himself to concentrate on these narrow visions definitive of his culture, he would overcome his paralyzing fear in classic Rivièresque style. The mystery, alive only in his mind, would dissolve. His newly acquired ability to remain calm would permit him to maneuver through the flak, and that night he would break bread with his loved ones: Q.E.D.

Such is most certainly not the account which Saint-Exupéry renders of his experience over Arras. Rather than retreating into the supportive confines of personal and cultural order—or rather than creating those confines ingeniously out of primal thunder and lightning (since the pilot-hero must re-create his culture from the void)—Saint-Exupéry clearly feels an awakening. He departs from his corporeal identity at the behest of some yet more intimate voice. The body, left behind, becomes a pitiful shell in his estimation: he is ecstatic, in the word's literal sense. He has discovered the infinite range of the soul—a revelation of sorts, announced not by angelic hosts but by the metaphor of the deadly fireworks. The consequences of such a revelation can, and usually do, change a person's life forever. The thousand natural shocks which flesh is heir to never again seem quite so shocking, for the flesh itself becomes a rather puny concern. Likewise, all the fetters which worldly circumstance twines about one's consciousness—race, age, gender, social class—have a looser hold ever after, for these superficial accretions do not result from free choice, but are as arbitrary an attachment as the cut of one's clothes. Even culture loses some of its gleam, for the interpreting of race, age, gender, and class is administered by cultural prejudice. While culture may also pass along values which any conscientious person can endorse in abstract, it tends to make its ethical system a repeated test of conformity rather than a recommended guide to integrity. How can anyone who has taken the full measure of this life's limitations intricately identify him- or herself with one culture or another?

How, indeed? How can Saint-Exupéry emerge from his revelation claiming to fight "pour un certain goût des fêtes de Noël"—"for a certain savor of Christmas holidays"—which filters through Europe from Norway and Finland (368)? Would it not have been far less frivolous, given the spirit's elevation over bodily concerns, to fight against murderous oppression in general, even when that oppression is directed at a culture from which France derives little or nothing?

Either Saint-Exupéry was not privy to the kind of awakening which he describes so accurately and inspiringly—and this seems quite impossible—or else he chooses to suppress the experience's proper moral insights in favor of an almost opposing moral argument. In the latter case (and surely the true one), his decision becomes all the more enigmatic in that it deprives his painfully arranged (and just as painfully resisted) rendezvous with meaning—his grand Wait—of its legitimate climax. Again, the descending god has no face . . . or the wrong face. The pilot returns to base as he left: a Frenchman fighting a hopeless battle for the sake of observing the rules. His sole comfort arises from having observed the rules, a comfort vividly renewed in circumstances like those recounted because a defection from the rules becomes so tempting then. In the same fashion, a dusty bureaucrat or brainless colonel might take pleasure in having shifted the day's usual volume of papers, despite an unusual number of distractions.

So why did Saint-Exupéry perversely misconvey the revelation which he received over Arras? We must assume, as earlier, that he was not yielding to any propagandistic motive. Though a revelation of the soul's transcendence over petty cultural bias might have sounded the wrong note to a vacillating American audience (after all, life can continue without a France), Saint-Exupéry wrote only what he himself believed. There is utterly no evidence to suggest that *Pilote de Guerre* was any less forthright than his other books. For that matter, the United States was at least as closely affiliated to Germany as to France from a cultural standpoint: hence most of its vacillation. An argument based on choosing moral obligation over circumstantial ties could therefore have been very appropriate and effective. Saint-Exupéry's declining to see his experience's intimate truth thus makes less sense than ever as the cold calculation of a political realist.

I have stressed that the awakening over Arras is the main sequence's only stage to lack a parallel within the book's other vignettes. While the message elsewhere is to cling fast to tradition, the message following the grand climax is to seek the truth beyond this world's material façade. Perhaps Saint-Exupéry was trying to obscure the divergence in order to preserve his work's harmony—a harmony which, while tidying up the work's aesthetic power, would more importantly validate its ethical system (in the author's "contemplation through action" approach). Might he have sought to squeeze the climax into the preexisting pattern subconsciously, thereby preserving the illusion that he had defined the basic motion of real lives everywhere?

The problem here is that, just as the materially transcendent moment over Arras might have been written out of the story, so similar moments could have been written into it elsewhere. In fact, Major maintains (quite plausibly, I think) that every extroverted moral lesson throughout the book has been drawn from essentially introverted activity:

> In all the experiences which end in fraternity . . . we notice that the fundamental preoccupation is of an individual order, first and foremost. The declarations of friendship and soli-darity no doubt express the author's sincere feeling; but relative to the literary situations from which they are

supposed to have drawn their justification, they often appear gratuitous. (231–32)

What did Sagon feel, crouched interminably on the wing of his flaming craft, if not the paltriness of a material existence which we mistake for the essence of life? Saint-Exupéry had brushed against death often enough (as in the hydroplane which almost took him to a watery grave) that he must have divined the body's inconsequence and material reality's shallowness. Even the childhood recollections of *Pilote de Guerre* (e.g., his brother's deathbed "bequest") offer him ample scope to measure the spirit's superiority to matter. Why, then—why in the world did he obstinately return to the conclusion that the arbitrary forms of culture must serve as our fundamental references in an otherwise shifting void?

As irrepressibly as this question imposes itself, we must ultimately be content to leave it unanswered. The tidy syllogisms of those biographies which presume to reconstruct a man's soul from a few stray "facts" strike me as highly dubious. As Renée Zeller has remarked of *Citadelle*, "one is always hoping that the name of Him who gathers together, who makes us whole as He is whole, will be pronounced. But the reader must finally write it in himself as the logical conclusion of these pages" (134). With just such trepidation must one supplement Saint-Exupéry's personal motives. The veil which conceals human beings from each other is often at least as opaque as that which separates them from God.

I regard Saint-Exupéry's resistance to a belief in some sort of independent metaphysical reality—some realm where the moral duties and aesthetic pleasures which so dominated his consciousness could take root more deeply than in the realm of culture—as the central enigma of a highly enigmatic human being. My own suspicion is that Saint-Exupéry's formidable capacity for puzzle-solving would not allow him to let the most important puzzle of all abide in permanent mystery. His life was a history of untying Sphinx's riddles—of dispelling mysteries, as he had said through Rivière. He even found a solution for the machine-guns that froze at high altitude, and he seems to have been on the verge of inventing the jet engine in 1939 (Cate 389–90). Pélissier (197–98) and Chevrier (255) list almost a dozen extraordinary ideas which he patented in his final years.

Could such a mentality resign itself to watching Western civilization unravel morally while putting its own house in order through private contemplation? As Léon Werth writes of his beloved Tonio, "He had a curiosity about vast systems, and he himself worked at fashioning one for his own usage and that of his friends" (136). The traditional wisdom maintains that everyone should be content to cultivate his garden, but this regimen is much abused by complacent do-nothings who would not improve the world even if they could. The right way to reconcile the life of the spirit with life in this world, no doubt, is to live both lives in the same motion: to make one's conscience as clean and thorough as possible while eagerly doing what little bit of good one can do for others. Indeed, conscience demands a turning outward to others—but its perfection does not demand a perfection of the outside world.

Hence a conscientious act may often seem what Saint-Exupéry called (in reference to French opposition of the German blitz) throwing glasses of water on a forest fire. One proceeds to throw the water not because one hopes to bring the outer situation under control, but because one's inner world recovers its harmony in the apparently futile blow against disorder. Were Saint-Exupéry not satisfied with so delicate a balancing act—had his spiritual peace depended instead upon the zealous exporting of its vision throughout humanity—he would not have been the first to fling himself into the conflagration. Surely everyone who takes his or her conscience seriously and seeks outlets for right action knows the sense of reluctance to walk away, bucket of water emptied, while the world continues to kindle.

For the revelation over Arras cannot, after all, save the world, but only those who concede that the world cannot be saved. Its burst of mixed metaphors reveals precisely that no material revelation is possible, and that all supposed revelation is only (as Derrida warns) veiled metaphor. The ecstatic moment contains nothing more expressible than a pity—verging on disdain—for expression; and to that ethereal pity one must cling as one is lured hourly ever after by fear, lust, envy, egotism, and the rest to stake one's life on what can be seen and touched. How many can cling to so little? An epic hero who should bear back these sorry-seeming seeds of eternal life would not only fail to redefine his culture, but would certainly be laughed out of town like Jack with his silly beans. It is *because* such revelation is already known to everyone—is already waiting on those ascetic enough to wait—that few will ever see its blank face. Most will believe, instead, that they missed the face, or forgot it, or saw their own. Patience is a rare virtue, and the revelation to which this wait admits us is that we must wait still more.

Add to this Saint-Exupéry's highly personal impatience with prophets who say much and do nothing, and you have the portrait of a man who would make a myth. Saint-Exupéry requires action *both* because it puts honesty to the test *and* because anyone, after all, may act, just as anyone may arise on any morning and be honest. The mythic act of creation is at once exclusive and inclusive, and in just the right ways. Unfortunately for myth-makers, honesty is only so laudable a choice because human beings are already predisposed to long for the truth—not conditioned by culture, which often mandates lies, but inclined by their very nature. The mythic hero must respect the *terra firma* beneath him whose immovable bulk gives his mighty strides their spring; but, having recognized as much, in what sense can he call his gait mythically heroic? Nothing comes from nothing, but the something from which all comes stretches incomprehensibly beyond its thin layer of "thingness." So with morality: though no one is fully honest who fears to act upon his or her beliefs, action itself cannot create sincere believers. Indeed, a fanatical kind of action is often the last gasp before apostasy.

What avenues remain open to the pilot-hero's questing after so disastrous a revelation? Not only can he no longer seek the Holy Grail, but he has discovered it to have been secretly in his possession all along—an embarrassing insight which turns his previous epic travail to comedy. As an author, Saint-Exupéry would never again race for the prize with such fervor and conviction. *Le Petit Prince*, instead of continuing to experiment with varieties of epiphany, would wearily entrust itself to death's ever reliable discretion. As for *Citadelle*, its rambling story would be conveniently interrupted after hundreds of pages of narrative tail-chasing by Saint-Exupéry's own death. The work's fully earthbound hero has become eerily resigned to mere convergence, as opposed to risk-fraught arrival. "For there is no storing of provisions," says the desert philosopher-king coyly, "and he who ceases to grow dies" (909).[47] In the wake of *Pilote de Guerre*'s evaded revelation, however, the monarch might more correctly have summed up his and his author's predicament by declaring, "He who never ceases approaching will never die to one state and grow into another."

NOTES

¹ Je suis triste pour ma génération qui est vide de toute substance humaine. . . . Il n'y a qu'un problème, un seul de par le monde. Rendre aux hommes une signification spirituelle, des inquiétudes spirituelles.

² . . . forger un langage pour penser le monde de son temps.

³ Mais il est une impression qui domine toutes les autres au cours de cette fin de guerre. C'est celle de l'absurde. Tout craque autour de nous. Tout s'éboule. C'est si total que la mort elle-même paraît absurde. Elle manque de sérieux, la mort, dans cette pagaille . . .

⁴ Chacun s'évertue, de son mieux, à faire que la guerre ressemble à la guerre. Pieusement. Chacun s'efforce de bien jouer les règles.

⁵ Et ce n'est pas que je ne pense sur la guerre, sur la mort, sur le sacrifice, sur la France, tout autre chose, mais je manque de concept directeur, de langage clair.

⁶ . . . choqué par une évidence que nul n'avoue: la vie de l'Esprit est intermittente.

⁷ Nous sommes nous-mêmes divisés en morceaux. Cette voix. Ce nez. Ce tic. Et les morceaux n'émeuvent pas.

⁸ On traverse, à cet instant-là, le centre même de ce désert intérieur dont je parlais.

⁹ L'angoisse est due à la perte d'une identité véritable.

¹⁰ Or voici que le temps a cessé de couler à vide. Je suis installé enfin dans ma fonction. Je ne me projette plus dans un avenir sans visage.

¹¹ Le combat entre l'Occident et le Nazisme devient, cette fois-ci, à l'échelle de mes actes, une action sur des manettes, des leviers et des robinets.

¹² L'amour de son Dieu, chez le sacristain, se fait amour de l'allumage des cierges.

¹³ La tentation, je connais en quoi elle consiste aussi bien qu'un Père de l'Église . . . c'est . . . , quand l'Esprit dort, de céder aux raisons de l'Intelligence.

¹⁴ . . . que ses paumes ont conduit vers le feu . . .

¹⁵ A l'instant même où vous connaîtrez qu'il y a combat, le chasseur ayant lâché son venin d'un coup, comme le cobra, déjà neutre et inaccessible, vous surplombera.

¹⁶ Sagon, ainsi, conserve le souvenir d'avoir, du début à la fin de son aventure, attendu. Attendu de flamber plus fort. Puis attendu sur l'aile, on ne sait quoi. Et en chute libre, à la verticale vers le sol, attendu encore.

¹⁷ Aucune circonstance ne réveille en nous un étranger dont nous n'aurions rien soupçonné. Vivre, c'est naître lentement.

¹⁸ La terre, malgré ses quarante-deux kilomètres par seconde, fait lentement le tour du soleil. Elle y use une année. Nous aussi, nous sommes lentement rejoints, peut-être, dans cet exercice de gravitation.

¹⁹ Ainsi j'avais trois fois . . . franchi les steppes vides et glacées de ma chambre.

²⁰ . . . un corps d'enfant accroché au sein maternel et accueilli et protégé, puis un corps de soldat, bâti pour souffrir, puis un corps d'homme enrichi de joie par la civilisation du feu, lequel est le pôle de la tribu.

²¹ Tout cela est absurde. Rien n'est au point. Notre monde est fait de rouages qui ne

s'ajustent pas les uns aux autres. Ce ne sont point les matériaux qui sont en cause, mais l'Horloger.

[22] Il faut que la signification de l'incendie du village équilibre la signification du village. Or, le rôle du village brûlé n'est plus qu'une caricature de rôle.

[23] N'était cette douleur au coeur qui me semble vivante, je sombrerais dans des rêveries vagues, comme un tyran vielli.

[24] Une civilisation est un héritage de croyances, de coutumes et de connaissances, lentement acquises au cours des siècles, difficiles parfois à justifier par la logique, mais qui se justifient d'elles-mêmes, comme des chemins, s'ils conduisent quelque part, puisqu'elles ouvrent à l'homme son étendue intérieure.

[25] Avant dix kilomètres d'ici elle aura déjà tamponné trois voitures, grippé son débrayage, crevé ses pneus. Alors, la belle-soeur et les sept enfants commenceront de pleurer.

[26] Arrachés à leur cadre, à leur travail, à leur devoirs, ils ont perdu toute signification. Leur identité elle-même s'est usée. Ils sont très peu eux-mêmes. Ils existent très peu.

[27] . . . l'incohérence générale qui les divise les uns d'avec les autres, et non par horreur de la mort. Ils n'ont horreur de rien: ils sont vides.

[28] . . . un déluge de morceaux dont aucun ne montre un visage.

[29] La défaite peut se révéler le seul chemin vers la résurrection, malgré ses laideurs.

[30] Je plonge vers l'armée allemande à huit cents kilomètres-heure et à trois mille cinq cent tours-minute. Pourquoi? Tiens! Pour l'épouvanter!

[31] C'était un peu comme des prières, puisque je ne la connaissais pas. . .

[32] Je suis entré dans ce paysage. Finies les vitrines! Je suis un maraudeur qui a sauté le mur. Je marche à grandes enjambées dans une luzerne mouillée et je vole des prunes. Paula, c'est un drôle de guerre.

[33] Je dispose de tous mes souvenirs et des toutes les provisions que j'ai faites, et de toutes mes amours. Je dispose de mon enfance qui se perd dans la nuit comme une racine.

[34] Voilà . . . un arbre. Cet arbre a pris Arras dans le réseau de ses racines. Et tous les sucs d'Arras, toutes les provisions d'Arras, tous les trésors d'Arras, montent, changés en sève, pour nourrir l'arbre.

[35] Je joue encore au chevalier Aklin. Vers mon château de feu je cours lentement, à perdre haleine.

[36] Il n'est pas question de danger! M'éblouit le luxe où je trempe!

[37] . . . le plus rustre, quand l'action l'empêche de choisir ses mots et qu'il laisse sa chair penser, ne pense pas dans un vocabulaire technique, mais en dehors des mots, en symboles.

[38] La vie a toujours démenti les fantômes que j'inventais. Mais il s'agissait, cette-fois ci, de marcher nu, sous le déchaînement de poings imbéciles, sans même le pli d'un coude pour en garantir le visage.

[39] Tu loges dans ton acte même. Ton acte, c'est toi.

[40] Je ne peux pas m'en empêcher. C'est mon corps.

[41] Et je commence d'éprouver un plaisir prodigieusement inattendu. C'est comme si ma vie m'était, à chaque seconde, donnée. Comme si ma vie me devenait, à chaque seconde, plus sensible. . . . Je ne suis plus qu'une source de vie. L'ivresse de la vie me gagne. On dit "l'ivresse du combat . . .", c'est l'ivresse de la vie!

[42] Le métier de temoin m'a toujours fait horreur. Que suis-je, si je ne participe pas?

[43] Si j'accepte d'être humilié par ma maison, je puis agir sur ma maison. Elle est de moi, comme je suis d'elle.

[44] Je comprends pour la première fois l'un des mystères de la religion dont est sortie la civilisation que je revendique comme mienne: "Porter les péchés des hommes . . ." Et chacun porte les péchés de tous les hommes.

[45] La contemplation de Dieu fondait les hommes égaux, parce qu'égaux en Dieu. Et cette égalité avait une signification claire. Car on ne peut être égal qu'en quelque chose.

[46] Je désire me souvenir de ce que j'ai vu.

[47] Car il n'est point de provision et, qui cesse de croître, meurt.

WORKS CITED

Anet, Daniel. *Saint-Exupéry: Poète, Romancier, Moraliste*. Paris: Corrêa, 1946.

Baudelaire, Charles. *Petits Poèmes en Prose*. Paris: Garnier-Flammarion, 1967.

Borgal, Clément. *Saint-Exupéry: Mystique sans la Foi*. Paris: Centurion, 1964.

Cate, Curtis. *Antoine de Saint-Exupéry*. New York: Putnam, 1970.

Chevrier, Pierre. *Saint-Exupéry*. Paris: Gallimard, 1958.

Crane, Helen Elizabeth. *L'Humanisme dans l'Oeuvre de Saint-Exupéry*. Evanston, Ill.: Principia, 1957.

Delange, René. *La Vie de Saint-Exupéry*. Paris: Seuil, 1948.

Devaux, André-A. *Saint-Exupéry*. Paris: De Brouwer, 1965.

Estang, Luc. *Saint-Exupéry*. Paris: Seuil, 1989.

François, Carlo R. *L'Esthétique de Saint-Exupéry*. Neuchâtel: Delachaux and Niestlé, 1957.

Leleu, Jean. "Pilote au 2/33." *Saint-Exupéry en Procès*. Ed. René Tavernier. Paris: Pierre Belfond, 1967: 79–92.

Major, Jean-Louis. *Saint-Exupéry: L'Écriture et la Pensée*. Ottawa: U of Ottawa P, 1968.

Pélissier, Georges. *Les Cinq Visages de Saint-Exupéry*. Paris: Flammarion, 1951.

Quesnel, Michel and Michel Autrand. "Préface Générale." *Saint-Exupéry: Oeuvres Complètes*. Vol. 1. Ed. Michel Quesnel and Michel Autrand. Paris: Gallimard, 1994: ix-lii.

Robinson, Joy D. Marie. *Antoine de Saint-Exupéry*. Boston: Twayne, 1984.

Saint-Exupéry, Antoine de. *Oeuvres*. Roger Caillois, ed. Bibliothèque de la Pléiade. Paris: Gallimard, 1959; volume contains *Courrier Sud, Vol de Nuit, Terre des Hommes, Lettre à un Otage, Pilote de Guerre, Le Petit Prince*, and *Citadelle*.

—. *Carnets*. Paris: Gallimard, 1953.

—. *Un Sens à la Vie*. Paris: Gallimard, 1956.

Schiff, Stacy. *Saint-Exupéry: A Biography*. New York: Knopf, 1994.

Webster, Paul. *Antoine de Saint-Exupéry: The Life and Death of the Little Prince*. London: Papermac, 1994.

Werth, Léon. *Tel Que Je L'ai Connu . . .* in René Delange, *La Vie de Saint-Exupéry*. Paris: Seuil, 1948: 131–86.

Zeller, Renée. *La Grande Quête d'Antoine de Saint-Exupéry dans Le Petit Prince et Citadelle*. Paris: Alsatia, 1993.

CHAPTER 6

LE PETIT PRINCE AND THE
IMPASSE OF DEATH

To all appearances, the conception and writing of *Le Petit Prince* was extraordinarily straightforward, not only by Saint-Exupéry's standards but by any author's. The cherubic figure with the flaming hair whom we now know so well from Saint-Exupéry's personal illustration of the book had apparently adorned napkins and marginalia in cafés and restaurants for several years (cf. Delange 88–89). Schiff has the pilot "scribbling a little man over and over, often with wings, or standing on a cloud, in one case menaced by a tiny devil representing a Messerschmitt" in his frigid billet at Orconte (324). Cate describes the particular occasion when a fellow French exile in New York encouraged Saint-Exupéry to write the boy's story in the form of a children's book (457–58). Saint-Exupéry seems to have been captivated by the idea immediately. Concerned as he was over the course of events in Europe, he nonetheless threw himself into the new project, and the book by which he is exclusively known among most readers today appeared in early 1943.

Never was a man less inclined to escapism, at least not of the conscious, self-indulgent sort. If Saint-Exupéry could spare the time to compose a story in so "frivolous" a genre, we must assume that he did not consider his work frivolous at all. In fact, we know from his musings in the later-published *Carnets* (e.g., 28–29) that he had admired the formula of the children's book throughout his career. Its utter simplicity—its distillation of experience into a few basic character types engaged in some prototypical course of action—verges upon

175

moral allegory. History, too, may be allegorized, of course; but young readers can hardly be expected to know about Hitler or capitalism or the Koranic (so he felt). Hence the semantic objective of a book intended for their consumption would have to be accessible to anyone with an uncluttered mind and an unpolluted heart. The universal patterns which history and culture *conceal* might therefore credibly represent the substance of a children's book.

Such transcendence of history used to be ascribed to ancient epics, fairy tales, and, in general, myths. These genres were actually considered suitable for young people by the Victorians—after occasional lurid or obscene details had been purged, naturally. Saint-Exupéry seems to have been negotiating a fusion of the pilot myth with moral allegory through a very similar kind of expurgation. If the comical, even tawdry self-delusion of human nature could be filtered out of the story, then a heroism sufficient for mythic action might remain. That is, if the slain dragon would stay slain—if its evil were exterior to the hero's nature and hence deprived of any chance at revival—then a brave victory over an alien mystery would fully close one cycle and begin another. Mankind would forever after rest a little easier on the dragon's bleached bones.

In religious terms, the hero of the myth, like the child of the allegory, must know no sin. Were someone to believe, for whatever reason, that sin does not exist, this distinction between myth's tragedy and allegory's comedy would vanish in a happy meeting at midway. As Saint-Exupéry's inexhaustible faith in social revival implies, he entertained just such a belief. Earnest individuals bearing the imprint of their milieu can always regenerate both themselves and their cosmos simply by asserting it in the void. The only enemy is entropy, that magnetic attraction which the void exerts from within as well as from without. At the same time, "within" does not mean "intrinsic" (so this profession of faith goes). The lethal attraction belongs not to our nature, but to our enemy's. That seductive call to surrender does not awaken some treacherously latent sympathy in our hearts, but only exploits our weariness of resisting the external assault. At any moment, we can substitute our own lines of force for it through sheer insistence—an accessible kind of heroism if ever there was one.

Thus *Le Petit Prince* is an even more profound statement about adult realities than we might expect. In this single regard—i.e., that the child's truth is the adult's truth—Saint-Exupéry resembles Rousseau, though he certainly would not agree with Jean-Jacques's notion of society as a necessary evil for modern humans, already too degenerate to recover their natural innocence. One of the Prince's (and his author's) most child-like and endearing qualities is precisely his selfless devotion to his circle of friends. Nevertheless, both Saint-Exupéry and Rousseau would concur that a typical education sadly lacks the emphasis on originality needed to make adult society vibrant, resilient, and sincere. If only the child could be kept alive in the adult, the world might function as it ought . . . and a strictly regimented, conformist upbringing is largely responsible for putting the child to sleep. A reawakening is possible at any moment, and would require not a radical alteration of the will, but only a few well-chosen words (or a great many, apparently, for Rousseau).

So deeply convinced was Saint-Exupéry that an essential body of truth for all people—the archetypal sequence of human life—could be found and formulated that he had toyed with allegorization even when naming the characters of *Vol de Nuit*. In his art, the approach to greater degrees of realism had become a withdrawal from the peculiar and the contingent, since the highest reality was moral and thus transcended the material world's quirks. The author of the unfinished *Citadelle* (for whom so many self-styled intellectuals are "myope et le nez contre"—"nose myopically pressed against [the evidence]") would surely have accepted Emmanuel Mounier's "personalist" assessment of realism in the narrow literary sense, and probably also his alternative version of artistic reality.

> Much so-called "realism," complacent and commonplace, is merely a compromise, and generally a cheap one, intended to reassure us about reality and not at all to reveal it. Art is, indeed, a protest against this mendacity, in the name of deeper realities that occasionally flash into our marginal consciousness. (78)

In short, Saint-Exupéry had been ready to write *Le Petit Prince* long before the notion of a children's book was planted in his conscious mind. The desert returns in its ambivalent role (already well developed in *Terre des Hommes*) of void without reference and elemental order whose few references the prevailing emptiness greatly enhances. Into this contradictory setting the pilot-hero is again introduced. Forced down by engine failure, he encounters the very predicament so often described by Saint-Exupéry in *Terre des Hommes*. The next step, of course, should represent the pilot's struggle to impose meaning upon his desperate, lonely situation; and, in accordance with the pattern celebrated in *Pilote de Guerre*, perhaps he would read the epiphanic writing in the stars.

In a way, both of these developments occur—but it might be more accurate to say that both are postponed as the hero suddenly dissolves into another pilot-hero, yet more forlorn and more deracinated. The Little Prince appears as if from nowhere (actually he hails from an asteroid which, as Schiff finely observes [383], bears the same number as Bernis's plane in *Courrier Sud*). He and the original castaway quickly forge a trusting friendship. The rest of the story virtually ignores the pilot's plight to trace the Prince's adventures. In a series of episodes which variously allegorize Saint-Exupéry's disdain for spiritual indolence, the miraculous boy relates his journey from asteroid to asteroid in search of a windscreen for his beloved flower. The Prince thus reenacts the pilot-myth himself as he penetrates, evaluates, and rejects one bankrupt order after another, always preserving his love of the rose and of his own tiny asteroid to guide him through all the confusion. He comes face to face with utter chaos in the rose garden on planet Earth: never before had he doubted his rose's uniqueness. Repressing his logical misgivings, however (thanks in part to the counsel of the fox, that revelation-peddling prophet whose intrusion we might have expected), the Prince remains true to his asteroid culture. So unassailable is his fidelity that he faces apparent death, through the serpent's bite, to return home. The distressed pilot cannot recover his body, and assumes that he must be among the stars, after all.

This desert, it seems, is as fertile in mirages as a hall of mirrors. We have seen all of these structural stages before in Saint-Exupéry's work (including the hero's death: viz., Bernis and Fabien). The only difference is that now they are catching up with each other, mingling, dancing, and trading places. Not only is the Little Prince more son than brother to the stranded pilot: he is more heavenly messenger than son, and perhaps more savior than angel—the charitable Bedouin of *Terre des Hommes* again, but now, behind the veil, an Exupérian Son of Man instead of Man. Rather than taking the pilot's sins upon himself, however, this savior simply takes over the pilot's mythic role, just as the Christ of *Pilote de Guerre*'s highly staged epiphany is all of us taking responsibility for all of us. The desert's mirages mirror back the traveler who walks into them, so that now anyone could be the real Bedouin, including the castaway he saves! When Zeller called the setting a reflection of Saint-Exupéry's internal solitude (44), she was more correct than she suspected.

In the same way, the Prince's beloved fox offers *him* a bogus message from on high in his struggle's critical moment; for that kerygma, too, is only a mirror set before the Prince, exhorting him to serve as and where he already serves. The Prince's conduct is really no better grounded or guided by the fox's moralizing than the pilot-narrator's—or our own—is by the Prince's parabolic story-telling. The little lad has already opted for his tarnished rose, whose disparity with the ideal goddess of his devotions was fully evident before he ever started heaping interplanetary sacrifices upon her. Not since *Courrier Sud* have we seen one of Saint-Exupéry's heroes immolate himself to a woman. Now, for some reason, all futile sacrifices ever attempted in any of his works seem to have found their way to a grand reunion. Frankly, the futility of the Prince's amorous excesses is interlaced so tightly with other misestimates, like waves of heat over the desert furnace, that one scarcely notices it. Or rather, what one notices is that serving a fading violet is no *more* absurd than serving a foxy friend or a boy stuck in childhood. The deceased infant who carried Geneviève's last hopes to the world beyond—and Saint-Exupéry's own brother who, when they were children, died bequeathing his favorite toys to posterity—makes no less wobbly a target for devotion than a flirt's favor: and the Prince, of course, commemorates these children, as well.

Which raises the question of death itself as that ultimate resting place of mirrored images, that haze or distance where illusion may safely retreat . . . is death not, after all, a little less wobbly an "omega point" or *grand Autre* (Lacan's "upper-case Other") simply because one's vision fails upon its threshold? Is this not why Saint-Exupéry dares to import such patently unworthy, previously discredited objectives as mistresses on pedestals back into the myth—that is, because the Prince must at last die to achieve reunion with the rose?

The trouble with hazy horizons is that they become less opaque as one treks toward them. Death is true fulfillment rather than arbitrary termination only if we believe our struggle with life's senselessness to be made good in another, *post mortem* realm, where all will be explained and justified. Helped by this kind of belief, anyone ought to be able to reach a compromise with existential absurdity. Such is most transparently *not* the world which awaits the Prince after his death. We know altogether too much about that world. We know that he will simply renew his material existence in its original form. His cherished rose will remain as vain and thoughtless as ever, we must suppose, and his former duties of weeding out baobabs and unstopping volcanoes will resume with the same monotonous regularity as besets the lamplighter on a neighboring asteroid. We know, in short, that the great mirror will merely reflect our view back into lesser mirrors. That angel winging toward us through the haze is only our own figure lurching toward an imaginary angel. Under the circumstances, a black hole would have been preferable.

An all-annihilating vortex, however, would amount to an admission that life's struggle really can mean nothing at all. Saint-Exupéry's strategy in *Le Petit Prince* has hence become a matter of obfuscating this uncomfortable conclusion rather than (as he had lately done in *Pilote de Guerre*) timorously stretching out a hand to pull the veil away. The important thing is to believe in the destination's reality—for no one would walk a step to arrive at utter nullity, and a life of torpor would violate as no other Saint-Exupéry's precious imperative to act. Thus delusion is not to be feared, or not as much as revelation. We should not be surprised, or even disdainful, if the pilot-hero at death's door cries, "What a relief! I have successfully beguiled myself throughout the days of my life—now I can drop the pretense and rest!"

Yet a person who could say this to himself would know that he had been his own dupe, and so would not be duped at all . . . where, then, would be the peace of death? Does embittered exhaustion qualify as fulfillment? Does Saint-Exupéry's image of death as the great storehouse (employed often in *Citadelle*) not deceive us—and him—as much as all the mirages it has gathered together? For the gathering and storing is itself an illusion, since these supplies will be put to no service whatsoever. They will not even have been cast into a pit whose bottom remains invisible: they will simply have been erased.

As always, I believe we must credit Saint-Exupéry with intellectual honesty: he has not knowingly and cynically set out to tease us. He appears, indeed, to have beguiled himself too well ever to celebrate his self-beguilement, even at death's door. Death naturally enjoys a certain terrible grandeur for all of us. One readily supposes that it must conceal some revelation, if only the definitive absence of anything to reveal; yet an intense anticipation of death also relieves one—very conveniently—of clutching at veils, because death's veil cannot be reached by any hand within this world, nor, once reached, can its face be named by any voice audible to this world. Its discretion is utter, and its tolerance of misplaced faith complete. Poet Pierre Reverdy, a contemporary of Saint-Exupéry's, had taken the full measure of death's obliging character:

> Life is only a succession of defeats. Some wear a pretty front, others do not. But behind the pretty ones almost as much as behind the others, defeat is always defeat—which doesn't prevent our singing a victory hymn, for in the end man is never really vanquished except by death—and then only because death deprives him of all means to proclaim (against the evidence) that he is not. Considering this, he has even made an ally of death, and he counts heavily upon it to give him all the glory which life refused him. (76)

Of course, Reverdy is indeed being rather cynical here, or at least heavily ironic. Saint-Exupéry would never have tipped his hat to death for absorbing the hero's lies. The hero does *not* lie: his assertions of cosmos ("against the evidence," to use Reverdy's phrase) constitute a moral truth, even though the culturally conditioned forms of his cosmos are wholly arbitrary.

But why not at least leave death to be the repository of that mysterious absolute value which makes the *longing* for absolute value universally valid? Why populate death with more customs and manners—with the same chain of falling dominoes, now curling its way back toward life? Why not keep silent in the presence of the ineffable? Why the mirrors?

Saint-Exupéry would write in *Citadelle* (during one of his final entries, in fact) that only an "ink-spitting pedant . . . celebrates in its universal abundance" the power of love (934).[1] This suspicion of immaterial, categorical ideals always burdened him as he labored to rise above the particular. Like Mounier, he had had his fill of "-isms." Bergson's words could also have been his (for Saint-Exupéry's work is riddled with Bergsonian notations): "God . . . has nothing of the already finished: he is incessant life, action, and liberty" (270). Yet Bergson saw behind biological evolution's grand puzzle a struggle to broaden the realm of action, thus valorizing the moment of choice over its Darwinian effects. Potentially, Bergson's God (like Teilhard de Chardin's) offers a loving ascent, a growth into understanding the metaphysical ground of choices. Why would Saint-Exupéry thrust such thinking into the province of the hair-splitting pedant?

To put it in the idiom which best expresses his self-contradictory narrative ambitions, Saint-Exupéry required a world in which heroic action was possible—was, indeed, within the scope of ordinary beings. He was closest to downright intolerance when faced with doctrines which seemed to license surrender, apathy, or paralysis, and his overriding ethical concern for the coming age was that its representatives might lose the will to act. A system founded upon the assumption of absolute values would threaten this primacy of action. It would involve humanity in a kind of moral fatality, wherein people could never rise above their own nature (or only, perhaps, by ones and twos, not on a scale that could change the world). What kind of hero saves himself but not the world, or what kind of hero thinks he has driven the dragon away from the castle only to find it awaiting him in the inner sanctum? These scenarios would never do: they belong to comedy or bitter satire, but not myth.

No revelation was safe, then, which unveiled the essential and irrepressible sameness of human beings . . . but what other kind of revelation can reach the hearts of all men and wormen? Trapped by this impasse, the pilot-hero watches each revelation become another trek across desert wastes, another revelation postponed; and the meaning of his quest ultimately recoils into death, where all journeys, no matter how heroic, must come to an end. Yet lest this mortal consummation hint at a grand fixity of cosmic power in whose lines of force life's call to action is soothed or muted, a new journey must begin on the Other Side, or an old journey must begin anew. In the chicken-or-egg conundrum of love and works, Saint-Exupéry would always conclude that no love can exist apart from its labor of love.

II.

It has become routine for commentators to observe that *Le Petit Prince* is a serious and mature statement of Saint-Exupéry's personal philosophy. We should also acknowledge the obvious: as well as a philosophical statement, it is a children's book. Saint-Exupéry's tongue-in-cheek dedication to Léon Werth "quand il était petit garçon"—"when he was a little boy"—and the first chapter's unforgettable vignette about a much misunderstood drawing from the author's boyhood (a boa constrictor digesting an elephant which adults always mistook for a hat) are plainly, delightfully intended to win over children. Of course, the maligned boa portrait does serve a purpose in the allegory. It represents the kind of stunningly original perspective which spiritually stale people dismiss out of hand. Beyond the shadow of a doubt, the dingy bureaucrats of Toulouse or the stuffy career officers atop the military hierarchy would have concurred with the "hat" interpretation.

Yet the mature myth resides in this vignette, as well. Since the "hat" people invariably inherit the principal means of cultural enforcement and transmission, culture is forever in danger, and the "boa" people must continually revive it from encroaching somnolence. The pilot-hero's alarm has thus already been sounded by the conclusion of chapter 1, in perfectly child-like terms. What better proof could we have of Saint-Exupéry's faith in human nature—in its innocence of willful disorder, specifically—than this earnest spiritual allegory which is also, from start to finish, an earnest children's story?

Chapter 2 introduces the narrator (and us) to the Little Prince, who is sketched rather than described in words. Evidently, words borrow too heavily from logic to communicate the presence of the celestial visitor, even the words of a professional who long ago gave up drawing in favor of writing. The Prince would surely agree. Indeed, his initial reason for approaching the downed pilot, who has at most eight days to repair the engine before his water supply runs out, is to solicit a drawing of a sheep. The pilot tolerantly obliges, astonished that the young stranger should recognize the elephant-in-a-boa of his first and last great sketch.

Again, a mild, pleasant irony so dominates this scene that many commentators have declined to analyze it, yielding in deference to Saint-Exupéry's hatred of academic rigamarole. Without presuming to dissect the chapter's charms, however, we may certainly note the role that artistic creativity plays in it. Perhaps no scene in the more "serious" works better shows the similarities of right conduct to aesthetic sensitivity in Saint-Exupéry. Being good is nine-tenths a matter of being energetically perceptive and receptive. The Prince wants a real sheep, yet he asks for a picture: his determined imagination will find ways to integrate the representation's two dimensions into reality's three. The ethos which will take shape around his "illusion" of having a sheep will justify itself independently of the sheep's objective value. As *Citadelle* affirms repeatedly, the service of a god is morally elevating whether or not the god actually exists.

Furthermore, we might remark that creativity is a social—and socially edifying—exercise. The Prince asks someone else, a stranger at that, to draw his sheep. Not content with the stranger's clumsy efforts, he finally accepts the sketch of a crate which, he is told, contains just the sheep he desires, and which features breathing holes for good measure. Each party involves the other in adumbrating a vision. The imagination of both must labor to produce a functioning image, and in the resulting harmony of expression they become the fastest of friends.

Within this artistic collaboration lies the quintessence of Saint-Exupéry's hope for mankind. The pilot-hero does not simply invent guiding coordinates out of a spontaneous impulse as he faces the vacuum; he re-invents his culture, rather—he revives a memory or plunders a familiar countryside now infinitely far away for a metaphor that imposes sense. By the same token, everyone who shares a common culture assumes the burden of interpreting it in such a way that his or her actions may fit into its context. Rivière's insistence on night flight might resemble the gift of an empty box to external observers (is a few hours' delay in the mail worth risking a man's life?), but those involved with him in the project undertake to honor a vital force behind the etched-in breathing holes.

All child-like simplicity aside, however, this box which might be empty—this *picture* of such a box—is not exactly the Arc of the Covenant. A child would not recognize its latent cynicism, but an adult ought to. Rather than a sacred space reserved for an inconceivable but spiritually necessary objective, we are given a fully material presence whose lowly powers temporarily justify an interminable pilgrimage. The sketch is thus the first of many "transparent obscurantisms" in Saint-Exupéry's fantasy.

Little by little, the pilot manages to piece together the boy's history (a projection of Saint-Exupéry's own personality, the Prince has no patience with routine questions aimed at establishing his precise position relative to "the norm"). The young wanderer must have come from a tiny asteroid—number B612, to be exact. At this point, Saint-Exupéry proceeds to recount the ordeal of the Turkish astronomer who discovered B612 only to be derided by European scientists for his quaint apparel. Fortunately, a dictator forced Western dress upon his people (under pain of death). When the now properly attired astronomer re-publicized his work, he won international recognition. The folly of the adults' belief that they have somehow explained an asteroid once they have pinned a number to it is so patent that the narrator apologizes to his young audience . . . but "les grandes personnes sont comme ça," he stresses (421): "grown-ups are like that."

The tone of these remarks maintains that wistful, dead-pan frankness which is unique to *Le Petit Prince* among Saint-Exupéry's works. The frankness is highly ironic, of course, in its concealment of an amused disdain. Saint-Exupéry had a distinct gift for irony, as his friend Léon Werth asserts in defiance of those who would quote *Citadelle* out of context (154–55). Nevertheless, the content of these same remarks may be retrieved from the priest's homily in *Courrier Sud*, when he warns his congregation that modern science can forecast the stars' movement but knows less of them, for all that, than a little child (45). Mathematics only measures perceptible exteriors. What a lot of truth—and what vital truths—must therefore escape it!

Another allegorical dimension of this vignette, more subtly stated but no doubt more grimly in earnest, is the political absurdity which surrounds the poor astronomer. Ignored purely because of his appearance, then threatened with death (along with his entire nation) for preserving the customary dress, he finds a "happy" ending which cannot withstand scrutiny. After all, fame is awarded to him by a bunch of cultural prigs and as a result of a potential genocidist's duress. Even mathematical truth, limited though it is, achieves a kind of purity unkown to the ruthless egotism of those who claim to serve the intellect and those who claim to serve the state. They are altogether a sorry lot, these arbiters of human destiny in the adult world. Saint-Exupéry must have had Hitler, Mussolini, and Stalin (whose tonsorial decrees he had witnessed first-hand: cf. Cate 275)— and maybe even De Gaulle and Pétain—in the back of his mind as he wrote. He was not forgetting their world: he was merely dismissing it with a few deft strokes so that he could advance into one more "real."

The ensuing chapters lay the foundation of what might be called the Prince's culture. Needless to say, every Exupérian hero owes and pays strict allegiance to some well-defined body of rituals and tastes. The Prince, as a pilot-hero par excellence, is no idle passenger in his ethos. Indeed, the shared fragility and mutual dependence of B612's customs is dramatic: the Prince is the sole surviving practitioner of his asteroid's culture. If he did not weed out pernicious baobab shoots and clean his three minuscule volcanoes (symbolic of faith, hope, and charity in Zeller's daring interpretation [83–103]), the whole asteroid would soon be overgrown and shaken apart. Says the Prince, "It's a matter of discipline. . . . When you've finished grooming yourself in the morning, you must proceed to groom the planet carefully" (426).[2]

Thus the Prince assumes the rigors of a custodial existence in full awareness of his personal responsibility, not as an artificial, temporary game. (We shall shortly see how drastically his struggle for survival differs from the fanciful charades played on neighboring asteroids.) His active participation is indispensable in sustaining a certain quality of life. On the other hand, his many duties are themselves part of that quality—or cannot be distinguished from it, at any rate. The necessity of attending the asteroid bestows upon him the gift of being the asteroid's attendant, a gift of dignity, purpose, and love. He himself would be the greater loser if he were to resettle on earth and find no further need for his daily regimen. He is "of" his homeland as the Saint-Exupéry who wrote *Pilote de Guerre* was "of" Group 2/33.

During their discussions, the narrator becomes increasingly convinced that his companion is holding something back. Yet only after a flare of tempers (as a result of which the narrator recognizes the relative unimportance of repairing his plane and surviving physically beside consoling a friend) does the truth emerge. The Little Prince is deeply concerned about the welfare of his asteroid's one flower, which he believes to be unique in all the universe. His crated sheep, intended to eat baobab shoots, might also have a taste for petals, he frets. For that matter, the true purpose of his voyage is not to obtain a hungry sheep—he could have held the baobabs at bay alone—but to find a windscreen for the demanding, persnickety rose. Not that he fails to realize the vanity of her whims: he divined that "she was none too modest" ("elle n'était pas trop modeste" [433]) from the moment she finally deigned to open in full bloom, precisely at sunrise. Always acutely conscious of her visual effect, she had more or less invented the complaint against breezes to accentuate her delicacy. She was even on the brink of imperiously requesting a glass cover to insulate her from B612's frigid climate, so inferior to her customarily balmy surroundings, when she suddenly recollected that she had never lived anywhere else!

The unflattering comparison which the rose began to draw was a patent lie fabricated in a spontaneous burst of self-aggrandizement. She is spectacularly unfit to represent the alpha and omega of any ethical system. Yet the Prince remains enthralled by her beauty. He consents to do her frivolous bidding, though she herself, astonished at her power over this innocent, later rationalizes away her discomforts in an attempt to forestall his journey. "Je t'aime," she tells him (438)—"I love you"—a word which the lad has shyly avoided, except to admit to the narrator that he is too young to know how such a coquette should be loved. Her vanity will not allow her to plead, or to confess that she really has no discomfort at all; and the Prince, confused and diffident, fears that renouncing his trip might appear to reflect a lack of dedication. Like a knight in the service of a haughty damsel, he departs on his quest through the unknown.

Saint-Exupéry probably intended the chivalric resonance, for he had read and admired the medieval *Roman de la Rose*. Not surprisingly, however, most commentators view the rose as a portrait of Saint-Exupéry's wife Consuelo, a self-styled bohemian artist *cum* hot-blooded Latin contessa. Schiff remarks, "She was as sensitive to the air around her as the Prince's globe-protected flower. Like the rose she hid her half-truths with a troubling cough" (381). The much-cited prayer which Antoine wrote for his wife to recite every evening (e.g., Migeo 150–51), though probably a tongue-in-cheek creation, certainly suggests a character like the rose's. Did Saint-Exupéry make the rose flighty and fantastical because his wife had such a nature, though, or did he select Consuelo to be his wife because she corresponded to his preconception of women? In his own words, the vivacious widow whom he courted in South America was a "grown-up, tempestuous spoiled child" (Robinson 61). Neither this description nor the general portrait of femininity found in the rose is particularly charitable, though both lack any malevolence. Self-centered, sedentary, boastful, pretentious, anemic, acquisitive . . . the picture shows the very inverse of the pilot-hero.

Yet ironically (and this irony could not have been intended), the quintessentially heroic Little Prince does not disdain his flower. He serves her the more confidently, rather; for like a star, a savage rite, or a stone idol, she can absorb infinite amounts of active devotion without ever fully recompensing him in tenderness, pity, or understanding. Such disastrous displays of humanity would deprive the servant of posture and purpose. His quest would fall slack, suddenly no longer magnetized by the arbitrary poles of a lady's inscrutable aloofness. Devaux's remarks about Saint-Exupéry's concept of God seem quite apposite here: "From this it follows that the *movement* of man in quest of God counts more than the impossible possession of God here below: God would vanish if he were attained, for he only exists because he is sought after" (79). In the same fashion, the Exupérian woman, while miserably two-dimensional as a human being, is not meant to function humanly, enjoying instead the glory of a goddess. This is so not only of the remote Paula in her icy Alps or the coy nymphs who silently smile around village fountains, but even of spiritually impoverished and materially extravagant objects of sexual desire like the rose. About all we may say on behalf of the rose's sensitivity is that, regaled with the Prince's virtual sacrifice of his life to her, she feels remorse and chagrin rather than pleasure. Her role of goddess turns out to frustrate her at least as much as it does her admirer.

To be sure, the Prince regrets his own part in this lavish sacrifice and recognizes his lack of maturity. If Saint-Exupéry had tried to dedicate himself to women during his years of youthful indecision, he had soon grown disillusioned with the strategy. Robinson (33) notices that in his letters to Renée de Saussine, he consciously confesses to having willed her into being the perfectly sympathetic creature (cf. *LJ* 61). The gap between the Renée of his imagination and the Renée who failed to correspond regularly could be narrowed to nothing, just as the stone in the Caïd's dream confirms his faith in God because it refuses any answer (*Citadelle* 683–85—cited earlier). Like Louise de Vilmorin, however, Renée eventually turned out to be a real person, and the gap between life and fantasy widened to irreconcilable proportions. Hence the young Antoine's first novel already shows Bernis unable to keep Geneviève on her pedestal; and Saint-Exupéry would later condemn all young men who squander their lives in a love-suicide over "quelque sotte petite fille semblable à d'autres"— "some foolish little girl just like so many others" (*TH* 167).

There remains in Saint-Exupéry's later works a faint bitterness about women which tends to assume the appearance of amused condescension, as if he could not forgive himself for having once elevated them so high—hardly the same sentiment as a sorrow for having made them shiver on a cold pedestal. Perhaps the rose, as a later construct, was his way of "putting in their place" the more composed, Geneviève-like women who had hurt him earlier. Even the Prince's regret over not knowing how to love the rose implies that a maturer course would have been to cajole her or ignore her. She cannot be taken at her word: she is not responsible for what she says, as any grown man should realize of any beautiful woman!

I do not wish to suggest on the strength of these female caricatures that Saint-Exupéry harbored a deep hostility toward the opposite sex which sheds light on his writing. Rather, the light comes from the failure of his fictional women as goddesses—as ever-receding objectives to whose pursuit one may dedicate one's life. No other asymptote of earthly endeavor is exposed by Saint-Exupéry to show less promise. Rivière's utter devotion to the postal line wins him the sobriquet "Victorieux" at the end of *Vol de Nuit*: we never witness in any sequel the extreme disillusionment which gnawed away at Didier Daurat (the probable model for Rivière, to whom *Vol de Nuit* is formally dedicated) and Saint-Exupéry himself when the former was fired and the latter demoted through shameless political slanders. *Pilote de Guerre* ends with the image of a grain about to "decay" into a glorious tree: we never see in any subsequent work the fungal growth of partisan bickering which rotted the tree's roots, and whose likely effect on Europe's future horrified Saint-Exupéry far more than fascism.

The point, then, is not that women fell singularly short of Saint-Exupéry's adoration, but that they constituted the single object of worship whose shortcomings he would declare in writing. That the Little Prince should be kneeling at just such an altar, and in full knowledge of its inability to raise him above his mortal state, proves that Saint-Exupéry was not so exhilarated by serving company, comrades, and ethnos as many of his biographers argue. The Prince's allegorical freedom from circumstance should allow him to sacrifice to any god he might choose—and he chooses a woman! Is not this Saint-Exupéry's tacit admission that the service of technical revolution or cultural tradition entails the same disappointment as the service of another human being? In every case, one lands back in the same humble dust which one had hoped to shake from one's heels.

The succession of asteroids which the Prince visits on his way to earth (numbers 325–30, to be exact) has been more thoroughly discussed by students of the book's allegory than any other section. Though no consensus exists about what each tiny domain signifies, Robinson reflects a certain agreement in observing, "He alone [the lamplighter] does not seem ridiculous, for he is concerned with something other than himself" (125); and Quesnel and Autrand are probably justified in recognizing images of "European democracies stifled by the Nazi monster" in these tableaux (xlii). I do not propose to append new interpretations of the Prince's individual hosts to an already long list. Clearly, the notion that they all exhibit spiritual deficiencies of one sort or another is sound. We should also note that each inhabitant, like the Prince himself, is his asteroid's sole occupant, and that each is a male. In other words, the king, the vain man, the drunkard, the businessman, the lamplighter, and the geographer all find themselves in the role of the pilot-hero (however ill they fulfill it), confronting the void in lonely isolation.

Indeed, Saint-Exupéry seems to have regretted a certain redundancy in these representations. He confessed to his friend

Georges Pélissier that the book "has 'a few too many planets,' by which he meant that he would willingly have done some trimming in the planetary voyages" (70). None of the lonely asteroid-dwellers simply surrenders to demoralization, yet neither does any of them (with the near exception of the lamplighter) offer a true affirmation by resisting the forces of disorder. The king allows the universe to work as it will and deludes himself into thinking that he has decreed its every motion. Self-delusion is no crime in Saint-Exupéry's work, as we know—but the king's sedentary style is another matter. In fact, passivity is the common denominator of these reprobates. The vain man self-indulgently bows to imaginary applause, while the drunkard shuts down even the imagination's delusive powers: he might as well be a vegetable. The businessman, like the king, relishes a kind of authority so abstracted from the real world that its lines of force do not send the slightest ripple into the stars which he claims to own—and, again, he is a do-nothing, lacking even the redemptive energy of a slick huckster. The geographer belongs to this group, as well. "He doesn't leave his desk" ("Il ne quitte pas son bureau" [457]) and busies himself recording sterile facts of no interest to anyone.

Only the lamplighter has an impact upon his environment. His tireless activity seems wholly absurd, yet at least it represents a duty which he performs punctiliously, thereby giving him a posture to assume in the flow of real events. The difference between him and the others is less a contrast between self-sacrifice and service (since all show a kind of dedication to their tasks) than between vigor and torpor. While the others trick themselves into believing that their impotence is action, the lamplighter is genuinely consumed in the vigorous cultivation of his surroundings. Indeed, there is very little reason to say that his routine is more absurd than that of a full-fledged pilot-hero who risks his neck to rush the mail along or to deliver useless reconnaissance photos. Perhaps his cosmos is rather more detached from reality. After all, the point of the hero's creativity is to resist strident incursions of nullity, not to rationalize himself into a cocoon while things fall apart. In Exupérian terms, the lamplighter may be in need of a life-or-death challenge to help him into becoming . . . yet the distinction remains a hair-fine one.

When the Little Prince reaches planet Earth, he is surprised to find it deserted (readers of *Terre des Hommes* will recollect Saint-

Exupéry's antithetical defiance of the common presumption that humans have tamed the whole world). The snake, his first encounter with a living creature, promises ominously that he can assist in the Prince's return to B612. Further on, a desert flower informs him that inhabitants of his shape do exist on the planet, but that they move by quickly in caravans. "They lack roots, and that troubles them a lot" (464).[3] Just when the Prince is beginning to feel distinctly alien in the strange land, he sees an all too familiar sight: flowers like his own—five thousand of them, all in one garden. "And he felt very sad. His flower had told him that she was the only one of her species in the universe" (466).[4] These flowers even have a generic name: they introduce themselves as roses. Smitten by the discovery of his plant's ordinariness, the Prince feels so cut off from his mission's purpose and his life's meaning that he bursts into tears. Says Major, "His delusion when he discovers the rose garden approaches that of anyone who finds himself in a world robbed of its particular meanings" (73). Now there are only things, no sense of things—only roses and no special rose among them.

The fox intervenes at this point, distracting the Prince from his grief by inviting him to undertake an unusual task. The fox wishes to be tamed. "If you tame me," he explains, "my life will become lit up by the sun. I will recognize one set of footsteps which will be different from every other. The others will make me return into my hole. Yours will call me forth from my lair, like a special music" (470–71).[5] Such taming creates friendships, and proceeds by establishing certain rituals. A friend tends to appear at a fixed hour, lending savor to the rest of the day as the time of his greeting approaches. Even the sadness of departure has its own special magic, for an absent friend transforms the world into an intricate network of hopes and memories.

Such is the gift with which the rose has endowed the Prince, as the fox climactically reveals. She is unique in the universe, after all, for the Prince has tamed her and she him. Because of their interdependence, each has oriented the other in time and space. The Prince always knows where he is in terms of distance from his beloved, and each hour of the day preserves the memory of some service or other which he would perform for her. The roses in the garden might have looked the same, but "what is essential is invisible for the eyes," declares the fox (474).[6]

No other character in *Le Petit Prince* (or in all of Saint-Exupéry's work) has a more ostentatiously allegorical function than the fox. Indeed, so aware is he of his semantic glory that he analyzes his own allegory before he executes it. He eulogizes taming's salutary effect on the spirit in order to enlist a tamer. Perched serenely on a spiritual plateau, he pretends to walk step for step with the Prince, decrying in highly cultivated terms his personal lack of cultivation. A pilgrim who carries his shrine handily in his pocket, this sly beast might as well be chasing his infamous red brush.

Normally, one would expect such a character to ring hollow to Saint-Exupéry. In *Pilote de Guerre*, he had remarked that "a child who would grow excited at the idea of grammar lessons would appear to me pretentious and suspect" (287);[7] and he would write much later at the end of *Citadelle*, "I mistrust any soldier who is too lyrical. If he wishes to die for his corporal, he will probably not die at all, overly occupied as he is with descanting his poem for you" (971).[8] What credibility would a soldier have who claimed to volunteer for dangerous missions because they taught him the value of life? If this outlandish *poseur* (disturbingly like the pilot-hero) had truly learned the meaning of things, why would he need repeated doses of jeopardy?

So with the fox: How can he speak in such fervent abstraction (those two words which Saint-Exupéry regarded as contradictory) about friendship when he has no friends; or, if he has friends, why is he so unfulfilled? How can he endorse domestication unless he is already tame; and, if he is already tame, why does he need domestication? For that matter, is the source of the rose's unique poignancy for the Prince really as simple as the circumstantial fact that he has slaved for her; and if so, would not another rose make as severe a slave-driver? Or if fidelity demands that he remain a one-rose cherub, then why not a rose in a box—a picture of a box—rather than the troublesome, arrogant, persnickety specimen on B612? Or if the rose's very lack of amiability calls the Prince's faith to higher levels, then why not seek out the thorniest variety in the universe? Why seek friends and lovers at all if one is in pursuit of no such ultimate, unconditional goodness as sometimes shines through the dark envelope of human egotism? What the fox offers looks suspiciously like what the king and the vain man offered: a game of "make-believe" whose roles have been so rigidly conceived that the player's individuality becomes irrelevant.

There is more to the fox's artificial mastery of his circumstances than an author's technical blunder. One might conclude that Saint-Exupéry the moralist—the Saint-Exupéry who would choose *Citadelle*'s monarch as his ultimate mouthpiece—could not resist having the fox preach "the wisdom of the sands (as the posthumous work's English translation was titled)," momentarily sacrificing the delightful naiveté of the previous episodes. Yet surely it can be no accident that the blunder occurs precisely where he had encountered the most discomfort in his other stories: the instant of salvation, of revelation, of mystical ecstasy. The Prince is facing his greatest crisis in the book. The rose which meant more to him than anything in the universe has just been shown to be as common in the universe as baobabs or asteroids. He might have moiled his way through this challenge by delving deep within himself to discover that his rose is not properly an object—on which basis she really would have been indistinguishable from thousands of other roses—but rather a subject, an originator of practical choices and hence a distinct moral being, a source of special talents and hence a distinctly gifted soul. In short, introspection could have taught him that the same richness of inner life which he enjoys should be extended to her. No two creatures possessed of intelligent volition are identical, whatever their appearance, yet all such creatures *may* (with a leap of faith) be viewed as sharing the same fundamental love of goodness and beauty.

This leap of faith Saint-Exupéry had consistently shunned in all his writing and throughout his life. It threatened that other faith of his, that greater faith in the utility of action: for if spiritual ties between humans preexist those memorable acts which anchor their various cultures, then intense contemplation rather than heady collaboration is the surest means to understanding the brotherhood of man. Even as early as Fabien's golden moon in *Vol de Nuit* (but *not* as early as Bernis's fatal flight in *Courrier Sud*), he had begun to externalize the discovery of the truth in his narratives. A heroic journey toward a hidden treasure now refined the pilot-hero's battle with chaos. When precious beads and ingots came spilling out over Arras, however, he again found himself face to face with mere symbols for a truth that could only be inwardly divined. He must have regretted prizing the lid open. As long as the lock was intact—as long as the Bedouin wore his veil—an enticing Otherness remained to justify still another vigorous deed.

So the fox's veil is off, and he must speak . . . Yet Saint-Exupéry's faith in action is so resilient that the fox's words, rather than betraying that mortal feet can approach meaning no nearer—that the heart must rest and wait—belie their own allegory, instead. They describe in foxiest fashion another journey to be stepped off. "What's essential is invisible to the eyes" . . . yes, but here only because the material causes of emotional attachment—the rituals which the fox recommends for taming someone—are so widely strewn over time and space that the eye cannot encompass them at a glance. Saint-Exupéry's spiritual reality, such as it is, still depends upon an ambassador from established tradition for its deliverance into less indoctrinated hands. If the eye which sees exteriors cannot perceive it, then neither can an eye turned inward. While other mystics have found themselves in the desert, and within themselves God, and through God humanity, the pilot-hero finds a messenger in the desert, and through the messenger mankind, and through the rituals of mankind a myth-like sanctity of strictly imposed limits. And the game becomes the god, the rules which make north good and south bad—such rules as no person could ever guess merely by examining innermost desires.

In contrast to the fox's visionary paideia, the human inhabitants of earth show none of the patience or endurance required to build and sustain a culture dense in personal commitment. The Little Prince has already heard of this giddy race's footloose ways from the desert flower. The reports of migrant caravans scarcely prepare him for what he sees closer to "civilization," however. In the blurred, thundering passage of commuter trains (technological extensions of *Terre des Hommes*'s abominable Toulouse tramway), he makes the acquaintance of a switchman, who expedites this machine-age herding of human beings in bland resignation. "No one is ever content where he is," he answers the puzzled lad, echoing the desert flower's judgment (476).[9] Only the children have preserved even enough curiosity to stare out the windows as they are shunted from nowhere to nowhere.

Immediately following this encounter, a nearby merchant boasts to the ever-inquisitive Prince that the thirst-quenching pills he peddles save consumers an average of fifty-three minutes per week in time not spent drinking. People can employ their economized hour, he concludes vapidly, doing anything they wish. The wryly understated absurdity of these two episodes, which dramatize the modern world's mania for saving time by annihilating the very social rituals responsible for the quality of life, not only shows Saint-Exupéry comfortably back in step with his allegorical myth, but hints at some of *Citadelle*'s most important and disturbing issues. Freedom for its own sake is a miserable acquisition. The freedom to do anything is a freedom from any potentially limiting kinship or obligation: the freedom, that is, of a corpse to lie still or a dust mote to spin in open space. That Western civilization's formal appearance in *Le Petit Prince* should be reduced to these two extremely brief and bitterly ironic chapters intimates much about Saint-Exupéry's ever more pessimistic assessment of the future.

The episode of the "anti-thirst pill" merchant being completed, the Little Prince has brought the narrator entirely up to date concerning his travels. It is the eighth day since the forced landing, and the narrator now faces his own crisis of thirst. His life is in the balance, just as the Prince's was when the discovery of the rose garden engulfed him in despair; and, just as the fox extricated the young alien from his spiritual crisis, so the Prince now steps in to relieve the narrator's physical anguish. Like a true disciple of the fox, he leads the docile, resigned pilot into the desert to seek a well. Futile as such a search would appear, the castaway pilot has learned to trust his little friend rather than the evidence of his eyes or the voice of reason. "Le plus important est invisible . . . ," he murmurs (480), reverently paraphrasing the fox's greatest maxim as he carries the sleeping Prince through the night.

Again, we find the life of the spirit made manifest not by a deeply introverted experience, but by an external agency (this time the Prince) who teaches the enriching bonds of culture. The narrator even recollects his childhood during the arduous trek—a formular invocation of innocence's golden age such as not only characterizes *Pilote de Guerre* but litters the pages of *Courrier Sud*. The legend of a buried treasure, he remembers, made the home of his youth a magical place, just as the supposed presence of a well transforms the desert and the presence of one rose on one asteroid transforms the starlit night. Childhood, buried treasure, secret wells, lost stars . . . is this what the

Prince has revealed? If so, the content of his celestial wisdom is as vacuous as the fox's, and he has no more saved the narrator than the fox saved him. In both cases, the thirsty pilgrim is sent traipsing through a shadowland which he has already traversed. The pseudo-messenger merely reshuffles the landmarks to disguise a well-known destination with its well-known disappointments.

The homiletic artifice of these passages continues until Saint-Exupéry's evasive parable reels to its head-spinning conclusion. The narrator and his companion rehearse how, when they reach the fabled well, they will engage in an elaborate communion ceremony. Together, they will drink of the water of friendship in a Land of Men (for a natural spring would not do: the setting must bear the orderly imprint of human culture). Sure enough, a well appears the next morning, as if by an act of faith (or of unhealthy imagination) and their behavior is nothing if not well rehearsed. The Prince goes so far as to break into personifying metaphors. "We are waking up this well, and it sings . . . ," he cries, adding an instant later, "I am thirsty for that water," as if he would have disdained a drink in less civil circumstances (482).[10]

In *Terre des Hommes*, a mysterious stranger called Man had brought the life-restoring water: in *Le Petit Prince*, the stranded pair finds Man's spirit among them, and then communal water materializes from nowhere. The latter scenario puts salvation more clearly in the hands of the questing pilot-hero. In the former, an allegorical hint lurked dangerously behind the Bedouin's veil—the hint that common humanity is not created by heroes but preexists them. Now a bucket and pulley join the heroic fellowship without stealing its thunder. As if he might have it both ways—both the self-sufficiency of effective action and the moral consensus which alone makes action effective—Saint-Exupéry has left this easy drawing of water to the autonomous hand of the thirsty. So restorative has been the bread and wine of collaboration, in fact, that the two may as well have discovered how to live on starlight.

Yet perhaps Saint-Exupéry sensed that he had had his water and drunk it, too. The profession of faith in cultural conditioning which we might expect about here is conspicuously absent. Rather, the Prince begins to speak of his impending departure before the narrator can ruminate too lengthily on the new gospel. The young visitor's asteroid awaits his return and has first claim on his heart, no doubt; but the proximity of his death to the well's theatrical epiphany almost makes the one seem a consequence of the other. Could it be that the pilot-hero took too much of his salvation into his own hands? Has bold action at last drawn its desires into such plain, bleak presence that an immediate retreat of the truly desirable is required? For to win this game is to lose: to complete a successful action is to negate the need of further action. How does a hero exist in such a state? Perhaps he need not sit paralyzed within a post-heroic sterility: perhaps, instead, we may envision him transfixed by the majesty of an eternal truth dimly grasped. But if truth may be thus contemplated, then it need never really have been chased, to begin with, and those proto-heroic create-from-nothing flourishes were a fraudulent slight of hand.

So the Prince must die. His weakness during the previous night and his paleness after making the necessary arrangements with the snake imply that he is losing strength even before the fatal venom enters his veins. He has incurred death so that the narrator might live—or, more honestly, so that Saint-Exupéry's ethic of heroic struggle toward an indefinitely regressive point will not lose its vitality. The narrator, at least, is truly saved this time, saved from having to confront the pitiful inadequacy of materialism as a possible ground for self-sacrifice. He is saved from the threat of a more spiritual salvation.

The Prince's salvation is quite another matter. As the critical hour draws near, he scarcely wavers. Repeating the sentiments (and some of the words) which Saint-Exupéry commemorated in *Pilote de Guerre* from his younger brother's death, the celestial traveler assures his friend that he will only give the appearance of dying—that he will only be discarding a cumbersome body too heavy for the return voyage. In a passage whose very simplicity elevates it above the senses, the Prince expires without a sound and with only the vaguest of visible gestures: "He fell softly, as a tree falls. Because of the sand, it didn't even make a sound" (493).[11] When the narrator looks for his body at first light, it is nowhere to be found. Obviously, Asteroid B612 has reclaimed it!

Thus the Little Prince has successfully preserved in himself his earthbound friend's omega point . . . but Saint-Exupéry had shifted the heroic role to the little cherub, and we cannot help but speculate about how this new incarnation of the pilot fares on the other side of beyond. Though we hear no further report of the rose's conduct, why should we assume her to have been so chastened by her lover's odyssey that she never nags or wheedles again? The narrator (to Saint-Exupéry's credit) does not seek to divert such curiosity. He focuses it elsewhere, though, and perhaps more critically. It seems that he forgot to sketch his friend a leather strap for the sheep's muzzle. Now he worries about the disaster which may have followed. "Nothing in the universe is the same if in a certain spot—no one knows where—a sheep which we have never seen has eaten a rose, or has not . . ." (495).[12]

Hence the stars above retain that multivalence which they enjoyed in Saint-Exupéry's earlier novels, sometimes laughing with the Prince's laugh (as the child had foretold), sometimes weeping for a virtuous order overturned . . . yet perhaps their quality here should be called contravalence. Though intended "to signify ulterior meaning, this sheep itself remains enigmatic" (Quesnel and Autrand xlv). Thanks to its potentially unimpeded jaws, the stars represent mutually exclusive states: the suggested richness of possibilities in them is in bad faith, since they can only *either* laugh *or* weep. In one interpretation, the stars smile on beatitude (which itself overlooks the rose's talent for trouble-making). In the other, they "cast down their spears/And water heaven with their tears," as Blake has it, lamenting the final subversion of cosmos and the triumph of chaos. The two interpretations cannot coexist: the truth of one requires the other's falsehood.

If we scrutinize the narrator's concern, then, we find that it has, after all, reinforced his old habit of life more than it has intuited the Prince's new one. Whether the Prince has been apotheosized by joy or annihilated by grief cannot be known in the dimensions of earthly reality—and that is all the pilot-hero requires in order to be able to continue the fight: insoluble ignorance. By the time his own death initiates him into ultimate truth, the narrator will have breathed his last, and that truth will have become irrelevant to life. The Prince has thus bequeathed to his friend (and to us as readers) an invincibly agnostic image which laughs *and* weeps before the obscured study of terrestrial nightgazers. For all they tell us of the truth beyond death, those stars might as well be the broken glass of a mirror.

The Little Prince's moving history, alas, has not brought him one iota closer to supreme fulfillment, and would not do so even if we could send him the strongest muzzle in the solar system. Whether he laughs or weeps, his spirit still belongs to the material world—but his legacy of deception allows us to persist in mistaking matter for spirit, at least if Saint-Exupéry has managed to confuse us as much as he did himself.

III.

Yet how well had Saint-Exupéry deceived himself—how well *could* he have? To be seduced by his story's child-like charm is easy enough; but if someone wished to make of the story a blueprint for living (as Saint-Exupéry did of all his stories), how could he possibly go about it? A fair lady, a beloved child, a lost homeland . . . such sources of longing, far from being new, are rather commonplace. Those of us who cherish a certain person at least as much as our own life, however, grow painfully aware of his or her vulnerability to worldly accident precisely because of our feeling's strength. How can we fool ourselves into believing that so fragile an idol can bear all the sacrifices of another's existence, let alone of an entire culture? We may make such sacrifices, anyway—and, if death robs us of our special person, we may throw ourselves into its arms to arrange a reunion; but our rational side will warn us all along that such reverence of a mortal being is a grotesque parody of healthy love, and that it gives little consideration to our beloved's common humanity.

And then, there is the very multiplicity of idols in *Le Petit Prince*: a fair lady *and* a child *and* a homeland, and much more. One might recall what Jacques Lacan once wrote of the baby's pacifier: "This is no more than an emblem, I say; the representative of representation in the absolute condition is at home in the unconscious" (312). Saint-Exupéry must surely have realized at some level that these various temporary hiding places for the utterly and eternally worthy objective were paper-thin, simply because he offers us so many of them. Yet if he understood that his successive Meccas were provisional substitutes for the City of God (reversals, one might say, of the *surenchères* or "higher bids" for which Derrida chides Freud [cf. 191–85]), should he not also have deduced that devoted pilgrimages to them merely mimicked the one real pilgrimage? And if that insight had confronted him and he had not turned away, how could his myth escape complete allegorization? How could the pilot-hero remain other than a pretend-hero, just as so much else in his child's game is pretend? Must Mecca not in fact precede the pilgrim who claims metaphorically that his steps create minarets on the horizon?

The old formula suddenly seems stale. A hero creatively enacts his cultural rites in free fall through the vacuum, thereby declaring a cosmos around which other errant atoms may cluster . . . but if the law of entropy reigns over all atoms by nature, then these newly ordered ones, too, must soon succumb to errancy. ("Life is something which resists the spread of entropy," Saint-Exupéry had once declared in a letter [Pélissier 196].)[13] So the colony weakens, first by units and pairs, then by entire networks; and dissolution into chaos at last grows irresistible. Back and forth the cycle gyrates. Social systems always teeter on the brink of oblivion, yet new heroes always step forth to reassert old lines of force or to impose fresh ones. Thanks to a mysterious gravity (or, in Exupérian terms, a love) which caresses loose members back into shared orbits for a while, civilization somehow survives . . . but where does the gravity come from? From the hero's will? But where does his will come from?

What is missing from this very ill-determined determinism is a *primum mobile*, an explanation for the atomic human being's fear of the void, or attraction to order, or both. If chaos is man's native state, why does he flee it? If order is native to him, why are there only contingent, arbitrary orders, all of them incapable of an inherent grounding in his intelligence?

Death is no answer to these questions: it may silence questions (at least to the ears of the living), but it cannot answer them. It is frightening, no doubt, and its monstrous amorphosis makes of it a sublime adversary for any hero who is running out of gorgons. But to suggest at the same time that it harbors the hero's ever-fleeting object of desire is inane. Either all possible meaning is material, in which case death is the ultimate enemy, or there are truths not subject to the laws of matter, in which case death hath no sting . . . but tears and laughter are of two different houses.

Perhaps the greatest irony in this little book of studied ironies called *Le Petit Prince* is the wholly unintended one surrounding the young hero's apparent death. No one reading the final chapters could conclude that their author believed only in the world of the flesh—that he accepted the end of the body as the end of all that ever existed. Yet Saint-Exupéry's treatment of the Prince's "resurrection" merely reintroduces him into a material and circumstantial environment. The star-child most decidedly does not ascend to a realm where all is explained, justified, forgiven, settled, squared, and blessed. On the contrary, he is plunged into a new round of existential *angst* by the narrator's negligently sketched sheep.

And yet, there remains all that talk about invisible things being the only things that count. The impasse is a real one.

Saint-Exupéry had played his final card and lost. From climactic revelation he had turned to climactic obfuscation; for a hero who creates everything around him can have nothing revealed to him, but the Exupérian hero keeps discovering things which preexist his deeds and contradict his creative powers. The author now threw shadows over the moment of truth, therefore—and no shadow is darker than death's. Yet the strategy only seems to have made his imagination proliferate with sketchy forms moving about well in advance of the hero's approach. In *Le Petit Prince*, myth has almost surrendered to allegory: act has almost yielded to word. Death was to have been the mythic hero's last window on chaos, a space from which no word proceeds. Perhaps it would indeed have been so if Saint-Exupéry had been able to characterize the state beyond this life as unambiguously chaotic. What he decided, instead, was that there are words which, like starlight, cannot be read but whose mood is unmistakably imperative.

NOTES

[1] . . . cracheur d'encre . . . célèbre dans sa plénitude universelle . . .

[2] C'est une question de discipline. . . . Quand on a terminé sa toilette du matin, il faut faire soigneusement la toilette de la planète.

[3] Ils manquent de racines, ça les gêne beaucoup.

[4] Et il se sentit très malheureux. Sa fleur lui avait raconté qu'elle était seule de son espèce dans l'univers.

[5] Si tu m'apprivoises, ma vie sera comme ensoleillée. Je connaîtrai un bruit de pas qui sera différent de tous les autres. Les autres pas me font rentrer sous terre. Le tien m'appellera hors du terrier, comme une musique.

[6] . . . l'essentiel est invisible pour les yeux.

[7] . . . l'enfant qui s'exalterait à l'idée des leçons de grammaire m'apparaîtrait comme prétentieux et suspect.

[8] Je me méfie du soldat trop lyrique. S'il souhaite de mourir pour son caporal,

probable est qu'il ne mourra point, trop occupé à te débiter son poème.

[9] On n'est jamais content là où l'on est.

[10] Nous réveillons ce puits et il chante. . . . J'ai soif de cette eau-là.

[11] Il tomba doucement comme tombe un arbre. Ça ne fit même pas de bruit, à cause du sable.

[12] Rien de l'univers n'est semblable si quelque part, on ne sait où, un mouton que nous ne connaissons pas a, oui ou non, mangé une rose . . .

[13] La vie est quelque chose qui s'oppose à l'accroissement de l'entropie.

WORKS CITED

Bergson, Henri. *Évolution Créatrice*. Paris: Félix Alcan, 1939.

Cate, Curtis. *Antoine de Saint-Exupéry*. New York: Putnam, 1970.

Delange, René. *La Vie de Saint-Exupéry*. Paris: Seuil, 1948.

Derrida, Jacques. *Archive Fever: A Freudian Impression*. Trans. Eric Prenowitz. Chicago and London: U of Chicago P, 1995.

Devaux, André-A. *Saint-Exupéry*. Paris: Desclée de Brouwer, 1965.

François, Carlo R. *L'Esthétique de Saint-Exupéry*. Neuchâtel: Delachaux and Niestlé, 1957.

Lacan, Jacques. *Écrits: A Selection*. Trans. Alan Sheridan. New York and London: Norton, 1977.

Major, Jean-Louis. *Saint-Exupéry: L'Écriture et la Pensée*. Ottawa: U of Ottawa P, 1968.

Migeo, Marcel. *Saint-Exupéry*. Trans. Herma Briffault. London: Macdonald, 1961.

Mounier, Emmanuel. *Personalism*. Trans. Philip Mairet. Notre Dame and London: U of Notre Dame P, 1970.

Pélissier, Georges. *Les Cinq Visages de Saint-Exupéry*. Paris: Flammarion, 1951.

Quesnel, Michel, and Michel Autrand. "Préface Générale." *Saint-Exupéry: Oeuvres Complètes*. Vol 1. Ed. Michel Quesnel and Michel Autrand. Paris: Gallimard, 1994: ix-lii.

Reverdy, Pierre. *Le Livre de Mon Bord: 1930–36*. Paris: Mercure de France, 1948.

Robinson, J.D.M. *Antoine de Saint-Exupéry*. Boston: Twayne, 1984.

Saint-Exupéry, Antoine de. *Oeuvres*. Roger Caillois, ed. Bibliothèque de la Pléiade. Paris: Gallimard, 1959; volume contains *Courrier Sud, Vol de Nuit, Terre des Hommes, Lettre à un Otage, Pilote de Guerre, Le Petit Prince*, and *Citadelle*.

—. *Carnets*. Paris: Gallimard, 1953.

—. *Lettres de Jeunesse (1923–1931)*. Paris: Gallimard, 1953.

—. *Un Sens à la Vie*. Paris: Gallimard, 1956.

Schiff, Stacy. *Saint-Exupéry: A Biography*. New York: Knopf, 1994.

Werth, Léon. *Tel Que Je L'ai Connu . . .* in René Delange, *La Vie de Saint-Exupéry*. Paris: Seuil, 1948: 131–86.

Zeller, Renée. *La Grande Quête d'Antoine de Saint-Exupéry dans Le Petit Prince et Citadelle*. Paris: Alsatia, 1961.

CHAPTER 7

CITADELLE AND THE SUCCESS
OF IMPASSE

I.

L ong before he had conceived of *Pilote de Guerre* or *Le Petit Prince*, Saint-Exupéry had completed a first draft of *Citadelle*. He had apparently begun work on the project as early as 1936 (Caillois 501), entitling it at this point *Le Caïd* after the narrator/protagonist (Chevrier, *Saint-Exupéry* 94 at n. 2). The phrase "first draft" may be misleading, however, for at no stage of its evolution did the manuscript ever display a coherent plot. Of course, Saint-Exupéry appears never to have favored a method of composition where a crude but dramatically complete original would be succeeded by fine-tuning of descriptions, dialogue, etc. Instead, the second and third writings tended to be voluminous overhauls of the first, starting from page one and retelling the entire story. Thus the 150–page edition of *Vol de Nuit* published by Gallimard was distilled from a 400-page text, according to Cate (230).

The same source also maintains that Saint-Exupéry wanted Monsieur Gallimard's opinion of an already enormous manuscript before leaving Europe in 1940 (413), which could only have been *Citadelle*. The author certainly made no attempt to keep his new creation under wraps, for he solicited opinions of it from several friends at various times. Caillois (501) mentions Drieu La Rochelle and Crémieux as test-readers. Migeo claims that this text was also at issue when Antoine wrote to the carefully concealed mistress of his final years (Nelly de Vogüé, alias Pierre Chevrier), "The question that at present agonizes me [is]: what will the reader think of my book?" (142).

In the ensuing years, the pages would swell in number despite Saint-Exupéry's continual immersion in more urgent matters. Even after he was able to resume the active military service so vital to his peace of mind, his attention was not utterly distracted from the work. A tape recorder purchased in New York had previously allowed him to dictate each new chapter late at night for a typist to pound out the next day (cf. Migeo 259). Unfortunately, the newfangled machine remained behind when he left for Algeria, as Pélissier reports, and his personal scrawl seemed to become increasingly illegible (72). The strain of these final months could well account for the messy handwriting—yet the work went forward, with a persistence quite beyond mere diary-keeping or doodling. Certainly the author's earnestness was clear to Madame de Vogüé, whom Schiff styles Madame de B and reports as saying to Antoine, "You are a little like Christ when you write your *Citadelle*." The lady in question was convinced that the manuscript to which Saint-Exupéry had so fervently dedicated himself at last became his sole reason for living (415).

For all of these reasons, we can hardly suppose (as some have argued) that *Citadelle* is a mere collection of impromptu scribbles never intended to merge into a serious creation. Saint-Exupéry's own comments about the text are as cryptic as they are oft-cited. He christened the work his "oeuvre posthume" ("posthumous work") in a frame of mind somewhere between self-deprecating playfulness and eerie clairvoyance. Some have adduced the remark in evidence of the author's intent to withhold the work from prying eyes as long as he lived (cf. Robinson 143). In other words, so the argument goes, he distastefully anticipated having his confidential papers ransacked and published after his death. Yet in that case, why did he also say to Pierre Dalloz, "beside this composition, all my other scribbles are mere exercise" (qtd. in Devaux 63)?[1] He would certainly not have wished a match put to his masterpiece—or, if he had, he might have left instructions to that effect, like Virgil.

For his part, Doctor Pélissier (who attaches no importance to the "oeuvre posthume" quip [159]), claims that his friend once urgently instructed him by telegram to keep the manuscript out of publishers' hands, not permanently, but until he could revise it, an undertaking whose length Saint-Exupéry then reckoned at about one year (73). The pseudonymous Chevrier possesses another letter in which Saint-Exupéry, now unmistakably serious, reiterates that he will not live to see *Citadelle*'s completion: "It will appear at my death, for I will never have finished" (*Antoine* 65).[2] The passage reflects, perhaps, the deepening depression of Antoine's later years (cf. Webster 253-57), but also a certain satisfaction that the work's eternal meanders offered the chance for "dying in action"—for self-consumption in a dutiful exchange—which the war had so far denied him.

On the balance, we clearly must conclude that Saint-Exupéry regarded this literary venture with the utmost earnestness (as if he could ever have been anything less than earnest in his writing). The manuscript's huge length and ill-focused rambling were, as has been said, typical of his compositions before editing. Hence we cannot avoid considering the unpublished work as potentially another—and a major—addition to a remarkable literary career. In Chevrier's apt words, "Whatever the controversies concerning the publication of this work may be, the fervor which Saint-Exupéry had consecrated to it justifies its publication all alone" (*Antoine* 67).

Furthermore, *Citadelle* reflects the lessons which Saint-Exupéry had learned earlier in his literary search for practical truth. The first-person perspective is sustained throughout every single chapter of the 219 (though perhaps these entries should be called sections, or even *pensées* after the fragments of Pascal's posthumous work, since some are only a few sentences long). The narrator is also the central participant in every major incident, and can thus vouch personally for any resulting moral insight. Indeed, he is the quintessence of authority: as a Berber chieftain (or caïd), he enjoys almost unlimited and arbitrary power over the lives of his pastoral tribesmen. Yet his decree remains only one man's voice giving law with mock-confidence in an inscrutable, unruly universe, as he is himself exquisitely aware. In this regard, he does not resemble the Rivière of *Vol de Nuit* to whom critics so often compare him; for Rivière benefited from a universe which, through literary accident (i.e., Saint-Exupéry's selective application of an omniscient perspective), always confirmed his suspicions, fulfilled his predictions, and moved at his beck and call. In *Citadelle*, the world "out there"—the desert surrounding the green city-state spatially, the future looming over its naive inhabitants temporally— shows no such signs of responding to the Caïd's interpretation.

The work's most fundamental tension, in fact, may be said to operate between the desert kingdom's pastoral confidence in an objective truth rigorously enforced and the Caïd's own belief that any truth is as fragile, artificial, and controvertible as its opposite. Trapped in this ambiguous position, the Caïd perhaps justifies Major's charge that he does not genuinely participate in the life of his people, just as the Little Prince's fox seems too aware of cultural artifice ever to become fully engrossed in playing the game.

> Saint-Exupéry withdrew from his subject in choosing as a narrator a king considering his people, and thus a man who is above common experience and does not truly participate in it. The reciter of *Citadelle* is in reality a moralist, and the work itself is taut with moral purpose. (178)

Finally, as is suggested by Major's comments above and by the mere fact of the work's *tabula rasa* setting (cf. Major 248) and monarchic protagonist, *Citadelle* seethes with allegorical potential. "The author's moral preoccupation invaded his works little by little, chasing away all their literary effects," summarizes Caillois (501); and he concludes that the unfinished manuscript is "a direct parable, without any temporal gap between image and evocation." As well as shunning the more obvious literary postures, Saint-Exupéry had for once cut loose entirely from his personal experience as a pilot. Even *Le Petit Prince* uses aviation to create a certain verisimilitude. This work, in contrast, reveals no overt connection to Europe, technology, or Christianity—nor, for that matter, to Algeria, nationalism, or Islam. It exists on an impregnable island beyond the reach of history and progress, as perfect a crucible for Saint-Exupéry's moral experiments as the Galapagos had been for Darwin's theoretical adumbrations.

In short, *Citadelle* is precisely the sort of work, though in very rough form, which we should expect to find next in the sequence of Saint-Exupéry's compositions. This is so even—perhaps especially—in regard to the labyrinthine complexity of the fragmented narrative's mythic impasses (though Borgal views the text as virtually complete and never intended to trace a story [158]). Belonging approximately to the same period as *Pilote de Guerre* and *Le Petit Prince*, *Citadelle* naturally shares the nervous concentration found in these two works (and in the climax of *Terre des Hommes*) upon the myth's dénouement. Revelation had always either failed as a concluding scenario or had succeeded in a way which ensured the myth's failure. The myth's active dynamism was undermined if too much was revealed: the oracle, lest it eclipse the hero's efficacy, must obscure its insight into human nature with tantalizing paradoxes (a confidence game at which ancient oracles excelled). The hero, not the seer, must be allowed to demystify the future. As a result, Saint-Exupéry's heroes seemed to keep finding a secret which had and had not preceded them. Whether in the Sahara or over Arras or somewhere between the planets, they reeled before a vision of infinity suddenly compressed into simple pattern, as if they had caught a genie in a lamp. That the genie was caught drew more attention—or was supposed to—than that he was a genie. It was the classically sublime encounter in reverse motion.

Yet Saint-Exupéry must have sensed to some extent that the process, as he had repeatedly insisted upon it, was backward. The agent of narrow ritual before whom the immeasurable universe gapes must surely discover his culture's pettiness and, simultaneously, the thrilling boundlessness of his own internal universe: such is the nature of life-altering revelation. If this hero of many contests then returns home feeling at peace, the sweetness of a warm light which he sees in a certain window scarcely explains his equanimity by itself. A far more important component of his new peace is the revealed knowledge that no homely menace, neither hunger nor war nor creditors, can threaten the stability of the spirit's eternal, unconditional truth. Something has changed for this home-bound adventurer; indeed, what has not changed?

In contrast, the Exupérian hero retreats to his pitifully puny domain with a new appreciation of its frailty and transience, glad only that he has kept so shaky a structure from toppling. All that has changed for him is his degree of sensitivity to the shakiness. There will have to be another sally tomorrow if things are to remain even so sound as he sees them now. Eventually, death will relieve him of his sentry duty—a death of dreamless sleep which will overtake him walking his rounds. He can hope for nothing better.

The failure of the pilot-myth, or (to put it another way) the fallacy in Saint-Exupéry's ethical system, might be stated with a mathematical precision. Doing something to which there is no end makes sense only if one is *approaching* an end. In such a way does a hyperbola approach its axis, assured of rest in time but not in space; and in such a way does a human being grow, never perfect but always a little better. We shall see that Saint-Exupéry explicitly subscribed to this perspective in *Citadelle*. On the other hand, if no point of intersection is conceived of as waiting beyond indefinite space, we have only perpetual motion with a cumulative value of zero; for how can one approach what does not exist?

The pilot-hero, then, is more like a circle trying to reach its focus by circling: let him proceed ever so fast, he will still only retrace his steps and make no ultimate progress. We also have Saint-Exupéry's explicit avowal of this perspective throughout *Citadelle*: i.e., that God's reality rests in motivating man, not in any objective, absolute quality brought to perfection in Himself. As Devaux encapsulates Saint-Exupéry's position, "God dies if man's ardor is extinguished: the truth of God is in the fervor of man" (72). Even so does the focus orient the circle's motion without the one ever coming a hair's breadth closer to the other. Such a focus could as justifiably be posited at the edge of the universe, for its purpose is merely in the energy which it anchors. Saint-Exupéry's myth succeeds in describing constant, Sisyphean striving toward an end beyond oneself (cf. "un but en dehors de soi," *Carnets* 23), but its failure to present progressive striving leaves it a grand story of moral futility.

Yet while *Citadelle* continues to present a hero who exults in the circular discovery of his own previous path, it remains different from any other work of Saint-Exupéry's. The manuscript is not only unedited, but—like the pilot-myth's most genuine form—in perpetual "take it from the top" reprise after interruption. Saint-Exupéry's massive rewritings do not tell the story from another angle, and another: none of them, rather, ever succeeds in telling any story to the end.

We can nevertheless identify several sequences of loosely related events easily enough. The work opens with the young monarch (or perhaps the aged monarch recollecting his youth) recounting his father's advice about human nature, governance, and the spirit. The father, obviously a practical philosopher himself, had been slain by an assassin, leaving a well-schooled heir ready and able to follow in his footsteps. The narrator ambles through numerous disconnected situations and meditations before informing us, thirty-three chapters into the work, that he is now an old man, ailing in body and dejected in spirit. What has happened to bring him to this state, and particularly to his dejection? Has he seen through the pseudo-epiphanies which were supposed to have revitalized his faith in human society? Is he the Saint-Exupéry who wrote of France's regeneration from the mulch of defeat, yet who foresaw the weed-like character of the post-war world?

Perhaps the narrator's jaded perspective, on the other hand, would merely have been the completed story's fundamental crisis, its primary source of tension. Perhaps the old king, reviewing his youth as Saint-Exupéry did in all his writings, was about to confront a great challenge which would restore his zeal. Subsequent chapters portray him struggling toward God in his dreams, desperately marching toward the well at El Ksour, leading an expedition (apparently in the same foray) to a marvelous citadel without gates, and even rethinking his attitude toward his wives. Would one of these situations have lifted him out of his mature despair? Or, considering Saint-Exupéry's peculiar style of rewriting, should we preserve the first and most obvious chronology, placing such active episodes in the narrator's middle years and assuming that their resolution, whatever it may have involved, no longer warms his heart as he waits for death?

And might this not have been the reason for Saint-Exupéry's enigmatically labeling *Citadelle* his posthumous work? That is to say, had the manuscript's resistance to closure not convinced him that its tensions had no solution? Knowing that the Caïd could only begin all over again as long as his "revelations" revealed nothing new—as long as they merely made him more aware of existing attachments and customs—Saint-Exupéry might have divined that death itself must conclude his literary experiment this time: not the Caïd's death, but the author's. Such a conclusion would not harmonize the tensions in the work of art, but it *would* stop the author's hand.

Thus, in a way, *Citadelle* is indeed complete, and was so from the moment Saint-Exupéry recognized its necessary incompleteness. The text acknowledges, as none of its predecessors had done, the impracticability of a myth which would spiritually save this world through worldly agencies. The pilot-hero cannot save society, after all, nor can society even save the pilot-hero. Were he to ascend from his cockpit to a throne and find before him not a control panel, but the reins of state, the hero could still not keep men and women from lapsing into complacent torpor; and were France to shrink into a pocket-kingdom of artisans, shepherds, and merchant caravans, the hero who might literally save the whole arrangement with one stroke of his sword would still awaken tomorrow in need of another battle. To undertake the construction of Utopia, even in one's imagination (if one has Saint-Exupéry's honesty), is inevitably a posthumous work, left incomplete when the limited resources of material reality finally run out.

Because *Citadelle* has succeeded in renouncing Saint-Exupéry's mythic quest insofar as it never fashions a coherent narrative, we cannot simply analyze the plot stage by stage, as in previous chapters. The following section, therefore, will examine bits and pieces of the manuscript that might readily have served in the assembly of a heroic *praxis*. Having looked closely at several such passages, we shall be able to draw certain conclusions about what pieces vital to a full assembly were missing from Saint-Exupéry's "test designs."

II.

The Nietzschean tenor of *Citadelle*'s opening chapters (and, indeed, of its opening line: "Car j'ai vu trop souvent la pitié s'égarer"— "For I have too often seen pity go astray" [507]) has been much remarked. My chapter 4 discusses at length Saint-Exupéry's penchant for antithetical argumentation at this moment in his career, and the strategy certainly implies the German philosopher's counter-conformist attitude toward virtue. In similarly shocking fashion, the Caïd urges us to abstain from romanticizing the misery of beggars, dying men, or grieving women: one must not hesitate to transform oneself into a better person even in death's presence, nor must one waste compassion on those who choose to dwell in their sub-human mire.

Yet for all its resemblances to the creed of the *ubermensch*, this sermon takes an abruptly un-Nietzschean turn in chapter 2. "I have decided to cure them," confides the king (514), speaking of every human being in his domain. He continues, "I forbid that one should ask questions, knowing as I do that no response can quench the thirst. He who asks questions is seeking, before all else, the abyss."[3] Far from creating a race of autonomous supermen, this philosopher-monarch wishes to subjugate his people to a certain set of rituals, an inviolable and unquestionable sense of things. In kicking their traces and asserting their independence, they would only plunge into an eternal chaos without gravity or direction. Thus he, the Caïd, has become a superman only to save others from the same fate. Though Zeller has perhaps gone too far in likening him to "the true Shepherd, the 'Good Shepherd' of humanity" (164), she does well to disparage the Nietzschean connection. The Caïd has rejected the dull squeamishness that commonly passes for pity only so that he might, in an act of monumental compassion, found an order wherein all common emotions are genuine.

In short, the Caïd is on the outside looking in, like Rivière or the fox of *Le Petit Prince*. Unlike the former, however, he has no narrative confirmation that his lines of force are really magnetizing other mentalities; and unlike the latter, he cannot enjoy the luxury of playing in the game whose rules he must dictate and enforce. Many readers interpret him as championing a patriarchal political order. In Ouellet's words, "The social order envisioned by Saint-Exupéry called for a unifying principle of authority capable of conceiving and orienting the vast enterprise of civilization. . . . Thus the author of *Citadelle* sets up . . . the dominant figure of an all-powerful chieftain" (146). I consider such readings misguided, and I shall suggest later that the Caïd's power much more narrowly resembles that of a literary creator over his creations than of a benign autocrat over his subjects.

Within this realm of salutary strictures, there is no room for a god who calls upon his faithful to look beyond what they can see, touch, and know. "Love must find its object," the Caïd warns. "I save that one alone who loves what exists and who can meet with satisfaction" (515).[4] The fulfilled citizen must delight exclusively in the material blessings and earthly rhythms of the given law. He or she must always preserve the ritual without peering into its artifice, for the structural gaps are too numerous and wide to withstand scrutiny. "For it occurred to me that man was [sic] entirely similar to a citadel. He overturns the walls to insure his freedom, but he is then no more than a dismantled fortress open to the stars" (516).[5] A person who strives after the inexpressible, immaterial fulfillment of the stars can no more be satisfied within the corridors of culture than a literary personage who refuses to suffer tension could find a happy ending in the tension's mere dissolution. In fact, a demanding god who impels people to dance to an inner drum is the ultimate enemy. "I am terrified when God moves. He, the immovable—let him remain seated, then, in eternity!" (517).[6]

Thus, within the first few pages of his manuscript, Saint-Exupéry has forthrightly stated the crucial insights which some sort of climactic confrontation had catalyzed before. The Caïd does not graduate to his appreciation of culture through a series of ordeals (though he will reminisce later about some of his more instructive struggles); he begins where the Saint-Exupéry of *Pilote de Guerre* and *Le Petit Prince* leaves off, inspired by a vision and determined to impose it benignly on his nation. To be sure, the imagery of revelation does have a place in these opening scenes, but not through the Caïd's personal experience. Rather, he and his father view from a distance—from the outside looking in, once again—a local woman whom the elders had condemned to be staked out in the sun, and who now hangs semi-conscious and delirious in the evening chill.

> Captured in this night without frontiers, she was calling for her house's evening lamp, and for the room that would have mirrored her, and for the door that would have been shut securely on her. Offered to an entire universe that presented no face, she was calling the child whom you kiss before going to sleep and who concentrates all your world. Submitted to the passage of the unknown on this desert plateau, she was singing of the husband's footfall which resounds each evening on the threshold and which a wife recognizes and finds reassuring. Exposed to the immeasurable and having nothing upon which to hold any more, she was supplicating the gift of those protective walls which alone permit one to exist, that bundle of wool to card, that special bowl to wash, that child to put to sleep and none other. She was calling out to the eternity of the home, encircled with the rest of the village by the same evening prayer.[7] (513)

This unfortunate woman, like the Saint-Exupéry who almost died of thirst in the Sahara and who was almost incinerated over Arras, retrieves from infinity's open prospect not a knowledge of unearthly spiritual realities, but animated visions of her daily routine. Surely she would have better things to think about! The equation of chaos with release from contingency is as disturbing here as it has been elsewhere. A woman hammered all day by the desert sun no more whimpers for her pots and pans than a man in the same situation babbles the phone numbers of clients or quotes stock prices (to accept for the moment *Citadelle*'s stereotypical gender roles). No doubt, when life's true necessities are interrupted, one tries to cling to one's circumstantial identity in a delirium; but if one recovers a measure of rationality, this superficial identity soon peels away to reveal whatever basic humanity it has not stifled over the years.

Many people in such predicaments (the classic castaway in the open boat or shipwreck on a barren island), having recognized the vanity of their frivolous worldly displays, also find a new identity in the eternal power ready to reabsorb them. Some do not. The journalist Decoud in Conrad's *Nostromo* is so disoriented by a week of hiding out along a wild coastline that he finally takes a trance-like, suicidal walk into the sea, fleeing to death from an intolerable void. The scraps of the artificial, culturally conditioned environment around which his spirit curled could not sustain him, any more than they will sustain the crucified adulteress if she should regain consciousness. In her observed state, she does not grasp after cooking and weaving because they constitute her truth, but because she is vainly attempting to keep a host of immensely greater truths from sweeping her into a self beyond time and place. Eternity, not death, is the enemy at her door, as the Caïd's own words imply. Once again, Saint-Exupéry's revelations utterly miss the point of revelation.

At least this time, however, the author's voice is not directly involved in the deception (cf. Borgal 165). As an onlooker, the Caïd need not grope for rhetoric to make the spiritual transformation appear genuine. Of course, he is a thoroughly interested onlooker. To him the ceremonies of cooking and weaving, and of every other civilized activity in the kingdom, owe their existence. He has intentionally created such rituals, "for it is good that the time which flows by should not seem to use us up and exhaust us, like a fistful of sand, but rather to perfect us" (518).[8] In the same way, he once ordered that a fountain be constructed in the middle of his ancestral palace "in order that one may be able both to draw near to and move away from something. In order that, here, one may be able both to go out and come in. Otherwise, one is no longer any place" (518–19).[9] Yet he himself necessarily remains aware that the rituals have no foundation beyond his arbitrary decree. He knows that the fountain creates an aesthetic illusion soon destroyed when, idling in the water's presence, one grows restless for new destinations. He grandly proclaims that his cultural citadel is "built like a ship" ("bâtie comme un navire" [524]) to carry his nation into eternity; yet he admits in a subsequent episode concerning a real voyage that, once the sea turns rough, the passengers lose their faith in tar and timber. "It is bad that the very frame around us should tremble," remarks an alarmed landsman in the ship's hold (527).[10]

The monarch, in short, does not act in the best of faith. Though himself knowing the truth of the sea, the desert, and the night—the mindless, tireless, inscrutable energy which surrounds all cultures and erodes them, sparing none—he would protect his subjects from this fruitless knowledge. They will continue to labor and grow if persistently, systematically deluded; but, once advised of their order's relativity and vulnerability, they will abandon the old strictures like a silly child's game and, in their aimlessness, come to naught. To be saved, they must abide in ignorance.

It is tempting to see in the Caïd's posture a new kind of Exupérian hero—a savior superior to the people he saves, who probably would reject the warm illusions nourished specially for them if he could somehow be given the option of entering his own creation. Such an interpretation of the monarch would be misguided. After all, Saint-Exupéry would spend the final years of his life seeking to obtain or preserve an appointment to active combat duty, even though he might have enjoyed some informal status as a social architect if he had taken care to survive the war. There is no room for doubt: the author saw himself as one of the Citadel's soldiers, a humble participant who embraced his culture's illusions—or who at least served them with such devotion that ecstasy would blind him (sometimes) to their limits. The young Saint-Exupéry who had displayed little patience with uninquisitive bureaucrats had slightly changed his tune. Though he still insisted upon an existence which would engage the elements, or at any rate something more elemental than carbon paper and clock-cards, he no longer seemed to value questioning as highly. He had apparently decided that atrophy was far less of a threat to social order than ostentatious, irresponsible mockery and rebellion.

What the drudge's atrophied imagination and the rebel's counter-conformity have in common is sterility. Neither can create, the former because he understands nothing but routine, the latter because he defies all routine (cf. 738–39). Since every creation extends convention—since nothing comes from nothing—the productive human being labors harmoniously within a social structure. Indeed, to be productive and to be fully human are the same thing: human fulfillment is only possible through the exchange of one's perishable envelope for some imperishable cultural imprint. "Those who do not exchange anything do not become anything," affirms the Caïd. "And life will scarcely have served to ripen them" (531).[11] Those who believe that they can stockpile creations, whether others' or their own, and live languidly off the wealthy accumulation are utterly mistaken; for, as the Caïd summarizes, "vain is the illusion of those sedentary people who believe that they can live at home in peace, for every home is menaced" (533).[12]

As noble as such sentiments appear, they again bring the monarch's reliability into doubt. In uttering these ostensible praises of human development as the key to right living, he has contradicted himself. Borgal says of such moments, "Here the Berber lord assimilates it [truth] entirely into the quest. . . . There he seems to see it shining like a flame at the end of his road" (165–66). Let us assume that the old women making lace, the sculptors chiseling statuary, and other proffered examples of successful human exchange are not pitifully nullified by the ravages of time (ravages with which Saint-Exupéry should have been only too familiar from the prospect of war-torn Europe): let us assume that Parthenons and Sphinxes will last a planet's lifetime. How can artistic masterpieces eternize one's spirit if one cannot in any sense abide in them?

Yet abide one cannot: the Caïd is quite clear on that score. The old women are deluded in thinking that their lace will exalt posterity, for the philosopher-king says that there can be no exaltation except through one's own efforts. Even the best lace-maker of them all, should she decide to rest her eyes in her final years after having created hundreds of intricate wonders, immediately becomes a *sédentaire* in the Caïd's judgment. Her life's work is insufficient at that moment to elevate not just its proud owners or eventual inheritors, but herself as well. No real exchange exists, therefore—only a mistaken belief in exchange; for which of these miraculous, exhausting crafts would ever have been undertaken if the laborer had not believed that it would long outlive him or her? The Caïd's chain of reasoning throughout chapters six and seven is fully circular and cruelly deceptive. To live properly is to exchange oneself for something more durable, but the durable creation has no value of its own; hence the *mentality* of exchange is the *desideratum* . . . but the cultivation of that mentality requires sustained delusion, for nothing on earth can preserve the human spirit. Thus a good person has necessarily formed a misconception of what is worthy in life.

How can the Caïd justify such profoundly misleading manipulations to himself? We can hardly suspect him of a Machiavellian self-interestedness: his ends are clearly altruistic, however confused his means may be. And here, I would propose, rests the crux of the matter. The Caïd is as deluded as his subjects, though on a grander scale. It is his most redeeming characteristic. Just as his soldiers honestly believe that the women of the enemy's oasis, "soft to the grasp, made as they are for capture" (535),[13] will fulfill all of their heart's yearnings, so the Caïd himself believes that a culture created out of sand through arbitrary laws and rites can contain more than was ever put into it—can contain the spiritual reality for which he pines.

Something made from nothing . . . a whole greater than the sum of its parts . . . but nothing is supposed to come from nothing—this is why the arbitrary referents of culture are invaluable! Aware of how cavalierly he violates his own logic, the Caïd (as we shall see) showers rational discourse with contempt. Yet to credit a system with having reached the truth just because it defies reason is the most devious rational ploy of all. The young Saint-Exupéry had lodged this very complaint against Père Sertillanges in his private notes: "I who knew in advance that this operation was possible, who see it succeed every day for delirious apologists when they arrange the universe judiciously to demonstrate their far stretches, I am entitled to remain disturbed"

(*Carnets* 37).[14] In the final analysis, Saint-Exupéry is tarred with the same stick. He cultivates poetic delusion through his Caïd, who, in turn, has built his human citadel not just to save others, but to save himself, as well.

It seems more than reasonable to suppose that Saint-Exupéry himself is the Caïd, not in the sense of a privileged aristocrat yearning for his eroded political powers, but in the sense of an author seeking to verify an aesthetic formula for practical application. He is the same man of thought and action toiling to fuse the two together perfectly as we saw in *Terre des Hommes* and *Pilote de Guerre*. To be sure, the airplane is conspicuously absent from *Citadelle*'s text—but it is virtually absent from *Le Petit Prince*'s, too, and Saint-Exupéry would never have identified his active, participatory side exclusively with aviation. "It's no more than an instrument of travel—and, in this instance, of war," he remarked of the plane in his "Lettre à Général X" (an unposted note to General Chambe found among his effects; *SV* 223).[15] Aircraft were but one means among many to serve creatively. For that matter, flying was often a more contemplative than active exercise for Saint-Exupéry (much to his own peril sometimes). Like the author, the pilot studies the world at arm's length, turning it slowly and following its travail with the profoundest sympathy but without vision-clouding passion. The Caïd has a predilection for just such vistas, it turns out: he frequently withdraws to a lofty eminence in the evening from which he may meditate upon the shrunken city lights. Indeed, he is the culmination of a long line of pilot-personae, a figure who can finally moralize about the planet at his feet without having to watch for ice on his wings (cf. Zeller 55).

Yet moralizing means artistically synthesizing for the Caïd: his most moralistic moments are also his most poetic. Is this not precisely the case with Saint-Exupéry himself? Why would authorship be so important to such a practical man unless he regarded it as morally valuable action? Hence the author contemplating his work which we find in the Caïd is at one and the same time a morally energetic human being charting the most responsible course to take ("For power . . . is a creative act"—"Car le pouvoir . . . est acte de créateur" [724]). In the Caïd's reign and in Saint-Exupéry's authorship, thought and action merge inextricably, as anyone can see—but also in a most unorthodox manner. Action becomes primarily artistic, while contemplation of the completed act stirs moral awareness: a reversal of the usual polarities. The best way to affirm goodness is to create beauty. Neither Bernis nor Rivière nor any of Saint-Exupéry's literary self-portraits could write such an equation so lucidly, immersed as they all were in material complexities and specific controversies.

The Caïd's essence is not his absolute power, then, but his aesthetic fertility. Any bullet-headed generalissimo can lord it over an entire populace. This monarch is a master craftsman of scenarios, a poet in time. He delivers to his people a paradigm for the beautiful life, ergo the good life. He is Saint-Exupéry insofar as Saint-Exupéry the Desert King, adrift in an internal desert which isolates him from fellow soldiers and fliers, brings back the Poem of Life to the Land of Men. There is really no arrogance, no aristocratic privilege, in either role, and certainly no lust for power. The poem will generate its own power over human hearts, if it is a good poem. As for the poet, he is blessed and cursed with simply having broader vision than ordinary people. He is as he was made, just as some are good mechanics and some good sculptors.

The Caïd explicitly remarks the power of a harmonious pattern over the lives of human beings on several occasions. When his soldiers grow demoralized during a long expedition through the desert, he seeks some means of reanimating them. The army has become sullen, almost mutinous. A poet transforms these lost, groping men (though whether to the Caïd's benefit or detriment is not clear) by developing an extended comparison between a tree and human endeavor. "For planted in the earth by its roots, planted in the stars by its branches," explains the bard, "it is the path of exchange between the stars and us" (544).[16] The Caïd further recalls (perhaps during the same crisis: the text establishes no clear sequence) his reverend father's use of a poet to revive a refugee camp. Having pitied the spiritual deterioration of so many men penned up like beasts, the old king "sent a singer to this putrefying humanity" (553).[17] Within minutes, the performer's words had so inflamed the captives that they were ready to die in rebellion.

It is just such fervor that the Caïd longs to create in his decomposing army. During one of his lofty evening meditations, he reflects that "nothing is more true or less true. But more effective or less effective" (554)[18]—a reasonable enough sentiment in an author fashioning a story. A thorough integration of action and atmosphere, of character and tension, etc., makes a far better yarn than a newspaper account exact in every detail. (Much later, the old king's recollected aphorisms will cast the relativity of truth in blatantly artistic terms: "Likewise, events . . . have no form but the form which the creator accords to them. And all forms are true in abstract" [856].[19]) The Caïd is trying to compose such a story: he is trying to enlist his men as actors in a drama, and will no doubt succeed if he can only define what they lack in terms of what looms just beyond their grasp. In quest of inspiration, he prays to God, "Can you not teach me a truth which may dominate their particular truths and gather them all to its breast?" (557).[20] Is this not the prayer of an author seeking the unifying principle of his tale, the program which will reconcile all the smiles and grimaces of his *dramatis personae*? Is it not the invocation which Homeric poets directed to the Muse when they desired a path, an *oimê*, through a chaotic mass of facts?

Naturally, the Caïd regards any plodding intelligence which insists on picking things apart as anathema to his rule by aesthetic stimulation. (By extension, of course, Saint-Exupéry harbored exactly such feelings toward pettifogging academicians, bureaucrats, and politicos for obscuring the life of the spirit.) The Berber generals, also concerned about the morale of the troops but lacking their lord's vision, propose various Procrustean measures for reasserting authority. "You are nothing but dense-headed onlookers," the Caïd proclaims, losing his patience. "And those obscure forces which press against the empire's walls will easily bypass a bunch of administrators to drown you under their tide. After which your historians, more dense than you, will explain the disaster's causes, and will label as the adversary's wisdom, craft, and science the avenues of his success" (560).[21] Such people (and the category has already expanded to include historians) take the word as gospel, but do not divine the spirit's motion before and after and within the word, which alone can give understanding. Some appropriate advice of the old king, his father, recurs to him.

> Learn to hear, not the wind of words nor the chains of reason which allow words to blunder. Learn to look farther. For the hatred [of those disputants] was hardly absurd. If each stone is not in its place, there is no more temple. And if

each stone is in its place and serves the temple, then all that counts is the silence born of stone and the prayer which takes shape therein. And who will understand the result as an issue involving stones?[22] (563)

Thus the Caïd continues to ponder the mystery of reanimation on his own. Of words he takes little stock: only the image behind the words matters. Indeed, far from explaining the problem, isolated words divided from their spirit have created it, in most instances. "Only an insufficient language opposes men to one another, for what they desire scarcely varies," observes the monarch. "I have never encountered a man who desired either disorder or vileness or ruin."[23] (What a stunning admission from a seasoned head of state! Léon Werth calls this remark too naive even for Rousseau [140]. We may infer from it just how far Saint-Exupéry himself was from conceding the influence of original sin upon human behavior.) The Caïd then concludes, "The image which torments them and which they would like to substantiate is similar from one end of the universe to the other, but the ways by which they seek to attain it are different" (567).[24] Original sin or not, this sounds very much like an artist's profession of faith in the innate human love of beauty.

In contrast, the well-intentioned but dull staff of generals sees every condition as a chain of causes and effects, "and from cause to effect, they make their way redundantly toward error. For it is one thing to climb back up a trail of effects to causes, and another to descend from causes to effects" (576).[25] The Caïd must point out to them that anyone can predict the next step of a caravan: the trick is to determine what makes men risk their lives in the desert, a quandary which no logic can resolve. He will use a very similar illustration later on to rebuff a troop of pseudo-intellectual geometers. In that episode, he poses the riddle of a man who leaves his tent in the middle of the night, walks straight to a cliff, and hurls himself into the abyss. The logicians succeed brilliantly in proving the necessity of his death, since one track in the sand leads to another, right up to the brink—but none can explain why he took his suicidal walk, to begin with (692–93: and cf. Carnets 158).

The Caïd's strategists, historians, logicians, and geometers, then, are nothing less than the enemies of poetry (to borrow a phrase from

W. B. Stanford). They take the *fait accompli* and attempt to reduce it to their level of understanding: "the spoken word falsifies to capture, simplifies to instruct, and kills to comprehend" (584–85).[26] But has the Caïd himself not become snared in the "logic" of his whimsy? Of his social order he claims, "it is the universal collaboration of all through one, and this order obliges me to create something permanent. For it obliges me to found a language which will absorb contradictions" (586).[27] Contradictory his universe surely is. Both boundless and bounded, it induces its inhabitants to exchange themselves permanently for the imperishable, the enduring identity beyond their own . . . but it also declares that no such identity really exists. Their artistic creations have no independent spiritual value, no ability to awaken the beholder to a vast and fertile inner realm, but instead are mere rituals of social participation. As for their moral "exchanges," these are precisely what the Caïd defines only in terms of artistic creation and social participation. All the energy which the community churns out to serve the Exupérian god simply goes back into the community to keep it churning, for that god is nothing more or less than the *illusion* of a worthy, enduring cause.

Writes Luc Estang, "For Exupérian humanism, too, 'God is dead'; but instead of proclaiming it and considering a replacement, if possible, he [Saint-Exupéry] designates as God the very signs of death: silence and absence" (150). Reason would insist that such contradiction be practically resolved by at least elevating God from an illusion to a supposition. After all, both art and morality strive not for illogical, but pre- or supra-logical objectives: the point where the trees become a forest, where good deeds become goodness. How *reasonable*, then, merely to concede that the universe is neither bounded nor boundless, but absorbed (to use the Caïd's excellent word) into unimaginable dimensions . . . Yet logic holds the monarch—and his literary creator—back. Saint-Exupéry mistrusts the unimaginable. People can only be content with what they see and touch: an immaterial end of action would prove socially disruptive. It would put redemption beyond the reach of those who cannot progress from a sensual experience to a properly aesthetic one, and even beyond those like Saint-Exupéry himself whose paradoxical aesthetic demands closure from life's most indefinite moments.

As skillfully as the Caïd averts his gaze from the reality beyond his tidy cosmos, he must come face to face with it at certain turns. One corridor which inevitably leads him back into the void is death. No amount of faith in the power of culture and community to animate can neutralize death's preemptive intrusions. It makes its way through the most honored ranks and most intimate families, releasing all such ties at a stroke. Of course, this very finality of death makes it attractive to the story-teller whose hero keeps chasing the horizon, as Saint-Exupéry well knew. Oddly enough, unlike the Little Prince, the Caïd is not much given to courting venomous snakes. He concerns himself exclusively with the living, the dead now being beyond his materialist reprieves, part of the outer darkness whose dim reality must never be allowed. The premature death of Ibrahim's son interests him less than the dying boy's ability to draw the village together. He observes that the household "keeps silent in order to tame the dying child" (532),[28] as if their stillness might lure him back to life as it would lure a wild creature to venture forth and accept food. The adults show themselves quite inept before this mystery, and the Caïd evidently approves, recognizing behind their futile coaxing his own aesthetic revulsion. For what could more outrage a young life's evolving story than a peremptory closure in the middle of chapter 1? This is not true closure at all, but an open end which all but defies metaphorical negotiation.

The death of a rival king elicits a very different reaction. Death is always a handy last chapter for those fully evolved adult stories that tend to grope for conclusions (cf. Fabien). Yet far from inviting the Caïd's mythos into some possible sequel beyond his imagination, this death merely poses a problem for the stories of still-evolving lives upon which it impinges. The worthy adversary had always provided the Caïd with an antagonist for his ongoing story—a force whose hostility gave his nation something against which to strive (cf. "a man who annihilates his enemy . . . used to draw life from him. Hence he dies of his enemy's death" [773]).[29] Now the villain of the piece (or, rather, the antagonist, since the only villainy to Saint-Exupéry is passivity) has vanished. The Caïd finds himself in desperate need of another antagonist so that he may resume "writing." In the meantime, he manufactures an artificial closure. Every year, he has a tent erected at the site where he and his *ennemi bien-aimé* would meet to parley.

With a full guard standing to attention, "I advance alone. And I raise the canvas of the tent and enter and seat myself. And a silence falls upon the land" (608).[30]

Silence again, as with Ibrahim's son—a silence which, like the open desert where the Little Prince seeks a well, might contain salvation somewhere. The Caïd has here ritualized death into one of his elusive (and delusory) treasure troves, the place which might contain just what men and women seek in life. He protests elsewhere that his ideas contain no such indefinite regression: "False is the distress of that man who tells you that satisfaction flees eternally before desire. For in that case he is deceiving himself on the object of desire" (597–98)[31]—as if fully material desires, far from being the most deceptive, were the only ones capable of not deceiving. Yet in the present instance, wherein he confronts the inescapable mystery of death, he all but cynically orchestrates hidden spaces and enforced hushes. Though this rite of the tent hints at some kind of incarnate union with eternity, it is complete slight-of-hand, lacking hypocrisy only to the degree that it succumbs to delusion. It is not a door opening on the ultimate enlightenment, but a door closed and locked to create mystery. How ironic that Rivière had declared war on the mysterious! His battles, at least, were waged against raw nature. In the ultimate act of *mauvaise foi*, the Caïd has imported mysteries ritually into the very heart of his culture, where they distract people from a greater, far less determinable mystery.

Thus Exupérian death is either a *trompe l'oeil* passageway right back into material existence (as it was in *Le Petit Prince*) or an utterly impervious blank upon which one imposes whatever is missing from life—not so as to chase it, but so as to leave it confidently deposited in an impregnable stronghold. In fact, the closed, locked door of death often merges poetically with megalithic walls whose outside is also their inside. The Caïd's own father is immediately petrified in sublime impassivity upon being slain, so the legend goes.

> They say that the assassin's hair turned white when his dagger, instead of emptying the perishable body before him, filled it with such majesty. Hidden in the royal chamber, face to face, not with his victim, but with the giant granite of a sarcophagus, caught in the snare of a silence which he himself

had caused, the murderer was discovered at daybreak reduced to a prostrate bow by the dead man's mere immobility.[32] (509)

Such turning to stone is the closest anyone comes in *Citadelle* to deification or resurrection. For those who remain behind watching mortal flesh turn to granite, the face of death presents a blank slate for writing or a clean canvas for painting, thus redirecting them to what they know best . . . but it also implies a contradictory outwardness, a repulsion, as we see here. The old king's assassin, kneeling in awe-struck reverence, has evidently beheld much more than his victim's life flashing before his eyes in familiar images of pomp and power. What other ideas could have filled his head? We know that characters in Saint-Exupéry, when thrust before the immeasurable, do not reel beyond time and space in a classically sublime experience. Instead, they recover the sense of things, the taste for tea and conversation and fine china . . . but mere recollections, whether fond or painful, do not blanch a man's hair.

Nor do they make rugged miners flee in panic. In a chapter where the Caïd rails against the facile logic of his generals, he offers in illustration of his point an event whose macabre unlikelihood far surpasses that of the assassin's overnight aging. He relates the story of "le grand exode." A group of salt miners awoke one day to find that the mountain under which they habitually labored had been transformed as by a thunderclap.

> For it chanced that the winds which had gnawed at the cliff over so many centuries had left a giant face sculpted there—a face expressing wrath. And the desert, the underground salt deposits, and the tribes . . . were now dominated by a furious black face sculpted in the rock beneath the depths of a pure sky, opening its mouth to curse. And the people fled, seized by terror, when they recognized it.[33] (577–8)

In a rout defying all logic, the miners and their families ran hastily into the desert, where they perished of heat and thirst to the last man, woman, and child. What face could the settlement have seen of such horrific delineation that it inspired mass hysteria? The Caïd only mentions the blasphemous mouth. No doubt, these miners had guilty consciences: perhaps the mountain was cursed of old, or sacred to another tribe. At any rate, their imaginations must surely have participated in creating the dreadful image—a creation of devastating consequences, to be sure, but one which nonetheless affirmed in the strongest terms the power of spirit over word, of inspiration over logic. Such, at least, is the Caïd's assessment of the catastrophe.

Yet in these two instances of what amounts to being struck dead by the sight of a stone, the Caïd—and Saint-Exupéry—have opened the Citadel's massive gate a crack rather than bolting it fast, as they seem to have intended. Neither the assassin nor the miners are recoiling into the finite sense of their traditions, any more than the tortured adulteress was likely to have been recalling her kitchen duties. These terrified people, while writing their own ghost stories on a blank slate (for none of the incidents involves immediate physical danger), are nonetheless writing about a ghost—about a form unknown to their cosmos which yet has risen above utter chaos. The stable reference points of culture are just what evades their groping hands as they tremble in the presence of the unassimilable; and a presence it is, for they see a face—something of their own face, something projected from deep within them. Whether they have recognized their own fundamental depravity or a basic goodness, rather, which their act has betrayed unpardonably, no one can say. After all, the author will not even consciously admit to any internal reality preexisting the imposition of tastes and habits from without.

In what must surely be an unconscious kind of progress, however, Saint-Exupéry's miraculous stone surfaces are indeed closer to genuine windows on the soul than to *Le Petit Prince*'s mirrors for prolonging quests. Also more perspicacious than the children's book is *Citadelle*'s treatment of women. As a mature man, the Caïd has taken the measure of romantic love long ago. He troubles himself very little about what women think of him (an attitude to which Saint-Exupéry himself may never have "graduated": the much-cited night which he passed in a friend's company conversing about God originated, as biographers invariably forget, in a quarrel with a woman [Pélissier 126–28]). Possessing many wives and able to acquire new ones at will, the Caïd has dissolved any mystery that ever lurked in a pair of dark eyes above a veil. He has not always been so imperturbable. In his youth, he was often caught "in the snare of female creatures, knowing that a particular one, formed in a certain foreign country and oiled with a perfection of scented balms, would possibly be within my reach. And this vertigo I called love" (598).[34] Once having obtained whatever *gazelle aux longues jambes* he craved at the time, he would invariably murmur to himself, "I have mistaken my prey, and I was mistaken in my pursuit. It was fleeing so quickly, and I stopped it to lay hold of it . . . And, once captured, it was no longer there . . ." (598–99).[35]

Finally, he realized what the Little Prince never seems to learn: that each woman for whom he pined only symbolized fulfillment because of her very elusiveness, and that he was thus closer to what he really sought while chasing his beloved than while enjoying her. Other men of his realm have still not comprehended the nullity of a woman won. He may entice them, therefore, with artfully imagined prospects of female spoils. The speech which he delivers to inspire his soldiers before an assault on the enemy's oasis (already mentioned) is frankly nothing less than a celebration of rape. They must grab their captives by the hair, he says. "They will still close their eyes to ignore you, but your silence will weigh upon them like the shadow of an eagle. Then finally they will open their eyes upon you and you will fill them with tears" (535).[36]

No doubt, the modern Western woman will find virtually every allusion to females in *Citadelle* objectionable, but we must distinguish between what is consistent and what is not in the Caïd's arguments if we mean to understand him. Casting women as wives, mothers, and home-makers is fully consistent with the Caïd's kerygmatic endeavor, for his message is precisely that people must limit themselves in order to construct a life which tends ever higher—that they must *be* before they may become. Men suffer the same kind of stereotyping in the book's allegory: they are either soldiers, artisans, or government functionaries. If women are condemned to slow death for disrupting their home, men are executed, too, for questioning their commander, challenging the Caïd's social vision, and falling asleep on guard duty. The game of life will have no drama, no sense, if people—men or women—find that they may break its rules with impunity. "I by no means sacrifice men to the empire," insists the monarch. "But I found the empire to fill men with it and animate them with it, and the man counts more to me than the empire" (633).[37] The good person is the fervent person, busily exchanging him- or herself for something more durable.

Yet if women are to be recipients of a man's exchange—if they are his work of art, claiming all his time and labor like marble statues rising from the sculptor's hand—how can they, in turn, effect an exchange? Herein lies the contradiction in *Citadelle*'s treatment of women. The Caïd speaks of women in just these terms at one point. "A woman, if she is beautiful, demands gifts and sacrifices," he assures us, referring specifically to a celebrated but vain dancer decked in jewels, "and she makes you drunk upon what you give to her—not upon what she gives to you" (615).[38] Like a marble statue, the dancer performs her function in life by posing on a pedestal before male worshipers; any attempt at a modest or compassionate gesture would only compromise her value as a receptacle of fervent offerings. Shortly thereafter, the Caïd explains to another woman unwise enough to have wed her worshiper that she has deprived her man of a creative outlet. Naturally, he has sought feminine company outside of his marriage. The ruler elaborates: "The woman of whom you speak was perhaps born of him. And that is why he is responsible for her. You owe yourself to your creation. He goes in search of her so that she may plunder him. He goes in search of her so that she may drink life from him" (617).[39]

This approbation of infidelity, let us remember, comes from a character who has fully appreciated the folly of sacrificing one's life to one's lady-love. Why does he countenance conduct which disrupts his nation's households and is also sadly benighted? Because, apparently, *all* sacrifice is benighted—but the *mentality* of sacrifice must be cultivated at any cost. A woman can no more contain all a man's answers for him than an exquisitely wrought chalice can bear its maker's soul through time; but the person who believes in the former delusion will labor as ecstatically, scorning food and sleep, as a person who accepts the latter one. As for all the pedestaled Galateas everywhere, Saint-Exupéry summarized his estimate of them when he quipped before Jean Leleu, "The prettiest girl in the world can only give what she has . . . but for me, that's enough" (88).[40] So uncomfortable was he with the female presence in a collegial rather than a symbolic role that, as Léon Werth revealed (170), he expunged the innkeeper's wife from the idyllic repast of *Lettre à un Otage*.

The foregoing observations apply just as well to subsequent passages about females. Without reviewing each of these, we may say that the Caïd's treatment of women is often very explicitly that of subject to object, not that of human subject to human subject in an assumed moral equality. "A woman . . . will always reproach you for what you give elsewhere than to her," he warns (641);[41] and, a bit later, he adds more generally, "it is possible to love only through a woman—not to love a woman herself" (645).[42] Meditating upon courtesans, he finds them, along with dancers, most typical of their sex's moral perspective. Their creed: to be elusive and always want more—precisely the attitude (not surprisingly) that men like the Caïd, ever seeking an altar upon which to sacrifice, require them to have. In this passage, however, the Caïd emphasizes his own disaffection with the altar. Its unworthiness has become too evident: for the goddess gives back nothing, and "there must be someone to receive" (661).[43] Now, the perfect god gives back nothing, either, and one must keep giving as long as one lives: hence the most divine gift is that impenetrable ungiving whose author we woo and attempt to soften. But the typical woman is too plainly squandering our gifts as well as refusing to return them. At least a mute, stony recipient might sustain the illusion of absorbing the donor's sweat and blood into something eternal.

More to the Caïd's taste is the princess whom the caravan, traveling for years, brings from the other side of the world. Her tutors have trained her in a dance which she has never danced before a man, and in a science of flower-arrangement which she has never practiced upon real flowers. Unlike a living, participating man who must constantly exchange and grow, her accomplishments are self-contained, a virginity "not only of womb and breasts" ("non seulement du ventre et des seins") but of the spirit (643). The Caïd concludes, "by reaching me in her total perfection, she could do no more than die."[44] The assassin who fancied that the old king had turned to stone scarcely monumentalized the body he had plotted to ravage more reverently and imaginatively than the Caïd does here.

It should be added that Saint-Exupéry may have been rethinking his views on women in one of Citadelle's final entries, chapter 204 (949–54). "But it has occurred to me that I was mistaken on the subject of women," announces the Caïd suddenly (950).[45] He proceeds to confess that he had always considered women before as so many separate gifts to be opened and then stored away, perhaps permanently. One has a certain poignant pitch of voice, another a certain longing look about the eyes: as many women as a man has moods. "But I was seeking to harvest the already-made honey from hive to hive, and not to penetrate that expanse which at first offers you nothing and requires step after step after step of you . . . ," he continues penitently (952).[46] The meditation closes as he gazes down upon his present bedfellow and muses, "Sleep peacefully in your imperfection, imperfect mate. . . . You are no end and recompense and jewel venerated for itself, of which things I would immediately tire; you are road, vehicle, and carriage. And I will never tire of becoming" (954).[47]

For all its indulgence, this chapter scarcely suggests that the Caïd has been cured of his tendency to seek the Holy Grail in other human beings, as its closing sentences prove only too well. His reassurances to the sleeping partner still lack any concession that she, too, might find a channel for becoming within him, let alone that they both might help to correct each other's faults in quest of a moral perfection beyond either one of them. Nevertheless, the chapter's tenor strongly implies that Saint-Exupéry, like his Caïd, sensed the need to develop further, and a more equitable attitude toward the opposite sex seems at hand.

If this attitude still strikes us as politically incorrect . . . well, nothing is more human than inhumanity. I have stressed the Caïd's cruel elevation of women to dumb idols who should receive offerings in solemn silence, not in order to revile him (or his author), but only to underscore why Exupérian ethics do not work. Human beings are never complete in this life, as the Caïd himself reiterates. They are unfinished even at the hour of death (a position *not* shared by the Caïd) insofar as no person can ever achieve moral perfection. As a result, the rest of an imperfect humanity has no right either to judge an individual or to worship an individual; for the former assumes that the person judged will progress no farther, while the latter cuts off the person worshiped from opportunities of progressing farther (cf. the Caïd's own dictum, "whoever gives himself to you separates himself from you" [683]).[48] Before, when the king was encouraging delusion in his people that they might find fervor, he was only guilty of withholding evidence. In this case, he is guilty of denying humanity—

both the idolized half and the idolatrous half—a chance to grow. That people are better off if spared certain knowledge is an ethically conceivable argument: that half of them are better off if allowed to deify or otherwise dehumanize the other half is not.

One might question, of course, whether the Caïd even deserves credit for sparing others an unsupportable knowledge. A deliberate deceiver may actually respect the truth, suppressing "objective" details lest they prejudice an audience against higher—but less expressible— facts. Yet the Caïd alternately honors truth and illusion without discrimination and deceives himself as well as others. He no longer idolizes women, but he is fully content to watch others do so who have not discovered the absurdity of their exchange. He sees through a whole class of things desirable only in their absence—or seems to, or should have—yet he is never moved to speculate about the perverse streak in human nature which tirelessly covets what is just beyond reach. Praising the elusive in whatever form it may take, he declares, "What matters is to go toward and not to have arrived, for one never arrives anywhere except in death" (644).[49] At the same time, he draws a fine distinction between those who know their objective to be imaginary and those who believe—deludedly—that it awaits them over the next hill. ". . . Those people waste themselves in utopia and in dream journeys who pursue faraway images, the fruits of their invention. For the only true invention is to decipher the present beneath its incoherent surfaces and contradictory language" (649).[50]

How strange it is to find a celebration of the here and now in the same author whose mystical fox told the Little Prince to mistrust his eyes! One must chase only that which exceeds one's grasp, because then the present moment's step vaults in anticipation of the capture. Let the objective become immaterial, though, and one's step slows to a despairing trudge. The Caïd never considers the possibility that the seeker, cheated of one prize after another, might graduate from despair to real insight. Ecclesiastes, the biblical personage most like this brooding desert philosopher, has exhausted every fantasy of man. Beautiful women in abundance, wealth beyond reckon, absolute power, arcane knowledge—all have been his, and all have disappointed him. His life preserves savor after so much disillusion only because he has finally accepted its limits, living each day by the rituals of work, rest, food, and drink, just as the Caïd recommends—but never believing for an instant that he is doing more than marking time in a world which cannot answer his questions or satisfy his desires. It is stunning to ponder what different conclusions the Caïd draws from experiences and observations so thoroughly similar. For him, the succession of gods served is a process of steady maturing. The suspicion that he might be staying the same through all these transitions—that he has resisted seeing the futility in them which alone might have broken his cocoon—could scarcely be further from his mind.

"From surmounted contradiction to surmounted contradiction, I make my way toward the silent subsidence of questions and hence to beatitude" (620), proclaims the Caïd in a moment of exhilaration.[51] In the text, this moment follows a scene where he confesses that old age has overtaken him, both physically and spiritually; but perhaps the Caïd's depression marks something like the end of a first draft, and Saint-Exupéry will hereafter circle back to restate or develop the sections of greatest interest to him. As it stands, the manuscript certainly offers no clear remedy to the aging monarch's demoralization, nor does any other scene portray him as so utterly devastated.

> And as I was admiring the design of the streets and plazas and, here and there, the temples standing like lofts for a spiritual harvest, and, all around, the slope's somber drapery, there nevertheless came to me the image of a plant which had dried out and been cut off from its roots, despite its ample flesh. There came to me the image of empty lofts. Here there was no more a living being whose every member resonated in the others, there was no more a heart collecting blood so as to pour it throughout the entire substance, there was no more a single flesh capable of rejoicing as one on holidays, capable of forming a single field of crops. There was nothing more than a bunch of parasites installed in alien shells, each one isolated in its prison and the whole collaborating in nothing.[52] (609)

Let us make no mistake about it: the Caïd here contemplates nothing less than the failure of his life's work—of his ultimate, chosen exchange (though Pélissier also sees in this section traces of

Saint-Exupéry's self-styled rheumatism [137]). A painter in time who uses men for colors, the Caïd has awakened to find his cautious strokes dribbling down the canvas and merging into a muddy blank. Had he ever really dominated any contradiction—the worship of vain, shallow women, the deathly struggle to win a rancid well—or had he simply suppressed them all in favor of a grander one, and then a still grander one (the Derridean *surenchère* again)? Now he has run out of heights to which he may advance, or retreat; for the earth has no higher prospect than leader of a nation, and no earthly cause can be more glorious than the molding of history for the benefit of mankind. The Caïd has done all that a man can do . . . and all for naught. As the Aeroposta Argentina had dissolved in vicious scandal, as European democracy had surrendered faint-heartedly to fascism (this passage could well date to 1940: cf. Schiff 337), and as the imminent triumph of freedom in the West would lapse into squalid self-indulgence, so the citadel built to keep vertigo from men's heads and emptiness from their hearts was being eroded from within by the mean egotism of their souls. Nowhere does *Citadelle* approach so closely the *vanitas vanitatum* of Ecclesiastes.

Could *Citadelle*'s intended ending have left the Caïd in such a state, the first Exupérian hero ever to let go of the material world and its cultural conditioning? Probably not. While no particular solution to the monarch's anguish is supplied, neither do instances lack of his resiliently snapping out of lesser demoralizations. Perhaps the best evidence, then, that Saint-Exupéry was at least vaguely aware of his myth's hopeless incoherence is not its failure to locate possible sources of meaning, but its success in locating so many such sources. There are altogether *too* many. A fertile imagination might indeed find God in any part of Creation . . . but the pilot-hero creates for himself, and hence can only see his mirror-image in his moments of revelation. The ubiquity of possible meaning thus becomes a prison, sealing him nonsensically within innumerable versions of himself. Even chaos must be a mere fable of his unseen part. Norman Austin (alluding to Lacan) has invoked an ancient myth to warn us away from such self-delusion: "Even Narcissus, who imagines that he can find himself without hazarding himself in the field of the other, is doomed to find only empty images of himself, and on the very face of the other that he shunned" (3). Under these circumstances, what might seem heroism can only be a kind of dementia, a war waged by the personality against itself.

Consider, for example, an extraordinary episode which I have already mentioned in several earlier chapters, and which reprises the iamge of the stone: the Caïd's dream of God as a great granite block. Though it appears in the text long after the doubts of old age cited above, this scene might easily be dovetailed into the weary monarch's spiritual crisis. Does it not hearken back to the same critical period? "I have discovered the people gathered around the golden calf—not selfishly, but stupidly," he explains in terms very like the earlier scene's. "And the children who are born these days are more alien to me than young barbarians without religion" (682).[53] Shortly thereafter, a strange vision visits the Caïd in his sleep.

> A slippery road along a cliff was overhanging the sea. The clouds had burst, and the night was flowing like a full wineskin. Stubbornly, I was scaling toward God to ask of him the reason behind all things, and to have him explain to me where the exchange was leading which had been imposed upon me so high-handedly.
>
> But at the mountain's summit, I discovered only a heavy block of black granite—which was God.[54] (683)

Darkness and storms, alone or in conjunction, had signified the chaos beyond culture in all of Saint-Exupéry's works. Now we find the Caïd wrestling with both, in the tortuous throes of creation. God the Inspirer, the blank slate awaiting an author, crystallizes before him. He prays for guidance but receives no answer. He prays for even the simplest of signs—for a loitering crow to fly away—just to reassure him that a god exists somewhere and hears him. The crow moves not a feather. From this encounter he comes away oddly comforted, more so than if a great voice had spoken to him: "For I had not touched God, but a god who allows himself to be touched is scarcely a god" (684).[55] His creative endeavor has succeeded, after all, and spectacularly; for without the slightest external assistance, he has himself produced nothing less than God. How could he have laid the foundation of culture any more securely in the void? Rather than a few childhood memories or a few rituals learned by rote, he returns with divine authority to build any structure he wishes and call it good. Moses descended with the Ten Commandments: the Caïd descends with a *carte blanche*.

If Saint-Exupéry needed an experience to lift the old ruler out of his doldrums, surely this could have been it. Zeller believes that the fictional dream grew out of a meditative exercise which the young Saint-Exupéry had often repeated while stationed in the desert, and insists that the passage therefore reflects a *bona fide* spiritual triumph (205–6). Yet the adventure is never rewritten, no later episodes appear to revolve around it or allude to it, and in general it composes just one more vignette in an endless sketchbook. May we not at least conclude, then, that Saint-Exupéry was less impressed than he used to be by this god whose stubborn inscrutability forces us to take his place? Is it not apparent that he hoped to find a genuine end—a fulfilling terminal objective—to right action, and not just another context for more action?

The Caïd continues to declare periodically that "you only make an apprenticeship to God in the exercise of prayers to which there is no answer" (639—and cf. 664).[56] He persists, too, in confusing God with the spirit of creativity: e.g., the circular formulation, "For God, above all, is the sense of your language, and your language, if it acquires a sense, reveals God to you" (701).[57] Here language is clearly not a rational but a tropological medium (the image of the sculptor immediately precedes this sentence). As Borgal keenly observes of *Citadelle*, "Man is an apprentice, and God is not his master, but the masterpiece which he must succeed in realizing" (184). This is another way, perhaps, of phrasing God's link with the moment of inspiration, for the imagined synthesis of the projected masterpiece is a motive force before the first word is written.

In fact, if this god differs from the classical Muse at all, it is in his licensing the individual's creativity with silence rather than intruding upon the creative moment with suggestions: a very fine distinction, indeed. Nevertheless, the Caïd will not let it pass. "As for the archangel's apparition," he explains, "I no longer place any hope in such claims, for he will either be invisible or not be at all. And those who hope for a sign from God are making of him a reflection in their mirror and perceiving nothing but themselves" (708)[58]—"which is something from a second-rate cartoon," he adds later of such perceptible epiphanies (810),[59] a cavalier dismissal which greatly disturbed Saint-Exupéry's friend Léon Werth (146: see also 978 and 991 of *Citadelle* for similar sentiments).

Yet in repeating to us so often that God is silent, has the Caïd not acknowledged that the comfort and profit of his own prayers lies only in their reflecting his meditations back to him? The difference between a bad cartoon and a good prayer, then, seems to be one of diminished dishonesty (or increased hypocrisy). One might at least admit, deep down, that the voice in the dark is one's own. But perhaps the sign-seers are honestly self-deluded—and since when has that affliction been any less than a necessary virtue in the Citadel's community? Besides, to make a special place for God's silence, apart from man's creative meditation and the universe's predominant nullity alike, is to concede the presence—however tentatively—of an absolute, eternal being beyond empirical reality. And is that not something quite new under *Citadelle*'s sun?

One might draw another fine distinction and say that the Caïd's god is not so much inspiration *per se* as the aesthetic satisfaction which pervades the creator contemplating his or her idea's potential form. The same satisfaction also overtakes other beholders, hopefully, when the form becomes objectified in a work of art. Such an understanding of divinity would unite both creator and beholder in spiritual elevation on equal terms, a notion essential to Saint-Exupéry's system. Originally, a face captures the sculptor's imagination or a metaphor the poet's, coming we know not whence in an unaccountable moment of wild energy. The face or the metaphor may prove too obscure or outlandish, however: it may fail to move the artist upon consideration and finally be rejected. In this regard, the beholder is also a creator. Beauty cannot exist as a purely objective quality: it requires the subject's participation. Hence, when the perceiver passes judgment on how well the object has integrated disparate elements of experience to form harmony, he or she, too, creates it. In the event of success, both artist and audience are moved by an impartial breeze of elation which touches their hearts. "And I only call truth that which exalts you," concludes the Caïd. "For there is nothing which is self-evidently for or against. Yet you have no reservations about the beauty of a face which echoes through your being" (771).[60]

It is not really possible to say which creator—artist or audience—these words are addressing. Both parties register an irresistible pleasure in the beautiful object's presence quite unaffected by any pride or envy upon which one or the other may ruminate later in analyzing their different roles. The aesthetic experience triumphs over egotism to bring them together, and can only do so by tapping a level of judgment even deeper than the awareness of material circumstance. That moment when both say, "This is beautiful," briefly puts in its shadow all that they happen to be by affirming something in their heart of hearts with no "happen" about it—something which simply *is*, whatever they may be or may ever have been.

And is this something, too, not another aspect of that unconditioned god, neither cultural order nor impenetrable chaos, who lurks on the fringes of *Citadelle*? Were Saint-Exupéry as much of a cultural relativist as he makes out, his description of the aesthetic experience would be indefensible. A person would approve of a work of art only to the extent that it confirmed his or her inculcated prejudices: there could be no tree whose roots turn earth and rock into love of the sun. As things are, art offers the greatest hope of bringing together the most inimical cultures. A poet can revive an army, soften an enemy, or incite a band of refugees with an image or two. In the Caïd's own words, "I know of no poem nor of any poetic image that is other than an action engaging you. What matters is not explaining this or that to you, nor even suggesting it to you, as the more subtle believe—for what matters is not this or that object, but making you become such and such a person" (799).[61] The artist's words do not encode secret commands which the well-programmed citizen subliminally recognizes and dumbly obeys: they *act* upon him—i.e., they transport him where he was not, awakening his faculties and changing his perspective so as to make him burst his former boundaries.

Why else would Saint-Exupéry's own extraordinary images be so purged of cultural allusions but that they strive to create culture from something deeper than contingency (cf. the examples offered by Pélissier [84–85])? Often his ambitious metaphors even lead him beyond the properly human realm into primal nature: e.g., the wild predator which roars to make the cringing inhabitants of the night sweat in fear. "For wild predators are guided by the sharp odor of anxiety, which can be carried on the wind. Scarcely has such a beast roared when all of his victims begin to shine before him like an illuminated mass of bodies" (830).[62] To the best of our knowledge, big cats do *not* roar for this brilliantly conjectural reason. The primal element here is human: that unique fear and exultation of the sublime. Art at such moments humanizes even more than it acculturates, and it acquires moral significance in doing so. Aesthetic formulas which evoke a basic human response can, with rather slight adjustment, be translated into a moral imperative to respect one's fellow beings as bearers of a common spark. The Caïd's *seul géomètre véritable* seems to understand that his career's essential accomplishment has been to behold two superficially different objects and say, "It's just the same" ("Il en est de même") for them as for his triangles. Even so does a poet develop a metaphor—and even so does a compassionate person divine the hearts of others.

But the old geometer, as a contemplative and (in his way) an artist, is hardly a manifestation of the pilot-hero. He looks within and discovers what was always waiting to be found. Myth raises and levels mountains: it leaves the cosmos permanently changed. The most energetic attempt to break out of allegory's predestination occurs in chapters 156–58, where the Caïd first leads a struggling expedition over the desert furnace to the well at El Ksour, then swoops down upon a mysterious city (apparently the expedition's objective) only to find it impregnably sealed by a seamless wall. The episode will end up combining many of *Citadelle*'s most heavily worked motifs. The death march toward a dry well, the confrontation with chaos, the awe-struck panic and ecstasy before a sublime stone massif—all are represented here, and with an intensity which appears nowhere else in the manuscript. If Saint-Exupéry were ever going to map a mythic act, surely this would be the moment.

And yet, as has become typical of this author's distinctive self-contradictions, no episode sounds more heavily allegorical. While the Caïd's desert ordeal may recapitulate several factual vignettes from *Terre des Hommes*, it far surpasses that work in representing archetypally the pilot-hero's journey into the void. An ominous wind rises from the desert's interior which carries innumerable birds to the encampment, inhabitants of a distant oasis now fatally stranded in a lunar landscape. Rudely wrested from the delicate framework suited to their vital needs, "they were perishing each day by the thousand, soon turned dry and crackling like a piece of dead bark" (834).[63] There is a hint of Dante's first ring of sinners (probably not intended) in this sad, arid migration through inferno. That the birds' fate has a human poignancy is further suggested as the Caïd's own army starts to rave and drop, one by one. Standing at the edge of a dry well, the monarch muses bitterly, "this well held us down like a nail in a bird's wing."[64] The stars "in the depths of a night at once bitter and splendid" (835)[65] seem to mock them that evening, ciphers grandly conveying the sense of things in a cryptic script across limitless chaos. Even here, on some of the last pages Saint-Exupéry would ever write, the star preserves the same symbolic ambiguity as it did in *Courrier Sud*. It announces order, but an order unsympathetic—perhaps hostile—to the human observer's . . . yet agonizingly beautiful, and so not at all inhuman.

Fortunately, the Caïd's advance scouts report that "the well of El Ksour . . . is a window on life," literally seeing a mirror in the earth and integrating it into their drama through poetry.[66] Another horde of birds—this time crows—attends the expedition's arrival at El Ksour, taking flight in the moonlight but refusing to depart the life-giving well. Their circling shadows lend a weird effect to the scene, yet are probably drawn from the author's actual desert experiences rather than specially designed as a symbol. At most, one might maintain that they represent an alternate culture, also tenuously sustained in the void, with which the Caïd's must compete. The notion of cultural clashes as inevitable, and even enriching insofar as an enemy poses a limit which both defines one's group and calls it to greater exertion, pervades *Citadelle*. Indeed, in a prayer of thanks, the monarch defends his army's imperialist mission. "I am leading them toward an oasis to be conquered. . . . These men who eat and drink and live only an elemental life this evening will hardly have shown themselves on the fertile plains when all will change, not only in customs and language, but in the architecture of ramparts and in the style of temples" (836–7).[67]

Thus, up to this point, the adventure encapsulates most of the pilot-myth's stages: a daring sally into the vacuum to assert the sense of things, a vertiginous fall into immense and deadly forces of resistance, and salvation by a hair's breadth. All that lacks is an epiphany.

This stage is not long in coming; but, as had happened in all of Saint-Exupéry's later novels, it quickly escapes and cancels the framework lovingly provided for it. The moment's heady surrealism can be appreciated best by reading the Caïd's own words:

> We were soon in sight of the city. But we could discern nothing about it—nothing except its red ramparts of extraordinary height which held turned toward the desert a sort of disdainful backside, stripped as they were of any ornament, of any redoubt, of any battlement, and to all appearances conceived on the principle that they would not be observed from the outside.[68] (838)

Obviously, here is one incident which could *not* have replicated one of Saint-Exupéry's experiences in the desert! The mysterious fortress insists upon an allegorical interpretation as much as any enchanted castle in a medieval romance. Is it the inverse of the Caïd's thriving, extroverted citadel, constantly participating in the cultural environment—or is it not rather that citadel's perfect image, but seen from a transcendent vantage which reveals its ruinous introversion? The alien structure certainly does not belong to the sensuous world, whether because it is dead to the living or alive to a truth beyond death. While studying it, the Caïd's army is invaded by the same paralysis as had struck him before the granite face of God in his dream. The general mood also recalls his father's spellbound assassin and the dumbfounded salt miners after the wind had transformed their mountain. In each case, a groping human consciousness runs upon something substantial in the void but too vast and silent to be comprehended. Says the Caïd, "a discomfort seized upon my men when the ramparts, having grown little by little at our approach, appeared so visibly to turn their back to us in a cliff-like fixity, as if nothing existed outside of the city" (838).[69]

The other "stone walls" mentioned in *Citadelle*'s earlier pages all forced the beholder to read into them his or her own hopes or fears, but this megalith harbors one more surprise. "From a distant rise which, while not abutting the ramparts, permitted us a slight peek over them, we observed a verdure as dense as cress. Yet outside of the ramparts, you would not have found a single blade of grass."[70] The god in the Caïd's dream had not deigned to set a crow flying, and even the blasphemous salt mountain must have been the subjective nightmare of lively imaginations. Within these Cyclopean walls, however, sits a genuine Eden. The green is truly there: the soldiers are not inventing a grimace out of a rocky depression, but remarking an objective reality. To be sure, they digest the discovery in very different ways. "One group of them was seized with fear,"[71] like the salt miners, because of the situation's utter defiance of every routine and ritual they have ever known; while others, "on the contrary, were tormented by an informulable, singular love. . . . How pretty it was, this darling city so jealously decked in its rare scents and its gardens and its customs!" (839).[72]

Thus, the irresistible, all-resistant fortress covers the gamut of everything to which men sacrifice, from inscrutable idols to lush oases to beautiful women sealed virginally in foreign ways—everything before which a man might fall terrified or infatuated—everything too perfect to touch but too perfect not to reach for. All is here; why take another step in any direction? Earlier visitors have apparently been seduced by the same Siren-song of unearthly silence, for "we discovered that all around this deaf and blind wall, the sand revealed an especially white zone, rich—too rich—in bones which surely bore witness to the fate of foreign delegations."[73]

What, then, are we as readers to make of this epiphanic vision? The Caïd is quite forthcoming with his own interpretation, once he has had time to deliberate. "As a result of having enclosed itself in its provisions, it has accepted death," he decides. "I fear those who nakedly ascend toward the north of a desert unmarked by fortresses, trudging along almost without arms. But . . . you are all mine, city too sure of yourself, as disposable as a honey-cake. Your sentinels must surely be asleep. For you are dilapidated around the heart" (848).[74] He has successfully reduced the threat to contemptible proportions—to something dead or something effeminate. Any city which is not vibrant enough to entertain curiosity about the rest of the universe cannot be worth capturing. Sustained by its own artifice, it has cravenly insulated itself from the challenges of real existence and their accompanying opportunities for growth.

Yet do these very words not accurately describe the Caïd's own citadel? Though he sends forth caravans and leads his soldiers on missions of plunder and conquest, he has raised a doorless wall around his people. The caravan's destination gives the merchant something to strive for; the woman who awaits the caravan's return bearing exotic carpets and scents has something to long for; the soldier who has no wife (or has tired of her) and expects to find houris in silk veils while sacking the enemy stronghold has something to dream about. None of these people knows it, but they are all walking in circles. Seeking the smallest fissure in a wall which keeps them from their heart's delight, they little suspect that they are caught in their own culture's labyrinth, carefully designed by the Caïd to turn them inward under the illusion of exploring the ends of the universe. When have they ever pondered the land beyond death, consumed as they are by the material world before them whose all too evident limits the Caïd has shrewdly, systematically effaced? In what regard have they ever shown themselves inquiring rather than acquisitive or aware of life's moment rather than engrossed in the present moment? Thanks to the Caïd, they are largely free of paralyzing self-doubt—not because they have rationally or mystically risen above their circumstantial selfhood, but because, like children, they have been too fervently immersed in games to stand back and be struck with an adolescent self-consciousness.

Now, facing the fortress's smooth shell, these benighted men confront a mirror-image of themselves for the first time. Now they know the paralysis of self-doubt—the petrifying, sublime stupor of discovering that all imagined ends are artificial, and that the ultimate truth cannot be imagined. The Caïd came to the same realization in his dream, but only to retreat to his former artifice, content that it could be proved no more absurd than any other arrangement of images. The same complacent resignation marks his eventual disdain for the eerie walls. Rather than concluding that what he really wants will never submit to any image, he concludes that a distinct image must more nearly approximate what he wants than eternity's conceptual abstraction.

But why the glimpse of Eden within the walls? If they truly enclose social decay, why do screams and wails not arise from within? Why are the stone foundations not strewn with carcasses of those who have jumped from the inside rather than with bones of those who have pined away on the outside? The adventure's imagery appears to have shaken loose the author's grip. Saint-Exupéry must have wanted so insistently to find a hidden paradise—a terminal meaning, a reward for heroic action not created by any hero's act—that he wrote it into the text as a streak of luminous green. The inhabitants of such a world would not need to return to the desert: they would have sealed it out forever, no doubt fearing gate-crashers like the Caïd who come, see, conquer, and move on. At no point in *Citadelle* does an image of independent and immobile serenity so belie Saint-Exupéry's pilot-myth, his lifelong ethic of imposing order upon chaos. Rather than admit the myth's subordination to a preexisting order not made by man, he turned away in the Caïd's person with a nonchalant shrug. His high regard for action continued to reject the inevitable answer which his spirituality intuited.

All the same, we observe that the Caïd must meditate for several pages before he succeeds in dismissing the citadel's mystery. Much of his thinking assumes the form of aesthetic rearrangement, as is typical of it elsewhere. "If there is, for example, behind the walls . . . such and such a musical instrument unknown to us . . . ," he reflects, "experience teaches me that, once this mysterious reserve has been forced open and my men dispersed among its riches, I will find them later, during the long evenings of pitched encampment, struggling to draw from our most exotic instruments some melody with a strange new appeal to their hearts" (840).[75] A little later, he wonders whether it is he or the impervious fortress—"qui menons [sic] la danse"—"who leads the danse" (845). Such reflections make us wonder why he does not order his men to play their flutes and cithers or import one of his young wives to dance before the walls. If his theory about the decadence within is correct, then faces should pop up along the parapets to catch forbidden glances of the visitors . . . but the fortress has obviously lured the Caïd (and Saint-Exupéry) to steal a forbidden, wistful peek inside. The strange new music which the Caïd has already heard—that green elysium—holds him spellbound, sweeping all thought of his own cultural riches from his mind. He stands upon his airborne eminence a poor man, indeed.

The Caïd's outlandish expedition all but leads him away from perceptible reality precisely by yielding a solid image. The verdant but inaccessible cress conveys not so much a material desire as the hopeless frustration of that desire. The vision could have reconciled him to confining his *Sehnsucht* within a disciplined wait for other dimensions. He might have realized that, while right action always strives after perfection, it also must accept in advance its certain failure to reach the mark in this life. He seems almost to hear the new music . . . almost. The harmony is finally suppressed, however, when he begins to chant his refrain yet again about the maturing effects of new quests. As he puts it several dozen pages later, "Mad is that man who would capture water in his urn because he loved the singing of the fountains" (887).[76] Yet mad also—or pitifully beguiled—he who chases the fountain's water downstream, since the essence of its beauty is the whispered suggestion of what cannot be grasped.

The manuscript's remnant never again comes so close to resolution: the old self-contradictions mount relentlessly, instead. "Seule compte la démarche," as the Caïd dutifully repeats: "Only the step forward counts." Even the desert, like a human enemy, is both dreaded realm of senselessness and beloved incubator of sense. One cannot live in the desert, of course—but one can walk in it: one needs only an oasis or a hostile border toward which to creep in hope of a ravishing fulfillment. And while "there is no end at issue, the pleasure being in progression" (894),[77] the end is indeed at issue; because he who wittingly, laboriously chases the next horizon can surely be no idle dreamer. "You scarcely go about looking for something of which you have no knowledge," states the Caïd confidently (906).[78] Yet the end is not really at issue, after all, because the seeker will never be so fulfilled as when he staggers thirstily up the next dune. "The desire for love— that is love" (912)![79] So the argument goes, back and forth. Such lubricity moved Estang to conclude (turning one of the Caïd's terms of mockery back upon him), "It must be said, as gently as possible . . . that *Citadelle* holds its own oriental bazaar, a *bazar d'idées*" (144).

Death, we have been told throughout *Citadelle*, is *achèvement* and *perfection* (e.g., 509 and 883). The provisions upon which one cannot live are suddenly transformed into an eternally self-replenishing cornucopia "only in the peace of death, when God stores his harvest" (852).[80] Conversely, anything which may be found in life of a completely self-sufficient nature must be relegated to the perfection of death. One can only wonder if the fully accomplished princess delivered to the Caïd by a long-awaited caravan was not immolated on some stone altar as a perfect sacrifice, since he speaks of her as fit for nothing less. Do such statements imply a sincere belief in an afterlife of reward, consummation, and bliss—or are they not, rather, yet another sign of the aestheticism pervading Saint-Exupéry's moral system? Is the perfection of death not simply the unity of a finished tale? One has only to organize the past, highlighting those moments when the deceased offered his or her variety of "exchange" and elevating to a climax, of course, the moment of ultimate exchange. Naturally, any person is self-sustaining in such a death—"the only place where provisions are of service" ("là seulement où servent les provisions" [925])—because no provisions are required. He or she becomes as immobile as an Egyptian pharaoh in a pyramid . . . or as a block of granite. The perfection is in the story left behind, which can now be punctuated, edited, and bound.

That death itself, viewed apart from its defining aesthetic contribution to life's sequence, holds utterly nothing of substance is intimated frequently in *Citadelle*. Absolute perfection, says the Caïd to the vexatious *prophète bigle*, "brings death with it" ("entraîne la mort" [973]). It is not an eternal reward, this perfection, or an aspect of a god in whose presence we stand after death—it *brings* death. Saint-Exupéry here regards the notion of absolute truth with open contempt for being disengaged from life. Beyond life is nothing. Just as the goddess who confers coherent and fervent motion upon a man's days may, when one follows her off her pedestal, turn out to be a silly strumpet, so death is mere nullity outside of its illusory terminal role in the pilot-myth.

Indeed, the two motifs—death and the strumpet—often merge in the Caïd's imagery. "For such a woman will never manage to be born," he says of a vain hussy who demands more and more without giving back anything (866).[81] A few words later, he adds, "She will remain an aborted grain, an unexploited potential, withered in heart and soul. She will grow old with funereal progress in the vanity of all she has captured."[82] The grain that will never germinate and the funereal romantic conquests clearly designate this woman as spiritually sterile; and, by association, they show that death itself is but a trash bin of things unalive, a Galatea on a cold slab whose Pygmalion has gone home for the day.

Further along and in the same vein, the Caïd warns his readers to beware of expecting to find their heart's content in possession. Were you to be painlessly transported to the mystical "isles of music, set before you like a wrapped gift" (892),[83] he insists that you would find no fulfillment at all, having been cheated of your creative struggle to raise land from the sea.

> As a result of having effortlessly awakened there, you will draw nothing from the embraces of native maidens except the ability to forget love. You will pass from one thing forgotten to another, from death to death . . . and you will say to me about the isle of music: "What was there in that land which could make life worth living?" when the same girl [as entertained you], properly instructed, would make an entire crew run the risk of death for her love.[84]

These few words explicitly declare that neither a beloved woman nor death itself has any meaning when taken out of the myth's aesthetic arrangement. How can anyone who ponders such passages maintain that Saint-Exupéry believed in a reality transcending and absorbing material existence rather than in a fully mortal reality enhanced by optical illusions?

And yet, how are we to explain what Zeller calls those "profound cries which contradict his resignation to waiting and demand the 'visage à aimer' [face to love]" (93)? One such passage, already cited, has the Caïd ecstatically anticipating a beatitude beyond life's contradictions. Using his formulaic images of death as a barn at harvest and God as a silence transcending all questions, he continues: "On that day when You store up Your creation, Lord, open to us Your double-leafed door and usher us into that place where there will be no more rebutting because there will be no more debate, but beatitude, that keystone of all questions, that face which fulfills desires" (620).[85] This vision is not necessarily inconsistent with the portrait of God as fountainhead of aesthetic truth (whether through inspiration or judgment or both) which we have seen elsewhere. Of death we learn here that life's labors may finally be stockpiled, that all questions will be resolved, and that satisfaction will not consist of a vile complacency but of a beatific peace. Much later, the Caïd even expresses the hope of meeting his *ennemi bien-aimé* and his cherished *géomètre* when God puts him to sleep "in the fold of his desert sands where I have labored well" (979).[86]

As aesthetic a construct as this beatitude may be, it remains somewhat otherworldly, too. After all, the science of aesthetics itself implies a supra-logical, immaterial realm of the thing missing, the thing sought: in short, a realm of love. "The being-in-itself of art is not an imitation of something real," observes Theodor Adorno eloquently, "but an anticipation of a being-in-itself yet to come, of an unknown that will determine itself through the subject" (qtd. in Iser 291). The fountain's music may not lend itself to bottling, but neither is it a mere slaking of thirst for the desert traveler.

Not every beautiful order is a good order, and right action sometimes calls for vigorous opposition to existing social structures; yet the good life does indeed toil toward an order of orders able to absorb a countless array of apparently contradictory acts. Cultivating a taste for art, a chore which demands that we divine purpose beyond diversity and diversity within purpose at the same time, is excellent practice for the good life. How could a person who took as much pleasure in the harmony of reconciled tensions as Saint-Exupéry manifestly did be said to have no inkling of a reality beyond this one, or of a loving god? "I have need of a god to receive me," confesses the Caïd (813).[87] Even if this admission reveals only a well-developed aesthetic sense, it necessarily reveals a fairly well-developed moral sense, besides. A god who gathers all loose ends together and grandly fuses all questions into one edifice is certainly not a god of lies, selfishness, enmity, despair, and chaos. As Huguet concludes his praise of Exupérian silence, "Across the 'human desert' devastated by the absence of God, this divine presence appears first to the restless spirit, steadily walking toward him, as the promised God of beginnings" (74).

III.

In effect, *Citadelle* rids society of sin by removing the two essential pre-conditions of wrong-doing: knowledge and freedom. A person cannot stray very far down the path of wickedness if he or she is discouraged from speculating about the ends of various conduct—is, indeed, encouraged to accept false ends. A truly evil act must be done with the knowledge that it celebrates disorder, destroying fertile disciplines and ruining lives by way of affirming its agent's ego at the center of the explosion. Just as evidently, no person can do moral wrong in manacles or under the influence of a secretly administered mind-altering drug. The Caïd's shackles are of the latter sort. To his credit, he relies minimally on thought-police and dungeons; but his intoxicating propaganda so incites his people that their range of conscious choices is effectively as restricted as if they lived behind bars.

Of course, to educate people about the consequences of certain common behaviors and then free them to choose among all possible behaviors would clear the way for some to degenerate miserably. Under the present regime, however, the Caïd has a nation of children in adult bodies, capable neither of great evil nor of great good. Fervent they may be—but fervent in the pursuit of what? Long conditioned to be unreflective, how many of them even stop to think that their suicidal battle charges or their *nuits blanches* over a bit of lace are exchanges of self for the eternal? More probably, they are excited at the prospect of plunder or eager to mortify their less artistic neighbors. All the fervor in the world cannot obviate the need to examine the *motives* behind the fervor, at least if right living is the desired objective. The Caïd's society, alas, can scarcely be said to create uniformly good people: it only creates uniformly busy ones.

The last hundred pages or so of *Citadelle* indicate a brief resurgence in the author's determination to frame a message both exhilarating and valid. Saint-Exupéry was probably little inclined to concede his myth's impracticability in formal, open terms even during his final months of life. The Caïd seems as vigorous as ever in his messianic single-mindedness when he declares, "I am he who inhabits. I am the magnetized pole. I am the tree's seed and the line of force working in silence . . ." (899).[88] Not only does this rapture reiterate his favorite images, but its style hearkens back to the text's beginning pages, where he announces that he has decided to cure the human race (e.g., "I am a green lawn verging on the abyss. I am the store-cellar which gilds the fruit" [517][89]). For that matter, the ecstatic priest of *Courrier Sud* had burst into the very same kind of rhetoric: "I am he who welcomes . . . I am he who carries the burdens of the world . . . I am the only one who can deliver man unto himself" (46).[90]

It has been said by more than one detractor that Saint-Exupéry saw himself as Jesus Christ, or at least begrudged Christ his role as savior. No doubt, to undertake a burden which has crushed every previous bearer—the salvation of all humanity from despair, no less—smacks of hybris. On the other hand, imitating Christ is supposed to be the solemn duty of all Christians, a duty which Saint-Exupéry, as an apparent unbeliever, might have ignored without fear of reproach. Instead, he devoted his life (and its moments of being shot at were probably much less anguishing than his literary labors) to finding cool water in a spiritual desert—for his own benefit, yes, but also and equally for that of his fellow human beings. He would have drawn little refreshment from a well meant only for himself or a select few. I believe that this is precisely why he could not accept a spiritual reality where good and evil vie for each individual soul.

"Utopia" literally means "no place." The inevitable shortcomings of human nature banish this Citadel to Baudelaire's "n'importe où hors du monde"—"anywhere outside of the world." But this world is where we must acquire and display our moral character, as unhealthy a place as it is. All the human beings in one culture will never exhibit, or even possess, great moral strength—not in any generation. In that regard, Saint-Exupéry's undertaking was doomed from the start.

Perhaps the more useful failure of *Citadelle*, then, was to demonstrate the pilot-myth's practical impossibility even on the level of individual conduct. One might protest that the two levels are inseparable: that the pilot-hero, by definition, sacrifices himself to save his culture, and that certain knowledge of his culture's eventual fragmentation into good and bad people would either forestall his sacrifice or transform its essential nature. Yet the hero need not grapple with such knowledge. We may follow the Caïd's lead in assuming that an individual, without compromising his worthiness, might deludedly believe that his immolated self will revive society's collective fabric. None of us can do better than to act upon the knowledge currently at our disposal. If it later proves to have been incomplete or mistaken, we must nonetheless be judged within the limits of what information was available to us before. Children should not be tried as adults.

The hero must be praised, surely, for daring the void, and also for remaining faithful to those whose fate rests in his hands. It is sorely tempting to give up the struggle sometimes, and even to embrace death, rather than to wage an apparently senseless war. But the pilot-hero insists upon sense, just as the existentialist insists upon nonsense, and the fact that he insists makes his cherished sense more formidable than it seemed at first. The void suddenly becomes filled with an invisible presence, a force of love surrounding the toils of the minuscule intruder. That such endurance bespeaks a virtuous character can rarely be held in doubt.

But how is this sequence mythic? Far from being superhuman, the Exupérian hero is punctiliously humanistic: he is Man. If every man may potentially swell to superhuman dimensions in the war with chaos—if such ecstasy belongs to Everyman's identity—then why does *chaos*, of all things, enjoy the power of defining human nature? Must not human nature precede chaos; and if this is so, must not the hero merely be borrowing chaos—creating it, in fact (far more than he ever created cosmos)—in order to express a part of his nature which he finds highly problematic? Is not his story really the Allegory of the False Myth—the old, old tale of the utterly new adventure?

If this pseudo-hero, this Don Quixote in us all, so loves his culture, why must he flee to its ramparts every morning to find new enemies? If he considers his inherited values as unconditionally true rather than circumstantially imposed, why does he not draw his greatest pleasure simply from living them—and what enemy could so suppress them, in any case, that they would not crop back up from the human heart wherein they are rooted? Or if his values are fully grounded in circumstance, why make such lavish sacrifice for them? Why be unshakably faithful to something inherently fickle? In the words of Shakespeare's Hector, "'Tis mad idolatry to make the service greater than the god."

Far more than in any of his other writings, Saint-Exupéry has conveyed in *Citadelle* the artistic character of this would-be heroism. Just as Don Quixote largely created a Dulcinea whose perfect beauty he served best when most remote from its secrets, so the Caïd creates longing, devotion, and sense from lace, music, and metaphor. At least Cervantes knew that his mock-hero had lost touch with reality (though perhaps the old knight's much-advertised, wryly lampooned madness was a clever ruse to render his fantasies a safe haven for incurable poets). Saint-Exupéry has less control: he is within an ace of losing himself in his art as he writes *Citadelle*. There can be no more mythic heroes. Basic human nature has grown too evident, and the very will to transcend it is perhaps its most evident parameter. Yet a creative mind can *pretend* that the conditions of such heroism obtain. The artist himself is not the hero—that would be sordid self-aggrandizement rather than aesthetic entertainment. He is, rather, the magician who nourishes the hero, a Charon or Merlin or Atlante. His reward resides simply in the luxurious dream of his fosterling's riding forth one day to change the world.

Even such introverted dreams are not always without social cost, however—even when a smiling Cervantes rather than an earnest Saint-Exupéry dreams them. "Dans chaque instant, je commence," the Caïd finally admits (969): "At every moment, I begin." There is a vast difference, though, between making a new start and resisting a second step—between broadening and narrowing one's vision through art. The Caïd cannot be born. With only ten short chapters left in Saint-Exupéry's lifetime as an author, *Citadelle*'s narrator has grown so accustomed to looping back that he is now his text's own literary critic. The Caïd may think that he is celebrating the many births (and many deaths: "To marry, you must die" [904][91]) which his identity has experienced over the years, yet he has indefatigably fought against any rebirth of consciousness which might have changed his fundamental philosophy. He has successfully evaded maturity.

How else could he fail to notice the grotesque dissimilarity of terms when he describes his community's ritual stoning of selected innocents? He likens the practice to "the throes of childbirth" ("la douleur de l'enfantement" [901])—a morally offensive metaphor if ever there was one! The only creature ever born from such travail is the already and eternally wizened, weary visage of a decrepit idol—the stone scowl of *Citadelle*'s salt mountain which frightens people back into mediocrity. Metaphor has been used to sanitize the situation's moral horrors; and has it not, in the process, brought its author (and perhaps its readers) one small step nearer to making those horrors real? Our art does not provide us with escape from our nature, after all, but immerses us in it. We must at last reject beauty without goodness, as Saint-Exupéry well knew, because beauty *with* goodness is so much more beautiful.

The ancient culture heroes whose cycle most closely approximates the pilot-hero's were ferocious non-conformists, to be sure, and sometimes displayed a moral originality which proved salutary. Society built temples to them and set them in the stars. Yet the constellations confer an ambiguous honor, as Saint-Exupéry's own novels demonstrate. They exact reverential gazes from mere mortals, but they also illustrate spectacular, unforgettable anguish. Society honors those who can cast off its rigorous programming, but it is also highly uncomfortable with them. Better to have them in the stars than next door.

Given this suspicion of genuine inner fervor and this tendency to anesthetize its individual members, society needs the pilot-hero—on that score, Saint-Exupéry was quite correct. Not only will the pilot-hero never win society to his own pitch of fervor, however, but he can never really hope to be accepted comfortably within its pale. He requires another home, a home in the stars, if he is to have a destination toward which to advance. If he is to help society at all, it must need what he offers far more than he needs what it offers. He must be able to create chaos within cosmos when the greater cosmos—the true, permanent cosmos whose imperative is inner—has been violated.

Let us concede that a visible, audible god is a material phenomenon representative only of material ends; and let us concede, as well, that an invisible, silent god, due to his very inscrutability, could never inspire people to right (or even wrong) action. This leaves the Caïd to choose between a god who is no god (in his own words) and a god who cannot animate his empire . . . but he overlooks a third option. A god of the spirit, whose perfection is not of this world or comprehensible in this world's terms, might nevertheless make ascent to that perfection after death conditional upon how well-intentioned (i.e., how faithfully) we behave in this world. Responsible action would thus enjoy the urgent importance which Saint-Exupéry always awarded to it, yet would not cease once its objective had been attained; for its objective would not be attainable in this life, and the agent's labors would necessarily become a genuine ascent, step building upon step, rather than an incessant series of waves and troughs.

Personally, I should wish to ask Saint-Exupéry what earthly objective could produce a responsible person even temporarily. A man who lives only to win the war will do anything to win the war, and a man who lives only to build the cathedral will do anything to build the cathedral. Which of these people may be trusted to guard a secret or keep a rendezvous? They will betray anything and anyone to serve their wars and cathedrals. Only a person who lives to serve goodness *in abstract* will understand that there exists a nebulous but spiritually real point beyond which his or her war is not worth fighting. Saint-Exupéry would never have challenged this conclusion, but its wording would have grated on him torturously. One can only join Zeller in marveling at "the simplicity of the step which remained for him to take" (192).

NOTES

[1] Auprès de cet écrit, tous mes autres bouquins ne sont qu'exercices.

[2] Ça paraîtra à ma mort, car je n'aurai jamais fini.

[3] Car j'ai vu trop souvent la pitié s'égarer.

[4] J'ai décidé de les guérir. J'interdis que l'on interroge, sachant qu'il n'est jamais de réponse qui désaltère. Celui qui interroge, ce qu'il cherche d'abord c'est l'abîme.

[5] Il faut que l'amour trouve son objet. Je sauve celui-là seul qui aime ce qui est et que l'on peut rassasier.

[6] Car il m'est apparu que l'homme était tout semblable à la *Citadelle*. Il renverse les murs pour s'assurer de la liberté, mais il n'est plus que forteresse démantelé et ouverte aux étoiles.

[7] Prise dans cette nuit sans frontières, elle appelait à elle la lampe du soir dans la maison, et la chambre qui l'eût rassemblée, et la porte qui se fût bien fermée sur elle. Offerte à l'univers entier qui ne montrait point de visage, elle appelait l'enfant que l'on embrasse avant de s'endormir et qui résume le monde. Soumise, sur ce plateau désert, au passage de l'inconnu, elle chantait le pas de l'époux qui sonne le soir sur le seuil et que l'on reconnaît et qui rassure. Étalée dans l'immensité et n'ayant plus rien à saisir, elle suppliait que l'on lui rendît les digues qui seules permettent d'exister, ce paquet de laine à carder, cette écuelle à laver, celle-là seule, cet enfant à endormir et non un autre. Elle criait vers l'éternité de la maison, coiffée avec tout le village par la même prière du soir.

[8] ... car il est bon que le temps qui s'écoule ne nous paraisse point nous user et nous perdre, comme la poignée de sable, mais nous accomplir.

[9] ... afin que l'on puisse et s'approcher et s'éloigner de quelque chose. Afin que l'on y puisse et sortir et rentrer. Sinon, l'on n'est plus nulle part.

[10] Il est mauvais que le cadre même nous tourmente.

[11] Ceux-là qui n'échangent rien ne deviennent rien. Et la vie n'aura point servi à les mûrir.

[12] ... vaine est l'illusion des sédentaires qui croient pouvoir habiter en paix leur demeure car toute demeure est menacée.

[13] ... douces à saisir, faites comme elles sont pour la capture ...

[14] Car le pouvoir ... est acte de créateur.

[15] Ce n'est plus qu'un instrument de déplacement—ici, de guerre.

¹⁶ Car planté dans la terre par ses racines, planté dans les astres par ses branchages, il est le chemin de l'échange entre les étoiles et nous.

¹⁷ . . . envoya un chanteur à cette humanité pourrissante.

¹⁸ . . . rien n'est plus vrai ni moins vrai. Mais plus efficace ou moins efficace.

¹⁹ Les événements . . . n'ont également de forme que la forme que le créateur leur accordera. Et toutes les formes sont vraies ensemble.

²⁰ Ne peux-tu m'enseigner une vérité qui domine leurs vérités particulières et les accueille toutes en son sein?

²¹ Vous n'êtes que témoins stupides. Et les forces obscures qui pèsent, elles, contre les parois de l'empire se passeront bien d'administrateurs pour vous noyer sous leurs marées. Après quoi, vos historiens, plus stupides que vous, expliqueront les causes du désastre, nommeront sagesse, calcul et science de l'adversaire les moyens de sa réussite.

²² Apprends à écouter non le vent des paroles ni les raisonnements qui leur permettent de se tromper. Apprends à regarder plus loin. Car leur haine n'était point absurde. Si chaque pierre n'est point à sa place, il n'est point de temple. Et si chaque pierre est à sa place et sert le temple, alors compte seul le silence qui est né d'elles, et la prière qui s'y forme. Et qui attend que l'on parle des pierres?

²³ Seul un langage insuffisant oppose les hommes les uns aux autres, car ce qu'ils souhaitent ne varie point. Je n'ai jamais rencontré celui-là qui souhaitât ou le désordre ou la bassesse ou la ruine.

²⁴ L'image qui les tourmente et qu'ils aimeraient fonder se ressemble d'un bout à l'autre de l'univers, mais les voies par lesquelles ils cherchent à l'atteindre diffèrent.

²⁵ . . . et de cause à effet, ils s'en vont, redondants, vers l'erreur. Car autre chose est de remonter des effets aux causes ou de descendre des causes aux effets.

²⁶ La parole fausse pour saisir, et simplifie pour enseigner, et tue pour comprendre.

²⁷ . . . c'est l'universelle collaboration de tous à travers l'un, et cet ordre m'oblige à création permanente. Car il m'oblige à fonder ce langage qui absorbera les contradictions.

²⁸ . . . faire le silence pour apprivoiser l'enfant qui meurt.

²⁹ Celui-là qui anéantit son ennemi . . . vivait de lui. Donc il en meurt.

³⁰ . . . j'avance seul. Et je soulève la toile de la tente et j'entre et je m'assieds. Et le silence se fait sur la terre.

³¹ Fausse est la détresse de celui qui vous dit que la satisfaction fuit éternellement devant le désir. Car alors on se trompe sur l'objet du désir.

³² Les cheveux de l'assassin blanchirent dit-on, quand son poignard, au lieu de vider ce corps périssable, l'eut empli d'une telle majesté. Le meurtrier, caché dans la chambre royale, face à face, non avec sa victime, mais avec le granit géant d'un sarcophage, pris au piège d'un silence dont il était lui-même la cause, on le découvrit au petit jour réduit à la prosternation par la seule immobilité du mort.

³³ Car le hasard des vents qui avaient mordu le bloc depuis tant de siècles y avait sculpté un visage géant et qui exprimait la colère. Et le désert, et les salines souterraines, et les tribus . . . étaient dominés par un visage noir sculpté dans le roc, furieux, sous la profondeur d'un ciel pur et ouvrant la bouche pour maudire. Et les hommes fuirent, pris d'épouvante, quand ils le connurent.

³⁴ . . . au piège des créatures, sachant que celle-là que l'on formait dans quelque contrée

étrangère et huilait de la perfection des aromates, il me serait possible de m'en saisir. Et j'appelais amour ce vertige.

35 Je me suis trompé de proie, et je me suis trompé dans ma course. Elle fuyait si vite et je l'ai arrêtée pour m'en saisir . . . Et, une fois prise, elle n'était plus . . .

36 Elles fermeront encore les yeux pour vous ignorer, mais votre silence pèsera sur elles comme l'ombre d'un aigle. Alors enfin elles ouvriront leurs yeux sur vous et vous les emplirez de larmes.

37 Je ne sacrifie point les hommes à l'empire. Mais je fonde l'empire pour en emplir les hommes et les en animer, et l'homme compte plus pour moi que l'empire.

38 La femme, si elle est belle, appelle les dons et les sacrifices, et elle t'enivre de ce que tu lui donnes. Non de ce qu'elle te donne.

39 Celle-là dont tu parles était peut-être née de lui. Et c'est pourquoi il en est responsable. Tu te dois à ta créature. Il va la chercher pour qu'elle le pille. Il va la chercher pour qu'elle s'abreuve.

40 La plus belle fille du monde ne peut donner que ce qu'elle a . . . Moi cela me suffit.

41 La femme . . . toujours te reprochera ce que tu donnes ailleurs qu'en elle.

42 . . . il est impossible d'aimer qu'à travers la femme et non la femme.

43 . . . il faut quelqu'un pour recevoir.

44 . . . en arrivant à moi dans sa totale perfection, elle ne pouvait plus que mourir.

45 Mais il m'est apparu que je me trompais sur le sujet des femmes.

46 Mais je cherchais à récolter le miel tout fait de ruche en ruche, et non à pénétrer cette étendue qui d'abord ne t'offrira rien et te réclamera des pas et des pas et des pas . . .

47 Dormez rassurée dans votre imperfection, épouse imparfaite. . . . Vous n'êtes point but et récompense et bijou vénéré pour soi-même, dont je lasserais aussitôt, vous êtes chemin, véhicule et charroi. Et je ne me lasserai point de devenir.

48 . . . ce qui se donne à toi se sépare de toi.

49 Ce qui importe c'est d'aller vers et non d'être arrivé car jamais on n'arrive nulle part sauf dans la mort.

50 . . . ceux-là s'usent dans l'utopie et les démarches de rêve qui poursuivent des images lointaines, fruits de leur invention. Car la seule invention véritable est de déchiffrer le présent sous ses aspects incohérents et son langage contradictoire.

51 De contradiction dominée en contradiction dominée, je m'achemine vers le silence des questions et ainsi à la béatitude.

52 Et comme j'admirais le dessin des rues et des places et çà et là ces temples commme des greniers spirituels, et tout autour ce vêtement sombre de la colline, il me vint l'image cependant, malgré la chair dont elle était pleine, d'une plante séchée, coupée de ses racines. Il me vint l'image des greniers vides. Il n'y avait plus là un être vivant dont chaque part résonnât sur l'autre, il n'y avait plus un coeur nouant le sang pour le déverser dans toute la substance, il n'y avait plus une chair unique capable de se réjouir ensemble aux jours de fête, capable de former un champ unique. Il n'y avait plus que des parasites installés dans les coquillages d'autrui, vaquant chacun dans sa prison et ne collaborant point.

53 J'ai retrouvé les hommes autour du veau d'or non intéressés mais stupides. Et les enfants qui naissent aujourd'hui me sont plus étrangers que de jeunes barbares sans religion.

⁵⁴ Un chemin escarpé et glissant surplombait la mer. L'orage avait crevé et la nuit coulait comme une outre pleine. Obstiné, je montais vers Dieu pour lui demander la raison des choses, et me faire expliquer où conduisait l'échange que l'on avait prétendu m'imposer.

Mais au sommet de la montaigne je ne découvris qu'un bloc pesant de granit noir—lequel était Dieu.

⁵⁵ Car je n'avais point touché Dieu, mais un dieu qui se laisse toucher n'est point un dieu.

⁵⁶ . . . l'apprentissage de Dieu, tu ne le fais que dans l'exercice de prières auxquelles il n'est point répondu.

⁵⁷ Car Dieu d'abord est sens de ton langage et ton langage, s'il prend un sens, te montre Dieu.

⁵⁸ L'apparition de l'archange, je n'ai plus l'espoir d'y prétendre car ou bien il est invisible ou bien il n'est pas. Et ceux qui espèrent un signe de Dieu c'est qu'ils en font un reflet de mirroir et n'y découvriraient rien qu'eux-mêmes.

⁵⁹ . . . laquelle est de mauvais guignol.

⁶⁰ Et je dis vérité cela seul qui t'exalte. Car il n'est rien qui se démontre ni pour ni contre. Mais tu ne doutes point de la beauté si tu retentes à tel visage.

⁶¹ Je ne connais point de poème ni d'image dans le poème qui soit autre chose qu'une action sur toi. Il s'agit non de t'expliquer ceci ou cela, ni même de te le suggérer comme le croient de plus subtils—mais de te faire devenir tel ou tel.

⁶² Car les fauves se guident sur l'odeur aigre de l'angoisse, laquelle charge le vent. A peine avait-il rougi, toutes ses victimes brillaient pour lui comme un peuple de lumières.

⁶³ Ils périssaient chaque jour par milliers, bientôt secs et craquants comme une écorce de bois mort.

⁶⁴ Ce puits nous tenait comme un clou dans une aile.

⁶⁵ . . . au fond d'une nuit amère à la fois et splendide . . .

⁶⁶ . . . le puits d'El Ksour . . . est une fenêtre sur la vie.

⁶⁷ Je les mène vers l'oasis à conquérir. . . . Ces hommes qui mangent et boivent et ne vivent ce soir que d'une vie élémentaire, à peine se seront-ils montrés dans les plaines fertiles, que tout y changera non seulement des coutumes et du langage, mais de l'architecture des remparts et du style des temples.

⁶⁸ Nous fûmes bientôt en vue de la ville. Mais nous n'en découvrîmes rien, sinon des remparts rouges d'une hauteur inusitée et qui tournaient vers le désert une sorte d'envers dédaigneux, dépouillés qu'ils étaient d'ornements, de saillies, de créneaux, et conçus de toute évidence pour n'être point observés du dehors.

⁶⁹ Le malaise s'empara des mes hommes quand les remparts, peu à peu grandis par l'approche, nous parurent si visiblement nous tourner le dos dans le calme de la falaise, comme s'il n'était rien hors de la ville.

⁷⁰ D'une éminence lointaine qui, sans surplomber les remparts, permettait un regard rasant, nous observâmes une verdure serrée comme du cresson. Or, à l'extérieur des remparts, on n'eût découvert un seul brin d'herbe.

⁷¹ Une part d'entre eux fut prise de peur.

⁷² . . . bien au contraire, furent tourmentés par un amour informulable et singulier.

... Qu'elle était belle, cette bien-aimée si jalousement cultivée dans ses aromates et ses jardins et ses coutumes!

[73] Nous découvrîmes que tout autour du mur sourd et aveugle, le sable montrait une zone plus blanche d'être trop riche en ossements qui sans doute témoignaient du sort des délégations lointaines.

[74] De s'être enfermée dans ses provisions, c'est qu'elle a accepté la mort. J'ai peur de ceux-là qui vont nus, remontant vers le Nord de leur désert sans forteresse. Déambulant presque sans armes. Mais ... te voilà mienne comme un gâteau de miel, cité trop sûre de toi. Doivent dormir tes sentinelles. Car tu es délabrée de coeur.

[75] S'il est, par exemple, derrière les murs ... tel ou tel instrument de musique ignoré de nous ... l'expérience m'enseigne qu'une fois forcée cette réserve mystérieuse et répandus mes hommes parmi ses biens je les retrouverai plus tard, dans les soirées de mes campements, s'exerçant à tirer de mes instruments peu usuels telle mélodie d'un goût neuf pour leurs coeurs.

[76] Fou celui-là qui enfermait l'eau dans son urne parce qu'il aimait le chant des fontaines.

[77] Il ne s'agit point d'un but, le plaisir étant de la marche.

[78] Tu ne cherches point ce que tu ignores.

[79] Le désir de l'amour c'est l'amour.

[80] ... dans la seule paix de la mort, quand Dieu engrange.

[81] Car celle-là ne naîtra jamais.

[82] Elle demeurera graine avortée et d'un pouvoir inemployé, sèche d'âme et de coeur. Elle vieillira, funèbre, dans la vanité de ses captures.

[83] ... îles à musique, comme un cadeau tout fait ...

[84] De t'y réveiller sans effort, tu ne puiseras rien aux seins de ses filles que le pouvoir d'y oublier l'amour. Tu iras d'oubli en oubli, de mort en mort ... et tu me diras, de l'île à musique: "Qu'était-il là-bas qui valût de vivre?" quand la même, bien enseignée, te fait qu'un équipage entier accepte, par amour pour elle, le risque de mort.

[85] Engrangeant un jour Ta création, Seigneur, ouvre-nous Ton vantail à deux portes et fais-nous pénétrer là où il ne sera plus répondu car il n'y aura plus réponse, mais béatitude, qui est clef de voûte des questions et visage qui satisfait.

[86] ... au creux de ses sables déserts où j'ai bien travaillé.

[87] J'ai besoin d'un dieu pour me recevoir.

[88] Je suis celui qui habite. Je suis pôle aimanté. Je suis graine de l'arbre et ligne de force dans le silence ...

[89] Je suis la pelouse sur l'abîme. Je suis le cellier qui dore les fruits.

[90] Je suis celui qui accueille ... je suis celui qui porte les fardeaux du monde ... je suis le seul qui puisse rendre l'homme à lui-même.

[91] Te faut mourir pour épouser.

WORKS CITED

Austin, Norman. *Meaning and Being in Myth*. University Park and London: Pennsylvania State UP, 1990.

Borgal, Clément. *Saint-Exupéry: Mystique Sans la Foi*. Paris: Centurion, 1964.

Caillois, Roger. Preface to *Citadelle* in *Antoine de Saint-Exupéry: Oeuvres*. Paris: Gallimard, 1959: 501–5.

Cate, Curtis. *Antoine de Saint-Exupéry*. New York: Putnam, 1978.

Chevrier, Pierre. *Antoine de Saint-Exupéry*. Paris: Gallimard, 1949.

—. *Saint-Exupéry*. Paris: Gallimard, 1958.

Devaux, André-A. *Saint-Exupéry*. Paris: Desclée de Brouwer, 1965.

Estang, Luc. *Saint-Exupéry*. Paris: Seuil, 1989.

Huguet, Jean. *Saint-Exupéry ou l'Enseignement du Désert*. Paris: La Colombe, 1956.

Iser, Wolfgang. *The Fictive and the Imaginary: Charting Literary Anthropology*. Baltimore and London: Johns Hopkins UP, 1993.

Leleu, Jean. "Pilote au 2/33." *Saint-Exupéry en Procès*. Ed. René Tavernier. Paris: Pierre Belfond, 1967: 79–92.

Major, Jean-Louis. *Saint-Exupéry: L'Écriture et la Pensée*. Ottawa: U of Ottawa P, 1968.

Migeo, Marcel. *Saint-Exupéry*. Trans. Herma Briffault. New York: McGraw-Hill, 1960.

Ouellet, Réal. *Les Relations Humaines dans l'Oeuvre de Saint-Exupéry*. Paris: Minard, 1971.

Robinson, J.D.M. *Antoine de Saint-Exupéry*. Boston: Twayne, 1984.

Saint-Exupéry, Antoine de. *Oeuvres*. Ed. Roger Caillois. Bibliothèque de la Pléiade. Paris: Gallimard, 1959; volume contains *Courrier Sud*, *Vol de Nuit*, *Terre des Hommes*, *Lettre à un Otage*, *Pilote de Guerre*, *Le Petit Prince*, and *Citadelle*.

—. *Carnets*. Paris: Gallimard, 1953.

—. *Un Sens à la Vie*. Paris: Gallimard, 1956.

Webster, Paul. *Antoine de Saint-Exupéry: The Life and Death of the Little Prince*. London: Papermac, 1994.

Werth, Léon. *Tel Que Je L'ai Connu . . .* in René Delange, *La Vie de Saint-Exupéry*. Paris: Seuil, 1948: 131–86.

Zeller, Renée. *La Grande Quête d'Antoine de Saint-Exupéry dans Le Petit Prince et Citadelle*. Paris: Alsatia, 1961.

CHAPTER 8

CONCLUSION

T hat Saint-Exupéry had foreseen clearly the spiritual crisis of Western civilization is no longer of much interest to the general reader. As it enters the twenty-first century, the West has become inured (or perhaps indifferent) to crisis, nor do the roots of its present malaise—whatever that may be—appear to have been more nourished by the fascism and totalitarianism of the thirties and forties than by the naive hedonism of the sixties and seventies or the cynical egocentrism of the eighties. Even the critical disputes which raged so hotly in the two decades after Saint-Exupéry's death concerning his relation to Christianity, existentialism, democracy, socialism, and so on are now a specialist's backwater. If we conclude that he was an agnostic, a Nietzschean, or a crypto-fascist, therefore, will anyone except the specialist care? Or if we claim that he was right to shy away from De Gaulle or short-sighted to praise technology, who in an age of political prattle bounced constantly around the planet by satellite can still remember the day when one man's writing deeply influenced a nation's conduct?

If there is any hope for us as a species in this material world, whether we hail from east, west, north, or south, it rests not in a superficial multi-culturalism or an indiscriminate liberalism, but in our common humanity. We of the postmodern world know that truth is relative to the position from which we observe it, and also that we are limited to occupying one position at a time: we have known this much since Einstein. In our zeal to universalize the relativistic after-glow of exploded universality, however, we have spread new falsehood. We have forgotten that, when a thirsty castaway sees a fluid mirage on the horizon, *something* outside the sufferer's teased senses is causing the mistaken impression: that is, our most idealistic illusions often strain at an objective, eternal reality. However inaccurate our notions of moral truth, both individual and collective, something beyond us must stir that strange loathing of selfishness which, in the desert silence of the soul, ignores the itch of animal need and overrules the call to political power.

Apparently—falsely—pointing at Polaris, the North Star (whose immobility is itself only an optical illusion), turns a constellation variously called The Great Bear, Charles's Wain, and The Big Dipper by members of Western civilization. A feminist critic might remark upon the brutality of the ancient myth which celebrated the victimized virgin Callisto. A Marxist critic, noting the stress upon wagons, crude utensils, and other working-class trappings in stellar imagery, might draw a wry conclusion about who spends nights indoors and who does not in this culture. A reader-response critic would delight in all three heavenly images, being sure to underscore the multiplicity of perspectives within this single cultural milieu. A deconstructive critic would go beyond tallying the number of possible alternatives for connecting the celestial dots, urging us also to notice how many nearby stars are excluded from the design lest they disrupt the emerging sense of coherence. All schools would agree that there is something high-handed about sustaining any given design. The meaning of the stars, they would concur, already resides in the benighted heart of each earthbound gazer who seeks to exploit them.

But all of these positions beg that very essentialism which they claim to repudiate. From where do feminists and Marxists draw the righteous indignation which so nobly fuels their championing of oppressed people? If only women may be feminists and only proletarians Marxists, and if the objective of both is to usurp rather than correct the traditional monopoly of power, then their ideologies lose all moral urgency. Their systems are simply the hoarse cry of a competing mob. What would redeem them from the self-serving egotism which they combat is a sense of common humanity. Why, then, are they so reluctant to acknowledge the universal human tendency to look into the stars for guidance, for warnings, for messages? Why do they fail to recognize that people all long for something which they cannot define in the terms of this world —which, when defined in worldly terms, becomes just another expression of egotism?

Richard Rorty, the pioneer of a new pragmatism, might have been discussing star-gazers when he writes that literary interpretation reflects "no more than the fact that somebody has found something interesting to say about a group of marks or noises—some way of describing those marks and noises which relates them to some of the other things we are interested in talking about" (97). Reader-response theory generally endorses such radical subjectivity. It differs from feminism and Marxism in asserting that even cultural conditioning cannot account for the innumerable shapes which an audience "reads into" a text. There are virtually as many opinions as people, in the words of Terence; or if schools evolve in which opinions tend to coalesce, they are nonetheless driven by shared interests far too specific to be held by an entire culture. Notes Jane Tompkins, "The phrase 'community of interpreters' or 'interpretive community' plays a crucial role in the more recent theories of reading advanced by Bleich, Fish, Culler, and Walter Michaels" (xxi). Such groups may obviously include cliques of armchair theorists as well as circles of poet laureates; otherwise, why distinguish between reader-response and culture-response?

This fragmented, almost anarchic species of community raises more questions than it answers. If interpretive communities result from mere conditioning, then why do they not embrace huge chunks of the cultural unit? If they result from a radical individualism, then why do they embrace even two people? Do these otherwise autonomous interpreters consent to come together for the furtherance of a political agenda with shared elements? But why, then, are they reading literature to begin with—why not pursue their political objectives more directly? By that very open-endedness which renders it susceptible to many interpretations, literature is a poor mechanism of propaganda (just as propaganda makes for bad literature—with all due respect to Chinua Achebe—because it allows only one interpretation). Is not one of the definitive qualities of a great literary text, rather, precisely that it licenses several readings at once without licensing every possible reading? Is this not a better explanation of why there may be numerous, but not innumerable, schools of thought about a work of art?

That a given school may wish to privilege its reading is another—and a very predictable—manifestation of human egotism; but does not the literary text's ultimate value lie in its ability to liberate us from our selfish objectives, our "pragmatic" concerns? And is such liberation to a between-the-lines limbo where ineffable truths may dwell not one of our highest needs as human beings? Surely the moot point about bears and wagons and dippers is *not* that they might as well be whales and pitchforks and spoons; surely it is that every such construct allows the mind to fabulize, to put an image in motion through time toward a destination which absorbs all images. Do we not all share the one great need (as Saint-Exupéry did so overpoweringly) to make action worthwhile—to make the stars into tracks of things done—to be offered, not necessarily the easiest or most flattering direction, but a *direction*? Is not the imperative to *respond* to creation the universal human substrate which precedes all reader-response? Emmanuel Mounier, the prime exponent of personalism, thought so: "Thus my freedom is never at my arbitrary disposal, although the point at which I espouse it may be hidden in the heart's most secret depth. My liberty is never mere spontaneity: it is always something regulated—better still, it is something called forth" (61).

Deconstruction, while claiming to have ramifications far beyond literary criticism, sometimes leads to a perspective indistinguishable from reader-response theory. Since every reading is supposed to be a prisoner of its own assumptions, any reading might be considered no less justified (or no more unjustified) than another. Norris thus summarizes Derrida's stance in this regard: "If interpretation is always caught up in a chain of proliferating sense which it can neither halt nor fully comprehend, then the critic is effectively absolved of all responsibility for limiting the play of his own imagination" (96). So chaotic an indulgence of all views in the infinitely echoing corridors of meaning's labyrinth is, if anything, a bit too audacious for the reader-response critic, who sees coteries irresistibly forming through common interest. To him or her, the bear in the sky may be a dog or a squirrel—but probably not the crumpled love letter back in the apartment's wicker wastebasket. Such a shape would hint at psychosis: it would license a militant solipsism which one just does not find in functional communities of any sort. It would belie the fundamental pragmatism behind any society.

The deconstructionist, though, is very like Saint-Exupéry in stressing the essential chaos of reality. The constellations in their entirety might as well be a single image—a representation of a million beads whose string has snapped to send them flying everywhere . . . but such a shape, of course, is unassimilable. Hence Saint-Exupéry maintained throughout his life the primary importance of defending a haphazard interpretation, a circumstantial set of values capable of generating a culture in the same way that clumping half a dozen stars into a bear requires adjacent ones not to be a bear, but perhaps the bear's prey or a hunter in pursuit. When pressed, Derrida is apt to concede that the self-contradiction of all systems does not mean that one can live without system. In his own playful words, "Emancipation from this language [of essentialism] must be attempted. But not as an *attempt* at emancipation from it, for this is impossible unless we forget *our* history. Rather, as the dream of emancipation" (28). He and the pilot-hero apparently share the same kind of agnosticism. The difference between them is the mood of their *différance*—of their postponement of meaning. Derrida finds the games we play with ourselves, though indispensable, highly amusing. Saint-Exupéry finds them the most serious thing we do, since they alone permit us to do anything. One senses that Derrida could not muster devotion-unto-death for any program of action (except, perhaps, for dissecting a program of action). To Saint-Exupéry, action has a unique redemptive power, for all its benightedness.

Which view is the more correct? Derrida's generation has been forced to mature on several truly sickening examples of action for the sake of action: a nuclear age in advance of whose demonic folly Saint-Exupéry was fortunate enough to die, genocide in Eastern Europe whose extent Saint-Exupéry never knew, and vast killing fields in Southeast Asia whose monument to doctrine might have made Antoine want to burn the *Citadelle* manuscript. On the other hand, had not the "appeasement" generation's inaction and passivity left the door ajar for secret police and stormtroopers? Is it better (to borrow a favorite Exupérian parable) that a hundred men should perish vainly in trying to rescue a trapped miner, or that the hundred should wait in safety counting their comrade's last breaths sympathetically?

The terms of that drama are deceptive, of course. Only the most eloquent of mystics or shameless of demagogues would undertake to argue that saving the miner will save humanity. The twentieth century has "saved" far more than its share of oppressed workers, if only that they might become tiny cogs in Stalinist or Maoist juggernauts. The fever of false altruism apparently reduces us to our most brutal level—but it is *false* altruism, let us remember. Isn't deconstruction at fault for encouraging us to smirk at any pretense of self-sacrifice? By demonstrating how the subject's special interests always lurk behind the "axiomatic," has not the New Historicism undermined the indignation which we should feel (and which it strives to feel) for clearly deplorable conduct? If a prophet with a holy book in one hand and a sword in the other slays myriads, should we come away believing that nothing is holy? Is not the proper message just the opposite: that there *is* a right and a wrong, and that those who murder meaning with words have died a death of the soul?

In exposing the ultimate self-annulment of all logical systems—all philosophies, that is, which place full faith in what the human mind can understand—deconstruction is well positioned to license certain assumptions about what our minds cannot understand. We cannot survive in chaos, yet we know that our human order walls out the truth astir in the inconceivable swirl of stars. Is not the obvious next step, then, to establish an order which leaves a sacred window open upon disorder (or upon an order invisible to our eyes)? Four points and a projection might be a wagon or a cup—or even a well-fed boa—but not a yet-to-be-invented flying saucer: the stars around B612 may be laughing or weeping, but not both at once. Even so is the preciousness of time—the immeasurable importance of action during life's one-way transit—a tie upon us which no amount of facetious fantasy can loosen. We must strive to live a story, even though we know that we (like Cervantes's Gines de Pasamonte) can never write its final chapter unless we would admit to lying. As Kermode concludes his own magisterial work, "Those [stories] that continue to interest us move through time to an end, an end we must sense even if we cannot know it; they live in change until, which is never, *is* and *as* are one" (179). Like the book that lives on, living authorship often indulges in lengthy digression, unexplained recurrence, and contra-diction—but it does so with as much determination as play, for we would not feel our own ludicrous absurdity if we did not feel the impulsion to live meaningfully. For us, at least, the stars *do* both laugh and weep.

To suggest with the deconstructionist that we play at living systematically, then, is as wide of the truth as suggesting with the pilot-hero that we should take in deadly earnest a silly child's game. We must live life in deadly earnest, for the stakes are greater than we can see or imagine; but we must also remember that the patterns and rituals through which we live life are mere games, since they cannot possibly capture life's invisible, unimaginable meaning. To treat our rules, customs, and traditions as silly child's play when they fail to accommodate our essential humanity is a matter of the utmost seriousness.

Were we to do otherwise, we would be attempting fundamentally new creation. We would be declaring that *this* rule, *this* time, is different. We would be trying to live a myth—to plant meaning in the universe where none had existed before. The deconstructionist invites such efforts at mythic heroism by not insisting (as he or she has every intellectual ground to do) that myth is dead, once and for all. When we knew ourselves less well—when we lived at the mercy of nature, fighting for another day's grace, unaware of pattern except as it was manifested in the deluges and drouths of our great adversary—then a man who could survive on his own in the wilderness was truly a god. In the twenty-first century, however, virtually every human being on earth will have leisure (whether or not it is so wisely spent) to ponder *human* nature. Indeed, one of the costs of *not* pondering that nature may be the irreversible poisoning of the other kind—the air we must breathe and the water we must drink. New technology will be exploited by old greed, and the greedy well know how to subvert brave new worlds so that the lustful, the lazy, and the fearful grow addicted to the pander's wares. The more things change, the more they stay the same . . .

The deconstructionist needs to remind us that we live in the post-mythic world, the new world where everything has suddenly become very old—not that old world where everything was new. To do any less is irresponsible: to suggest that one may simply toy with systems while fully aware of their artifice as a "wired" techno-consumer surfs television channels and the Internet is preposterous. Our electronic toys concentrate too much power for a sane person to start assuming that now, at last, the dragon will be slain. The essential human problem—the human mind's ineptitude for grasping the essential—will never change, and the illusion that such change is at hand can only usher in the kinds of disaster which it always has—the Allegory of the False Myth again.

Saint-Exupéry himself could not ultimately resist allegory, though it canceled out the type of heroism which he had dedicated his literary career to portraying. He tried to pretend that the desert and the stars contained rapturous truths open only to the pure of heart—a promise which, if true, might have convinced all of us to purify our hearts. Yet the only rapture he ever described was that of being a child rather than an adult, a flier rather than a bureaucrat, a Man of Men rather than a prophet in the wilderness. As he sat writing, in fact, he was all that he most dreaded: an adult, an ink-stained scribbler, and an isolated contemplative. "He never found repose," Léon Werth recalled. "In each of his triumphs was hidden a taste of cinder" (178). No wonder: for the rapturous epiphany was required to be of this world—how could such ecstasy end but in ashes? Yet an epiphany not of this world would be imperceptible to our minds, which can operate only on worldly images; so those who claim real ecstasy purvey a lie without the excuse of honest illusion. Is there, then, no ecstasy?

For those of us not spared by angels, the closest thing to moral ecstasy—to oneness with God—may be the temporary inner truce of a good deed well done. What other moment on this earth can so unite flesh and mind and spirit? But why should we perform good works for ends beyond our conception? By doing so, we may be tricked into believing ourselves saints. To escape such hypocrisy, then, should we serve only worldly ends? As long as Saint-Exupéry could not understand the mere *longing* after goodness (i.e., the acceptance of grace which breaks this vicious circle) as itself evidence of a magnetic source pulling upon our hearts, he could only orbit false sources which always proved pitifully unequal to the heart's lines of force. As long as he evaded the allegorical structure of his pseudomyths—the patent necessity of a power precedent to all possible human creation, which alone could explain human creations by undergirding them with its benign pre-logic—he could only keep rebeginning his quest at the climactic moment which should have solved it. Werth concludes of his celebrated friend, "Was not the life of Saint-Exupéry but an ever-disappointed aspiration to serenity?" (179).

"This myth carries a weight of sadness," wrote Estang of the pilot-hero's cycle in terms unconsciously close to Werth's, "even when it forces itself to achieve serenity" (167). A sacrifice to an unworthy god could scarcely help but be sad: would a sacrifice to an unknown one necessarily be disingenuous? Perhaps so, if the god were completely unknown; but if this god were the author of an innate need to sacrifice—to exchange oneself for a universal and eternal self—then his nature would be far from unknown. Here, too, of course, there is a sadness. One must feel some pain at being separated from the source of one's true identity; but the separation is no more complete than the seeming ignorance which inspires sacrifice, and it is compensated by the satisfaction of not being satisfied, of not making do with mere presence. In the words of poet Pierre Reverdy, "It is through the despairing need of plenitude which distinguishes man that he would best be able to define what he calls his soul—a desire never fully satisfied. All things tallied, it makes of the soul a lack, a void, which nothing palpable and definable in worldly terms may be applied to supplementing" (49–50).

I do not suggest that Saint-Exupéry's sadness is of this latter sort—but neither should anyone confidently assert that his sadness was fully benighted. "I don't care for people whom happiness has left satisfied, and who will develop no further," he wrote his mother. "We must be a bit restless to see what's going on around us" (157).[1] Has this man not deeply plumbed the paradoxical nature of moral truth? At least he knows that true believers refuse to believe implicitly in anything visible, even though he thinks he knows that only the visible can justify belief.

And he knows something else, as well. He knows that although the essential motive force behind apparent chaos precedes, outlives, embraces, and absorbs any possible human attempt at creativity, human beings must still act. It is this truth, indeed, which he knows best of all, and which has obscured the other truth behind logical contradiction. There is no comprehensibly sufficient reason to act; but action, as he intuits, cannot be divided from its motive, any more than creatures can ultimately be divided from their creator. A pure heart acts with the speed of thought: it acts in thinking action. It clears a space for the unknown god in a gesture of often stunning physical vigor, since that god is well known to need more space than the material world can ever offer. Derrida has written sublimely in his essay, "Force and Signification," "Only *pure absence*—not the absence of this or that, but the absence of everything in which all presence is announced—can *inspire*, in other words, can *work*, and then make one work" (8).

If we fashion forms in the chaotic whirlpools of stars overhead, perhaps it is not, after all, because we must have finite forms upon which to execute the practical functions of living. Perhaps it is so that we may rejoice in straining, splitting, and recombining those same forms as a sacrifice to a greater form yet beyond our grasp. Perhaps we have been created both to weave and to unravel, over and over, in our search for an inconceivable unity—a law which fits each litigant, a story whose end concludes all stories. When a man like Saint-Exupéry insists upon cosmos, yet continually returns to seek it in chaos rather than dwell within limits of his own design, we should be slow to condemn his volatility. Those who earnestly seek order never take rules too seriously.

NOTE

[1] Je n'aime pas les gens que le bonheur a satisfaits, et qui ne se développeront plus. Il faut être un peu inquiet pour lire autour de soi.

WORKS CITED

Derrida, Jacques. *Writing and Difference*. Trans. Alan Bass. Chicago: Chicago UP, 1978.

Estang, Luc. *Saint-Exupéry*. Paris: Seuil, 1989.

Kermode, Frank. *The Sense of an Ending: Studies in the Theory of Fiction*. London, Oxford, and New York: Oxford UP, 1967.

Mounier, Emmanuel. *Personalism*. Trans. Philp Mairet. Notre Dame and London: U of Notre Dame P, 1970.

Norris, Christopher. *Deconstruction: Theory and Practice*. London and New York: Routledge, 1991.

Rorty, Richard. "The Pragmatist's Progress." *Interpretation and Overinterpretation*. Ed. Umberto Eco. Cambridge: Cambridge UP, 1992: 89–108.

Reverdy, Pierre. *Le Livre de Mon Bord: 1930–36*. Paris: Mercure de France, 1948.

Saint-Exupéry, Antoine de. *Lettres à sa Mère*. Paris: Gallimard, 1955.

Tompkins, Jane P. "An Introduction to Reader-Response Criticism." Ed. Jane Tompkins. *Reader Response Criticism*. Baltimore: Johns Hopkins UP, 1994: ix–xxvi.

Werth, Léon. *Tel Que Je L'ai Connu . . .* in René Delange, *La Vie de Saint-Exupéry*. Paris: Seuil, 1948: 131–86.

INDEX